Date: 5/14/19

**BIO BAILEY
Duffy, Peter,
The agitator : William Bailey and
the first American uprising**

THE
AGITATOR

*William Bailey and the
First American Uprising
Against Nazism*

PETER DUFFY

PUBLICAFFAIRS
New York

PublicAffairs
Hachette Book Group
1290 Avenue of the Americas
New York, NY 10104
www.publicaffairsbooks.com
@Public_Affairs

Printed in the United States of America

First Edition: March 2019

Published by PublicAffairs, an imprint of Perseus Books, LLC, a subsidiary of Hachette
Book Group, Inc. The PublicAffairs name and logo is a trademark of the Hachette Book
Group.

The Hachette Speakers Bureau provides a wide range of authors for speaking events. To
find out more, go to www.hachettespeakersbureau.com or call (866) 376-6591.

The publisher is not responsible for websites (or their content) that are not owned by the
publisher.

PRINT BOOK INTERIOR DESIGN BY JEFF WILLIAMS

Library of Congress Control Number: 2018052360

ISBNs: 978-1-5417-6231-2 (hardcover), 978-1-5417-6232-9 (ebook)

LSC-C

10 9 8 7 6 5 4 3 2 1

To El

CONTENTS

Prologue 1

Chapter One 9

Chapter Two 21

Chapter Three 35

Chapter Four 43

Chapter Five 53

Chapter Six 67

Chapter Seven 75

Chapter Eight 85

Chapter Nine 97

Chapter Ten 107

Chapter Eleven 125

Chapter Twelve 137

Chapter Thirteen 151

Chapter Fourteen 169

Chapter Fifteen 189

Chapter Sixteen 211

Acknowledgments 225

Notes 227

Index 253

PROLOGUE

"**A**ND THEN," AS Virgil wrote, "were portents given of earth and ocean."

New York City had been suffering for three weeks under the worst heat wave in thirty-four years. Hundreds of thousands were flocking each day to the beaches at Coney Island and the Rockaways in search of a little relief. The newspapers printed lists of those who died from the heat, drowned attempting to escape it, or were so overcome they had to be revived. At least one suicide was recorded. A Riverside Drive physician, "his nerves worn ragged by his inability to get cool," leaped to his death from a fifth-floor apartment.

But the weather had broken. A series of rain showers swept through the city followed by a blast of cool wind from the north. By nightfall on Friday, July 26, 1935, the temperature hovered around 70 degrees. There was a slight breeze in the air.

Bill Bailey, dressed uncharacteristically in a dark suit, striped tie, and Panama hat, was ready for his mission.

Bailey was a young merchant seaman with the grittiest of proletarian occupations, working with the "black gang" in the belly of a ship, "eating, drinking, and breathing in the smoke and gas of the engine room," as he later wrote. In this primordial epoch before his nose turned bulbous and his face craggy, "Big Bill" was towering and handsome, if salty of demeanor and tattered of clothing. His accent identified him as a New York Irishman of shanty lineage. He would orate from his soapbox about wealthy capitalists enjoying filet mignon while "we're down here eating *boint liva.*" This, in his heavy Jimmy Cagney brogue, was how you pronounced "burnt liver."

Just twenty, Bailey had been a shoeless newsboy, grammar school dropout, juvenile delinquent, panhandler, turnstile jumper, insubordinate dockworker, stowaway, hobo, vagrant, thief, reformatory inmate, drunk, "lyin' son of a bitch," apprentice sailor, and connoisseur of the pleasures of the harbor. His life was transformed when he was working as a fireman (operating the oil burners to generate steam to power the ship) on a freighter traveling between New York and London. He was so outraged over the mistreatment of a stowaway of color, "so naïve, so trusting, so beautiful at heart," that he joined the Communist-led Marine Workers Industrial Union and, shortly thereafter, the Communist Party itself.

During the torrid days of July 1935, Bailey was mired "on the beach" without a ship. Broke and homeless, he was sleeping on the benches of the old International Workers Order hall on Union Square.

He had plenty of time to huddle with fellow unemployed seamen of leftist bent and discuss the civilizational assault that Adolf Hitler was conducting before the eyes of newspaper and radio correspondents who were relaying the news to the world. Over the previous few months, the Nazi state had launched its second major anti-Jewish onslaught since Hitler was elevated to power two and a half years earlier, proof that the initial-stage actions against Jews in March 1933 were just the beginning of the promised eradication of an existential foe. The Hitler government was also attracting international attention with strictures against the last vestiges of antiregime sentiment, targeting groups as varied as far-right paramilitaries of non-Nazi allegiance and professional comedians who lacked proper deference for regime leaders. The front pages blared the news about a months-long drive against the

Catholic Church. Of particular note to the radicals on the water-front, the Nazi government seized an American sailor from a US-flagged liner in Hamburg and threw him in a concentration camp for plotting to circulate antiregime printed materials.

"Something had to be done," Bailey said.

═══════

The SS *Bremen* was the flagship of Hitler's commercial armada, a technical and aesthetic marvel regarded by the world as the water-borne embodiment of German nationhood. It was the most pop-ular of the European passenger liners, the "floating palaces" that traveled between Europe and the United States in the first half of the 1930s, boasting the highest percentage of berths filled of any competitor on the Atlantic run. The ship was a "vast seagoing cathedral of steel," in the conception of its builders. "The Great Pyramid of Gizeh out for a stroll," declared the *New Yorker*.

The *Bremen* steamed twice a month into New York Harbor, easing with slow-moving grandeur into the Hudson River slip re-served for the Fatherland's premier vessel along what was known as "luxury liner row." The area around Pier 86, which extended a thousand feet into the river from the foot of West Forty-Sixth Street, was a tiny province of the Third Reich with bars, restau-rants, shops, and newsstands catering to a German-speaking cli-entele. Here, on the western edge of Manhattan Island, European civilization touched American soil (or cracked cobblestone) in the era before the standardization of air travel, before the transat-lantic jets at LaGuardia and Kennedy.

On the night in question, at the height of the Great Depres-sion and more than four years before the start of World War II, the *Bremen* was hosting a "midnight sailing," a cherished tradition of the European superliners during interwar New York. A few thou-sand guests paid a nominal fee to come aboard and imbibe with departing passengers like it was New Year's Eve. The bon voyage party lasted until the last woozy guests were shoved ashore and the ship backed into the river at the celebratory height of the gaiety at midnight. Anyone properly attired could join the bash whether they had an acquaintance on board or not. The topside areas with views of the shimmering cityscape resembled a packed subway train at rush hour.

It would later be estimated that 4,800 nonpassengers had boarded the ship for the affair. With the addition of 1,300 passengers and a thousand German crew members, the population on the *Bremen* hovered around 7,000. The revelers included a Hollywood movie star, a delegation of Protestant clergymen, a Rockefeller heiress, the new US ambassador to Norway, a future secretary of the navy, a collection of wealthy financiers, the governor of Pennsylvania, a Honduran nobleman, a Chicago meatpacking mogul, and the two-year-old grandson of the president of the United States.

On the stretch of shoreline under the looming bow of the forward-facing ship, a few thousand anti-Nazi activists gathered to protest the mounting crisis in the Third Reich, chanting slogans, holding signs, and delivering speeches. "Arise ye prisoners of starvation!" they sang, using that era's translation of "The Internationale." "Arise ye wretched of the earth!" The ranks included communists and socialists, anarchists and social democrats, high school students and old-timers, concerned citizens and cranks, gentiles and Jews, and, a rarity in those days of bedrock racism, blacks standing alongside whites.

Surrounding the demonstration was a New York Police Department (NYPD) contingent of more than three hundred officers, including a hundred undercover detectives and a few dozen "ten-foot-cops" on horseback. A private security firm hired by the German shipping line deployed an additional fifty uniformed men and five plainclothesmen.

Another several hundred people at least, curious onlookers out for a stroll on the pleasant summer evening, lined the waterfront to get a glimpse of the spectacle.

All eyes were turned toward the centerpiece of the evening's festivities, the swastika flag that waved from the short staff at the nose of the *Bremen*, hovering 50 feet over the stretch of unfenced shoreline where the rally was occurring. The flag was illuminated by a high-powered arc lamp beaming down from the ship's bridge.

Bill Bailey was one of about a dozen itinerant seamen disguised in stylish clothing who slipped through police lines and crossed the visitors' gangway onto the *Bremen*. Joining the covert operation were a few dozen Communist Party activists, women and men, who were assigned to support the seamen's operation. The plan: a few of the seamen were to march to the front of the ship, remove the swastika from its honored perch, stride off the boat, and make a presentation to the speaker, who would set the flag on fire to the delight of the crowd.

Up on the A deck, a midship position that seemed miles from the flapping swastika, Bailey feared the whole project was doomed. The women assigned to create a diversion by handcuffing themselves to the mast were having trouble with the cuffs. A battalion of imposing *Bremen* sailors and a 6-foot-high gunwale impeded the path to the flagstaff. He didn't know the worst of it: Two undercover detectives from the NYPD's Red Squad—a tabloid-famous slayer of one of gangster Dutch Schultz's henchmen and a *Jewish* luminary of the force who once took a bullet to the chest during the arrest of a drug dealer—had been aware for hours that something was afoot. Concealed in the crush of partygoers, the detectives were leaning in close enough to overhear the seamen discussing an improvised scheme to get close to the flag.

"It looked like it was going to be a tough job," Bailey would remember. "We had almost given it up that we would ever make it. But we had one dedication, that at least we would make a try. We knew we were going to get stomped and beat up and everything. But at least nobody could say when it was all over that we didn't make a try."

What followed was one of the most stirring acts in American political history—the first blow landed against the Third Reich by foreign adversaries, delivered without guns or bombs, years before

America, or any country, chose to take military action against a regime that was already signaling its treacherous intentions.

The action on the *Bremen* precipitated a diplomatic controversy that engaged the highest levels of the American and Nazi governments. It led to a fiery trial in the non-Supreme setting of Magistrates' Court in Manhattan. The case against the so-called Bremen Six framed the dilemma facing the world in the years leading up to World War II: Should we take the path of our protagonists and challenge the well-publicized injustices of the Third Reich? Or should we follow popular opinion and appease—no, collude with—a foreign despot who makes no secret of his malignant intentions?

The answer given by the avuncular judge who presided over the trial, a moderate Democrat with a deep connection to his Jewish lineage, thundered across the globe, causing a second international incident just as hundreds of thousands of Nazis were traveling to the Nuremberg Rally of 1935. Adolf Hitler was so incensed by the two-part "insult" from New York that he delivered an historic response on the penultimate day of his festival of hate. The twentieth century had arrived at a hinge moment.

This book is about unacknowledged nonelites who spoke clarion truths to a worldwide audience, acting with an urgency that we now recognize as proper and just. They were nuisances, the kind of public actors whose impolite advocacy inspired eye rolling in the salons of conventional wisdom. Yet they wouldn't have to issue apologies, explanations, or evasions as have so many others in the decades since the end of the Third Reich. They understood the threat. They saw the future. And they issued a call to action.

At the center of our story is Bill Bailey, who dedicated his life to what he called the "never-ending uphill battle to bring about a more rewarding way of life for all humankind." He served as a vaunted member of the Abraham Lincoln Brigade during the Spanish Civil War. He would toil as an engineer on Liberty and Victory ships in the Pacific theater of World War II. He became a celebrated labor activist, tireless in his devotion to the cause of the struggling worker. During the McCarthy era, he was blacklisted from his work as a merchant seaman and hauled before the House Un-American Activities Committee. ("Well, frankly, Mr. Chairman, I don't think that is any of your business.") He quit the Communist Party following the suppression of the Hungarian Uprising and found his place as a longshoreman on the San Francisco waterfront. In his retirement, he marched against Ronald Reagan's economic policies, protested US intervention in Central America, demonstrated against nuclear weapons, and urged young people "to save the universe from smog, filth and disease; to protect the ozone, and prevent the disappearance of the greenbelt."

Bailey was a spellbinding storyteller, a Gaelic *seanchaí* with a Toity-Toid Street accent, a wisdom-imparting man on the mountain who lived for decades in a tiny rustic cottage on Telegraph Hill with a spectacular back-window view of the San Francisco skyline. He had many tales to tell about "getting his head batted in" for the causes of peace and justice in his lifetime of activism. But when he surveyed the record of his accomplishments, he understood the resonance of that July night on the *Bremen*. For a brief instant, he became the personification of a prophetic minority, an "inspired servant of the people," in philosopher Jacques Maritain's description, whose primary work is "to awaken the people, to awaken them to something better than everyone's daily business, to the sense of supra-individual task to be performed."

"I asked Bill once if he thought he'd be remembered after he died," a friend of his, Maria Brooks, told me. "He took the question seriously. He thought for a few moments and said the only reason he might be remembered is that he had been the sailor off the *Bremen*."

CHAPTER ONE

Remember that rainy evening
I drove you out,
With nothing but a fine tooth comb?
Ain't that a shame,
I know I'm to blame,
Bill Bailey, won't you please come home?

—OLD POPULAR SONG

THE FIRST THING to know about Bill Bailey is that Bill Bailey wasn't his given name, a biographical detail that he never disclosed publicly and was only known to a close few. He was born in Jersey City, New Jersey, on June 13, 1915, to an Irish immigrant family living in dire poverty. He was christened Michael Bailey.

In his autobiography, which he self-published with financial help from friends and comrades in 1993, he wrote that the Bailey children were "Isabella, the oldest, followed by John Patrick, Kathleen, Mike, William, and Alice." But according to the 1920 census, the birth order was Isabella, John, Kathleen, *William, Michael,* and Alice. William's age was listed as eleven. Michael was five. At a pivotal point in our story, Mike Bailey will assume the identity of his older brother, but we are getting ahead of ourselves.

The stouthearted matriarch of the family was Elizabeth (née Nolan) Bailey from the outskirts of Waterford in southeastern

Ireland. She arrived at Ellis Island in 1904 with her husband, William Bailey *père*, who had served a stint with the British Army in India. The couple settled in the first city they came upon after passing through immigration, Jersey City, the gritty port on the west bank of the Hudson River across from Lower Manhattan.

Mrs. Bailey—"this beautiful woman," our protagonist called her—gave birth to thirteen children at home with the aid of neighbors or a local midwife. Seven of the children didn't survive infancy. "I only remember one of them," he told an interviewer. "I remember him sitting in a chair. She had placed this little kid in a chair, to keep an eye on him, and I, I think his name was Edward. And she went to the kitchen and all of a sudden this little kid started to shake somehow. And I hollered, 'Hey, Mom, there's something happening,' you know. She come runnin' in and picked the kid up, and that's all I ever saw of him. She took the kid to the hospital, and it was, apparently, I found out years later, something called spinal meningitis." Young Michael had his own bout with infectious disease. He contracted polio, spent several months in the hospital, and emerged with one leg a half inch shorter than the other. He walked with a slight limp for the rest of his life.

The elder Mr. Bailey was a manual laborer with a drinking problem who was always looking for a fight. When he heard a group of impromptu musicians performing the song-and-dance number "Won't You Please Come Home, Bill Bailey," written by Hughie Cannon and published in 1902, he had to be convinced they weren't taunting him. He always found someone to scrap with in bars, at least the ones that allowed him through the door. The police showed up at home the time he bit off half of Stephen O'Riley's ear. The kids would cower in hiding spots when he turned his practiced fists on Mrs. Bailey, who would sometimes have him arrested but wouldn't go so far as to testify in court. She was fearful of losing the scant help he did provide.

Sometime before the 1920 census, Elizabeth Bailey marched the six kids across Jersey City to a tenement a block from the waterfront in an industrial zone called Paulus Hook. Mr. Bailey didn't follow. He will not be heard from again.

The Hudson Street building had no running water, gas, or electricity. Kerosene lamps provided the only illumination. A wood-burning stove generated heat. Across the street was a machine shop that employed hundreds of workers, filling the air with the constant racket of steam hammers, rivet guns, and compressors. The Baileys moved into the top-floor apartment, the farthest from the tenement's lone toilet in the backyard. The neighbors, just slightly better off, were so moved by the family's plight that they donated tattered blankets, scuffed pots and pans, and an old spring mattress that was turned into a makeshift bed for Mrs. Bailey. The kids slept on the floor.

The windows of the decrepit hovel looked out upon an astonishing vista. The Baileys had a view of the busiest maritime hub in the world, a frenzy of barges, floating derricks, sludge boats, coal colliers, lighters, freighters, sightseeing craft, ferries, scows, railroad-car floats, oil tankers, junk boats, and, the most impressive of them all, transatlantic passenger liners cutting through the haze with the entitled air of high-born aristocrats.

Michael was transfixed.

━━━

In the 1920 census, Mrs. Bailey's occupation was recorded as "janitor" for "houses." She was a freelance washerwoman and cleaning lady, toiling day and night to buy the sacks of potatoes, onions, and flour that kept the family alive during the lean times. With help from the older children, she would collect laundry from middle-class families in a nearby neighborhood. The clothes would be boiled in a tub on the Bailey stove, scrubbed by hand on a wooden washboard, and hung out to dry on the line. Sometimes Mrs. Bailey would ride the ferry into Manhattan to work as a cleaner for Wall Street businesses. She also took employment as a kitchen helper at the Catholic parish six blocks inland, St. Peter's, where she retained her faith in God but grew disgusted by his servants.

The priests were "drunken pigs" who would pinch and grab at the nuns.

She made enough money to buy two beds, which were used not for the children but for rent-paying boarders, salty characters who worked maritime jobs on the harbor. There was an old tug-boat captain with a fondness for drink who never made a sound and always paid his rent on time. A ship's fireman from Portugal nicknamed "Spick" was a favorite of the kids, handing out pennies and, after a few drinks, performing the trick of pushing a hatpin through his hand and bicep, which left the youngsters chatter-ing for hours. With the extra money, Mrs. Bailey was able to sup-plement the family's meal plan with the gnarled remnants of a pig—tail, feet, or neck bone—which aroused the interest of the large water rats that were indigenous to the neighborhood. The children would fall asleep listening to them scratching through the wall-pipe recesses in search of a bit of sustenance.

The older boys—John and William—contributed to the family welfare by becoming juvenile delinquents. They began by stealing milk and bread from corner grocers. The middle girl, Kate, found a job in a slaughterhouse, where she pilfered meat products until she was caught one day with a ham underneath her apron. Michael joined the brigade of newsboys selling the *Jersey Observer*. His best day was July 2, 1921—he was six years old—when thousands of boxing fans arrived via the ferries to attend the championship bout between Jack Dempsey and Georges Carpentier at Boyle's Thirty Acres arena in Jersey City. "Read all about it!" he shouted. "All the facts about the big fight!" The family was thrilled when he returned home and dumped handfuls of coins on the table.

Michael learned his first lessons in politics from his mother, a proud Irish patriot with a deep-seated loathing for the British. Her brother back in Ireland, Patrick, was killed by the Black and Tans, the British unit notorious for its criminal brutality, during the Irish War of Independence of 1919–1921. The story went that Patrick was dragged from the family home, stood up against a door, and shot for being a suspected member of the Irish Repub-lican Army. "She told me that as far as she knew the bullet hole was still in the door," Bailey said. On the St. Patrick's Day after the establishment of the Irish Free State, Mrs. Bailey spent money earmarked for food to purchase an Irish flag, which she hung on the end of a flagstaff that extended 10 feet out over the street. "It was my mother's way of shouting her defiance to the New World, which had promised so much but delivered so little."

The young boy was raised on the myths and legends of Irish nationalism, a fighting faith with a tradition for bracing feats of revolutionary theater—the hunger strike (which dates to pre-Christian Ireland), the swearing of an illegal oath in a bogside shebeen, the stirring speech from the dock on the eve of execution. To be an Irish rebel was to be one of the select few with the righteous bravery to rouse the masses from their poverty-induced torpor. In a famous nineteenth-century ballad, which adorned many a tavern wall in the diaspora, Thomas Davis imagined the peasants of Ireland's most impoverished regions emerging into consciousness:

> And if, when all a vigil keep,
> The West's asleep, the West's asleep—
> Alas! and well may Erin weep,
> That Connaught lies in slumber deep.
> But hark! some voice like thunder spake.
> "The West's awake, the West's awake!"
> We'll watch till death for Erin's sake.
> The West's awake! The West's awake!

The Baileys were truly hard-luck. Mrs. Bailey found a second husband, an Irish native who had served with the US Army in World War I, but he was just as drunken, shiftless, and violent as her first. John and William graduated from pilfering milk and bread to stealing much of the inventory from a chandlery, which sold supplies and equipment for ships. Caught by the police, each was sentenced to the youth prison at Jamesburg. John would escape after a few years, fleeing to the western United States and changing his name. He eventually found work on an oil rig and then as a merchant seaman. William would remain incarcerated for the next ten years, leaving his birth certificate and other vital documents behind in the Bailey family apartment. Kate planned to marry a Polish barge worker, but he was killed in a pier accident. She briefly considered joining the convent. Isabella, or Bella, the oldest daughter, suffered from ill health, which made it difficult for her to work very long in the foul conditions of the Paulus Hook factories. She would be in and out of hospitals for years.

Michael had the distinction of being the only child to attend St. Peter's without shoes, which did not endear him to the pugnacious nuns who rapped students' knuckles for the slightest infraction. Informed of the dress-code requirements, Mrs. Bailey told the sisters that Michael would have proper footwear within a few days. But the family couldn't afford it. His shoeless condition was tolerated until he showed up with his legs and feet splattered with foul-smelling mud and grime, the result of an ill-advised shortcut through a polluted canal. The teacher scrawled out a note and told Michael to return to his mother.

Mrs. Bailey, who was illiterate, took the letter to the bartender at Paddy's saloon. Her body stiffened as she listened to him read the message. Michael, the note said, would not be allowed back in class until he was properly clothed and bathed, as the law required. She charged to the school in a fit of rage. Michael trailed behind, just barely able to keep up. Throwing open the door of the classroom, she confronted the nun and demanded to know whether she wrote the note.

"Who the bloody hell do you think you are, with your God Almighty airs, to tell me that I don't keep my boy clean?"

She added: "If you keep whipping my boy the way you have been, I'm gonna come up here and lay that rubber strap across your ass so you know how it feels!"

A conclave was convened in the Mother Superior's office, where a settlement was reached: Michael could come to school without shoes so long as he cleaned up in the washroom before entering class. And Mrs. Bailey would no longer enter classrooms uninvited or use such words as *hell* and *ass* in front of the impressionable students.

A reckoning was thus postponed until Michael was ready to receive his First Communion in the second grade. The preparation period, as any Catholic school kid will tell you, went on for months. Two weeks before the big event, Michael was informed he wouldn't be allowed to receive the sacrament unless he was suitably dressed and shod. A barefoot boy would not be allowed to defile the altar. Mrs. Bailey was so infuriated that she stormed directly to the Mother Superior's office. "The Lord ran around with a burlap sack on his ass," she said. If it was good enough for Jesus, it was good enough for her son. "If you want him to be dolled up, then you get him the clothes and shoes because I can barely get the money to feed him."

A few days later, one of the nuns pulled Michael out of class and took him to the uptown shopping district. He was outfitted in the formal attire necessary to receive the holy Eucharist. The poorest kid in St. Peter's school had his first pair of shoes.

Yet the nuns saw potential in the urchin from Hudson Street. His star shone when a teacher assigned him to sit in front of the class and tell a story from memory. Michael recounted the plot of one of the books that had been read to him by his older sisters. Even he was surprised by his photographic memory. The class was enthralled. Instead of asking another student to perform the assignment on the following week, the teacher urged Michael to recount another of his tales.

His tale-spinning ability was impressive enough to earn him a tryout as an altar boy, which, as the first step to the priesthood, was regarded by poor Irish families as an honor-conferring initiation into the middle class. But Mike Bailey wasn't about to be tamed by the strictures of the Church. He and a few of his fellow trainees, no more than seven or eight years old, were expelled from the ranks when they got drunk on sacramental wine. His profane indiscretion became so notorious that adults sneered at him on the streets of Paulus Hook.

═══

From Jersey City, the Baileys (along with the indolent stepfather) moved to the next town upriver, Hoboken, where Michael was freed from the tyranny of the nuns and enrolled in public school. His favorite teacher, Miss O'Rafferty, recognized him as a talented boy constrained by economic circumstances. She did what she could to keep him off the streets, offering gifts of food and clothing and assigning extra reading projects. The effort was doomed. He fell in with a small gang of fellow troublemakers, young hoodlums who provided initiation in the ways of petty larceny. They unscrewed 100-watt lightbulbs from streetcars, extracted lead pipe from abandoned houses, and pried copper sheeting from municipal depot roofs. The materials were sold to junk dealers for enough hard currency to buy pizza and charlotte russes. Cops had little trouble busting up the syndicate. Upon his first offense, Bailey got two weeks in the Farm for Wayward Boys, where he was treated for diphtheria. The second time he was nicked, he was sent to Wayward Boys for a month of digging ditches. "Shake hands with a pick and shovel," he was told. Before he could be sentenced for his third offense—stealing a suitcase full of silk shirts from in front of a fancy hotel—the Bailey family packed up and crossed the Hudson River to Hell's Kitchen in Manhattan. The Hoboken cops were happy to see him go.

They found a ground-floor apartment in a tenement on West Thirty-Eighth Street between Ninth and Tenth Avenues, in the heart of the infamous neighborhood long reputed to be America's toughest, the cutthroat quarter of warehouses, piers, factories, and rail yards that was a traditional breeding ground for organized crime. Mrs. Bailey arranged to work in the building as a part-time custodian, which meant a substantial break on the rent. She continued to take cleaning jobs wherever she could find them. One callous boss insisted she use lye in the mop water, which, when a splash got in one of her eyes, caused years of sight problems, eventually leading to partial blindness. The stepfather, who felt most at home on a barstool, made every effort to avoid work. He would come home from the taverns and wage drunken battles with Mrs. Bailey, who gave as good as she got. During one violent argument, she pulled a stiletto from a bureau drawer and plunged it into her second husband's lower abdomen. He stumbled out into the street and hailed a cab to take him to Bellevue Hospital. Although seriously wounded, he survived to drink again.

Michael resumed his knockabout ways. He would crawl under the pushcarts on Ninth Avenue and steal shopping bags of fruits and vegetables, which he either sold for a profit or brought to the family table. Sometimes he returned home with nothing more fortifying than a kick in the ass, administered by angry merchants who had caught him in the act. He would walk over to Times Square and hail cabs for theatergoers after the shows let out, pleading for a tip in return. On a good night, he could make a few dollars, which he invariably handed over to Mother. He picked up work as a newsboy. He recalled selling the "Extra!" edition that announced the executions of Sacco and Vanzetti, the Italian anarchists from Boston, on August 23, 1927. He was twelve years old. For fun, he and his pals would sneak into movie theaters through a bathroom window or unlatched back door. In the summer, they would dive off an open pier into the slum version of a swimming pool, the Hudson River. When one of the neighborhood kids drowned after getting his head stuck in a large milk container on the riverbed, Michael swore that he would never again wade into the garbage-strewn waters of his native river.

School interested him less and less until he stopped going altogether. But he would rather be anywhere than the dysfunctional chaos of the apartment. He twice attempted to hitchhike to California, only to be turned around by cops before he got more than a few miles into New Jersey. After his stepfather lunged at him during a family quarrel, he escaped into the subways, spending a few months panhandling, selling papers, and fare beating. He found shelter in the Sixty-Sixth Street station on the IRT line, which he determined was the warmest spot in the system. When he attempted to bum a nickel from a man who turned out to be a police detective, he was arrested for vagrancy and hauled into Magistrates' Court on West Fifty-Fourth Street, the venue of convenience for the small-time crooks and con artists who had been nabbed from Harlem to the Garment District, from Times Square to the piers on the Hudson River. The Tammany Hall magistrate—he didn't recall his name—was unusually sympathetic to Michael's concocted tale about how he raised himself on the streets without the aid of a mother or father. The court officers were stunned when the judge dismissed the charge and ordered the young man to be given an award of five dollars. It was not Bailey's most improbable victory in that gray stone courthouse, nor his last.

By the time he reached his early teens, Michael was 6 feet tall, broad-shouldered and imposing. He was never challenged when he exaggerated his age by five or six years, which was a regular habit. His mother decided it was time for him to get a real job. She cajoled a longshoreman boss who lived in the building, a man named Flynn, "to do something for your own kind and put my lad to work." Michael spent three or four months loading and unloading cargo from ships at the West Side docks, struggling to operate a large hand truck stacked with heavy crates while refusing to pay the kickback money necessary to get a good assignment at the shape-up each morning. He was outraged and humiliated when waterfront toughs demanded a portion of his wages for Flynn's nonexistent "Retirement Fund." His refusal to participate in a corrupt system earned him a defective hand truck, banishment to the worst jobs on the pier, and the contempt of the bent-nose thugs, who sputtered at the young punk: "You think you're better than us?" He quit in disgust.

And anyway, Michael wanted to go to sea. "Ships had always wormed their way into my soul." He'd read every sea story he could lay his hands on. Jules Verne's *Twenty Thousand Leagues Under the Sea* was a particular favorite. He'd dreamed of smoky dens in Port Said and rickshaw rides in Shanghai. "He belongs on a cattle boat going to Australia," a visitor to the Bailey household once said of the idle teenager, which sounded like a good idea to him. But he was also living in a perpetual state of hunger. He knew a seaman's job came with three meals a day, a luxury that was about to grow even more rare with the onset of the global economic crisis.

Left: Mrs. Bailey, holding dog; *right:* Bailey and his mother. (Michael Bailey)

Probably in late 1929 or early 1930, when he was fourteen years old, Bailey decided to visit every pier on the Hudson River waterfront until he found a ship that would take him on as a crew member. He started uptown and worked his way south. No one was interested. Finally, he arrived at his last chance, Pier 1, "way the hell down in the Battery," at the tip of Lower Manhattan. An old freighter named the *Lake Gaither* was preparing to embark for the sulfur ports in Texas and Louisiana.

"So I just happened to go aboard the ship at that time," he remembered. "I guess the mate had an argument with an ordinary seaman. I don't know what the beef was. He fired him and I just happened to be at the right place at the right time. And I stood there lying like hell. Told him I was an experienced seaman, been on all seven seas including the Dead Sea. I could do anything on a ship, blah, blah, and I'm 21 years old. And I've already been on so many ships. And I started naming them off, including Belgian and English ships. And the guy just said, 'Yeah, okay. Come back at 5 o'clock and at 6 o'clock take over the gangway watch.' And from then on I had a job as an ordinary seaman."

Bailey appears in the March 1930 census of merchant seamen as a crew member on the SS *Lake Gaither* of the Newtex Steamship Corp. The entry says he was able to read and write, was born in New Jersey, and hadn't been married. His name was recorded as "Bailey, William."

Michael Bailey had ceased to exist. Bill Bailey was born.

CHAPTER TWO

The ships built in that period surpassed all others in grace, luxury, speed, and size (and have since been bested only in the last category). They were the technical marvels of their time, "the greatest of the works of man," in one writer's phrase, and subjects of intense public fascination. Even people in landlocked little prairie towns—folks who would never see the ocean, much less an ocean liner—knew the ships' names and could tell them apart in photos with ease. The big ships were international celebrities in a way that no man-made object is today. Owners, builders, passengers, and spectators alike assumed that their ascendancy would continue forever.

—MICHAEL ANTON

I N THE YEARS leading up to World War I, Germany emerged as a formidable maritime power, challenging the supremacy of even the mighty ruler of the waves, Great Britain. Kaiser Wilhelm II's naval fleet grew to include more than three hundred modern warships, a fearsome arsenal of battleships, cruisers, destroyers, torpedo boats, and U-boat submarines. The German merchant fleet—the array of civilian ships carrying cargo and/or paying customers under the national flag—was led by two of the most impressive passenger liners on the seas. The 52,000-ton *Imperator* was the world's largest ship upon its maiden voyage from Hamburg to New York in 1913. A year later, its sister ship, the 54,000-ton *Vaterland*, seized the crown as the grandest expression of industrial and scientific might on the planet.

Then came the Great War. By the end of four years of conflict, Germany's oceangoing capacity was reduced to next to nothing. According to the punitive strictures of the Treaty of Versailles, signed on June 28, 1919, the German Navy was permitted eight obsolete battleships, eight aging cruisers, sixteen destroyers, sixteen torpedo boats, and a handful of auxiliary ships. U-boats were forbidden. The merchant fleet was decimated by 90 percent, its vessels lost during hostilities, confiscated in foreign ports, or seized under the terms of the treaty.

The two venerable German shipping companies—Norddeutscher Lloyd (North German Lloyd line, or NDL) and Hamburg-Amerikanische Packetfahrt-Actien-Gesellschaft (Hamburg-America Line, or Hapag)—were left with little of value. The North German Lloyd's *Kronprinzessin Cecilie* was seized by the United States government and turned into a troop transport ship, the USS *Mount Vernon*. NDL's *Kaiser Wilhelm II*, once the fastest ship in the world, became the USS *Agamemnon*. The great *Imperator*, a Hamburg-America Line property, was eventually taken over by the British and rechristened as the Cunard liner *Berengaria*. Hapag's *Bismarck*, which wasn't completed when the war broke out, became the White Star Line's flagship, *Majestic*. The masterwork of German shipping, the *Vaterland*, was seized from the Hamburg-America Line and transformed into the luxe passenger liner of the United States Lines, the *Leviathan*, remaining in service until the mid-1930s.

If a nation-state's strength can be judged by its presence on the world's waterways, Germany was pitifully weak in the aftermath of its defeat in the First World War.

Yet even as Germany struggled through the early years of the Weimar Republic—the unsteady experiment in democratic governance that followed the abdication of the Kaiserite monarchy—the rebuilding project commenced. National pride was at stake.

With the help of government subsidies and American loans, both Hamburg-America and North German Lloyd began placing orders for new vessels. "Resuming service, their small ships seemed merely to dog-waddle in the water while fabulous German-built ships under new names, with new oil burners, raced past them en route to New York or Southampton," according to one writer. By the middle of the decade, a handful of German passenger liners in the 20,000- to 30,000-ton range had entered transatlantic service. Then, in December 1926, North German Lloyd announced the beginning of construction on two superliners, the *Europa* and the *Bremen*, both of which would have the capability to cross the Atlantic at an average speed of 27.5 knots, a record. Shipping experts scoffed. "They claim that in addition to the tremendous cost," explained the *New York Herald Tribune*, "a liner equipped with engines driving propellers developing 27.5 knots would be subject to terrific vibration which would not only interfere with the comfort of passengers but would lessen the life of the ship."

The *Europa* was built in the Blohm and Voss shipyard on the Elbe River in Hamburg while the *Bremen* was fabricated in the A. G. Weser yard on the Weser River in Bremen. Thousands of workers in each port were employed in the immense task of assembling the frames, shaping the hulls, erecting the decks and superstructures, and installing boilers, shafts, and propellers. Security was tight to prevent prying eyes from getting a glimpse of the showpieces before they were ready for public inspection. On successive days in mid-August 1928, the ships were launched into their respective rivers following festive naming ceremonies attended by cheering thousands.

In recognition of its position as the new flagship of the German nation, the *Bremen* was christened by Paul von Hindenburg, the revered field marshal from the First World War, with large, drooping mustache, who had been elected to the presidency of Germany three years earlier. He arrived in an open car with his state secretary, his son (a major in the German army who served as his aide-de-camp), and the director general of the North German Lloyd line. The city of Bremen was resplendent in flags and bunting. Stores and factories were closed for the occasion. The crowd gathered along the banks of the Weser was estimated at 100,000. The old general, who was wearing a dark overcoat and top hat, strolled with his entourage up a ramp to a dignitary-filled reviewing stand perched next to the ship's bow.

"When the hard conditions of the Treaty of Versailles robbed Germany of its entire merchant marine, German shipping, supported by the Reich with great sacrifices, went to work with unbroken courage and in a firm trust in the future, rebuilding what had been destroyed and taken," President Hindenburg intoned into the microphone in a deep, calm voice. "German shipping has never lost faith in the new German future on the sea, even in the most difficult times.

"May this ship convey the German will of friendly cooperation to peoples over the ocean and may it be another bond uniting us with transoceanic lands," he continued. "May it remind us that only united in strength and dedicated to a single aim will we guarantee for ourselves an independent position in the world.

"I christen thee with the honorable name *Bremen*," he said. "Happy voyage!"

The newspapers offered conflicting accounts over whether President Hindenburg, then age eighty, smashed the champagne bottle against the bow using his own strength or pressed an "electric button" triggering a mechanical device that performed the function instead. Either way, the ritual was completed.

"Like a thunderclap, a shout of joy arises from the crowd in a holiday mood," according to an official history of North German Lloyd. "Slowly the giant steel moves. Majestically it slides into foaming water amid noisy acclamations, the waving of handkerchiefs and applause. The most magnificent ship ever to cross the seas under the German flag has entered her element. Days of popular festivity begin in the city of Bremen."

At this moment in history, Adolf Hitler was a regional demagogue writing a sequel to his poorly selling manifesto *Mein Kampf*. He wanted to cleanse German society of Jews, "the bacillus and fermenting agent of all social decomposition," and establish a

"The most magnificent ship ever to cross the seas under the German flag has entered her element." (Deutsches Schiffahrtsmuseum, Bremerhaven)

racially homogenous utopia populated by biologically superior exemplars of the "Aryan" race. He dreamed of rebuilding the German military in defiance of the Versailles Treaty and launching wars "to secure for the German people the land and the soil to which they are entitled on this earth." But his Nazi Party had garnered a mere 2.6 percent of the vote in the most recent federal elections. The annual party rally in Nuremberg had been canceled. Even propaganda chief Joseph Goebbels was skeptical when Hitler claimed that the public's opposition to the Nazis' message was an "almost mathematical reason for the eventual, certain triumph of our movement."

Both the *Europa* and the *Bremen* conducted brief river tests before being placed in fitting-out berths for the nearly yearlong job of finishing construction, which focused significantly on interiors. The rumor was that both ships would embark on their maiden voyages together, crossing the Atlantic side by side and breaking the speed record as a tandem. But in March 1929, a fire broke out on the *Europa*, causing such massive destruction that there was talk of scrapping the ship altogether. Although the *Europa* was saved, its completion date was pushed back by several months. The center stage would be occupied solely by the *Bremen*.

The hype built throughout the spring and early summer of 1929. "Every day 7,500 men are at work on her, hammering, polishing, carpentering, and painting to get the ship ready for service before the end of the midsummer ocean traffic," it was reported. Articles were published about the *Bremen*'s high-tech innovations and leisurely comforts. It would have its own seaplane, which would be catapulted from a launch pad on the top deck, enabling stacks of mail and perhaps a distinguished passenger or two to be delivered to port several hours before the ship docked. Bets were taken on whether the *Bremen* would have enough kick to seize the Blue Riband—the award given to the passenger ship in regular service with the fastest crossing of the Atlantic—from Cunard's stately *Mauretania*, the glory of Great Britain, which had held the honor for twenty-two years.

On June 24, the *Bremen* was completed. It left its fitting-out berth and made the passage 40 miles downriver to Bremerhaven, the small harbor on the North Sea that would be its homeport. Over the next few weeks, the ship conducted sea trials in preparation for the big day. "It was breathtaking—a once-in-a-lifetime experience, but far, far too short," wrote a traveler named Wilhelm McLean, who caught sight of the beauty during its preparation runs. "It was hard at that first short meeting to really describe the *Bremen*, other than that she was a gigantic greyhound—modernistic, dynamic, long and low, the most advanced ship on the oceans, the only express liner to have only two squat funnels." On July 9, the ship was hauled into dry dock for one last finishing touch, a final coat of paint on its underbelly.

The ship weighed 51,656 tons, was 938 feet long (more than 3 football fields), and 98 feet wide. Its most prominent exterior features were the bulbous, drag-reducing bow, which one commentator felt was suggestive of a *gemütliche deutsche Hausfrau* (cozy German housewife); nearly 7-foot-high electrified letters spelling out BREMEN on the sundeck; and two short, wide smokestacks (later heightened) that exhaled so much soot and grime that some thought they resembled the snout of an angry sea monster. Many observers used martial metaphors to describe the look of the new ship, which, a leading maritime author wrote, had the "cut and audacity of a destroyer."

The interior was lauded for its modernist cool, which was conceived by a team of architects and decorators led by such German luminaries as Paul Ludwig Troost, Bruno Paul, and Fritz August Breuhaus de Groot. Forgoing the ostentation of an earlier generation of German steamships, the *Bremen* took its inspiration from the geometrical austerity of the Bauhaus school. Indirect lighting, dark-hued mosaics and murals, and modish furnishings enhanced the ambience. This was not an overstuffed stage set for a Wagner opera. We were now in a Germany that was meticulous, efficient, and, some felt, unwelcoming.

The ship featured a bowling alley; a palm-filled winter garden; a children's recreation space with lacquered wooden slide; electric and Turkish baths; a rifle range that projected motion picture images of flying birds onto a target screen; a hair salon; a barber shop; a writing room with quotations on the walls from American authors; a billiard room; six dining rooms; a series of lounges, smoking rooms, ballrooms, and cabarets; top-deck tennis and shuffleboard courts; an à la carte restaurant; a saltwater swimming pool illuminated with underwater porthole lamps; a printing shop that published a daily newspaper with a circulation of two thousand; a library stocked with the finest in world literature; a gymnasium; a hospital with operating room and medical ward; a movie theater; and a long avenue of fancy shops likened to Fifth Avenue or the rue de la Paix in Paris. A forbidding oil painting of Hindenburg, scowling, adorned the wall along the main stair-case. "Bars rather predominate throughout the ship, there being a bar even in the swimming pool," noted a reporter. The final tally: Twelve bars.

The *Bremen* could accommodate 2,200 passengers—800 in first class, 500 in second, 300 in tourist, and 600 in third, where passengers were lodged in cabins containing two to four berths. With the exception of a few of what were known as bachelor rooms, the cabins in first class came with such amenities as private showers and toilets. The ship had four bronze propellers (each weighing 20 tons) powered by four single-reduction steam turbines (generating a total of 130,000 horsepower at full speed) fed by a battery of oil-fired boilers housed in two large plants below decks. "If muscles alone drove this ship, as once they drove the triremes of Rome, the engine rooms would have to house all the population of Philadelphia," wrote the journalist Eric Hodgens. The fourteen watertight bulkheads made the *Bremen* "practically unsinkable."

A crew of 950 kept the entire enterprise afloat under the paternal gaze of the much-respected captain, Leopold Ziegenbein, who first went to sea as an apprentice on a sail-powered barque during the last decade of the nineteenth century. They were officers, petty officers, navigators, stewards, pursers, helmsmen, cadets, carpenters, electricians, deck clerks, repairmen, wipers, firemen, oilers, machinists, watertenders, pumpmen, storekeepers, joiners, locksmiths, coppersmiths, boilersmiths, braziers, fitters, plumbers, laundry managers, secretaries, maids, upholsterers, butlers, mess boys, chefs, sous chefs, butchers, bakers, ice carvers, scullery boys, waiters, doctors, nurses, orderlies, radio operators, fitness instructors, hairdressers, and bellboys in brass-buttoned jackets and pillbox hats. Franz Koennecke was the bandmaster, responsible for directing his musicians in the oompah-pah classics and stirring choral ensembles required for German social gatherings. A dashing twenty-seven-year-old Lufthansa flyer named Baron Jobst von Studnitz was assigned to pilot the seaplane. Gertrud Ferber was listed as head of the travel office, but her real job was hostess and personal secretary to Captain Ziegenbein, a title that possibly might require a wink.

On July 16, 1929, the inaugural journey began with another round of celebratory pomp. The on-deck band blasted out the German national anthem. "*Deutschland, Deutschland über alles, über alles in der Welt,*" the crowd sang ("Germany, Germany above all—above everything in the world"). The *Bremen* maneuvered into the North Sea and steamed to the English port of Southampton, where 118 passengers joined the 1,375 who had boarded in Bremerhaven. Heavy fog delayed the trip across the English Channel by several hours. When the ship reached Cherbourg on the Cotentin Peninsula in northwestern France, another 175 passengers boarded. The vessel then turned toward the New World. At just after noon on Thursday, July 18, the *Bremen* crossed the Cherbourg breakwater and the race for the Blue Riband was on.

The whole of Germany was following along, listening to updates via the novelty of ship-to-shore radio transmission. Several American newspaper correspondents had booked passage and were sending wireless dispatches back to the States, which were read with avid interest from coast to coast. "A message to the *Evening Post* from Russel Crouse, the columnist, who is aboard the *Bremen* told today of the great ease with which the ocean greyhound is slipping through the Atlantic," read one incisive report. Over the first twenty-four hours, the ship experienced a stiff northwest wind and rough waters but still crossed 687 nautical miles, which beat the *Mauretania*'s best single day (676 miles) by 11 miles. After the turbulent start, the *Bremen* cruised to the record. From Friday (the 19th) noon to Saturday (the 20th) noon, the ship traveled 704 miles. From Saturday to Sunday (the 21st), the distance was 706 miles. On the fourth and final day, Monday, July 22, the *Bremen* traversed 713 nautical miles, a breathtaking accomplishment. After the ship passed Nantucket Light at 7:52 a.m., Russel Crouse sent a dispatch to the *Post* announcing that "Germany's new queen of the seas" was "nearing the end of the fastest voyage across the Atlantic Ocean ever made by a passenger vessel."

The ride was so smooth that Dr. William O'Neil Sherman of Pittsburgh performed emergency abdominal surgery on a

Mrs. Edward Adams while the liner was zipping along at more than 28 knots. It was "like operating in a hospital," he later testified.

At 1:05 p.m., 20 miles east of Fire Island off the southern shore of Long Island, the seaplane was catapulted from the top deck. Studnitz (assisted by radio operator Karl Kirchoff) piloted the silver-winged Heinkel on a half-hour flight to Pier 4 in Brooklyn, where the *Bremen* would dock for the next three years until moving to a custom pier on the West Side of Manhattan. Studnitz waved to the crowd below, flew across the harbor to dip the plane's wings in respect to the Statue of Liberty, and then returned for another pass. He dropped the plane into the oily waters, taxied to the pier, and stepped ashore to loud cheers. US Post Office employees grabbed six mail sacks from the cockpit and hauled them into the back of a truck bound for Manhattan, from where they would be mailed even before the ship arrived, a PR coup of the first order.

"The catapult worked perfectly," the flying baron told the waiting press. "In less than eighty feet we had been impelled to a speed of sixty miles an hour."

At 3:02 p.m., the *Bremen* reached Ambrose Channel Lightship at the mouth of the Lower Bay of New York Harbor, which marked the official conclusion of a transatlantic crossing. The trip from Cherbourg breakwater had taken 4 days, 17 hours, and 42 minutes, which bested the *Mauretania*'s record by eight hours and 52 minutes. The average speed was 27.83 knots but that was nothing, said Captain Ziegenbein. "We did not extend the ship's engines at any time," he said. "We hope to make better time on future trips."

Dozens of boats sounded their whistles and sirens in a cacophonous gesture of welcome as the liner pulled into the quarantine station off Staten Island, a necessary first stop for every arriving steamship. A pennant-and-banner-bedecked cutter was waiting with the city's official welcoming committee (led by Police Commissioner Grover A. Whalen) and the Street Cleaning Department band. "The reception given to the *Bremen* at anchor off the Quarantine Station was the most spectacular from the number of craft present since the late President [Theodore] Roosevelt returned from his big-game hunting trip to South Africa in the liner

Kaiserin Auguste Victoria in 1910," reported the *New York Times*, which, like the rest of the New York papers, gave voluminous front-page coverage to the ship's arrival. After the ceremonial sonorities and medical inspections were completed, the *Bremen* passed through the Narrows into the Lower Bay and steered to Pier 4 on the Brooklyn waterfront, where thousands of spectators crowded the streets hoping for a glimpse. The cheering didn't stop until the first gangway was jostled into place.

At 7:16 p.m., a nationwide musical program on the Columbia Broadcasting System (CBS) was interrupted so that Captain Ziegenbein could address the radio listeners of America.

"I am happy," he said, "to be the commander of a ship which I believe will be a splendid addition to the fleet which connects America and Germany. Good night."

Over the next four days, the *Bremen* was host to a glittering profusion of functions and receptions. So many visitors wanted to tour the Germanic wonder during its layover that ticket sales were halted at fifty-two thousand, which led to a brisk trade in counterfeit passes. James J. "Jimmy" Walker, the flamboyant and corrupt mayor of New York, was ushered aboard for an exclusive luncheon in the ship's nightclub with North German Lloyd brass, the German government's consul general, business leaders, and various Tammany Hall *machers*. Since Prohibition was the law of the land, Walker christened the seaplane with a bottle of ginger ale, but everyone knew that alcoholic beverages were readily available on non-American ships. The mayor, who was famous for his disregard of Prohibition laws, was having such a good time that he cleared his schedule and spent hours reclining in the bosom of the ship's comforts.

On Friday, July 26, 1929, the *Bremen* commenced its first return trip with the custom observed by all the European passenger liners servicing the world's busiest port. Instead of departing before noon, which would require travelers coming from out of town to find overnight accommodations, the ships threw midnight sailing parties. Hangovers were thus nursed somewhere approaching the Newfoundland banks. The galas had become boisterous adjuncts

to Metropolitan nightlife, chic diversions from the mundane celebrated in a popular song by big band maestro Tommy Dorsey.
"You're sailing at midnight," warbled singer Edythe Wright in a
slow dance tune that featured the mournful lowing of Mr. Dorsey's
muted trombone. "I'll be on the pier . . . ."

First-class ticketholders zipped through the darkened streets
in a phalanx of motorcars, heading toward the glowing vision on
the river's edge. They arrived in formal wear following a night
that already included a visit to the theater and/or supper club.
The men might be outfitted like an Irving Berlin song—"dude-in'
up my shirt front / Puttin' in the shirt studs / Polishin' my nails."
The women were in full-length evening dress with ermine wraps,
pearls, and perhaps a tiara or two. They jostled through the terminal, passed through customs, endured the check-in procedure,
and deposited stacks of luggage (steamer trunks, tennis rackets,
hatboxes, golf bags) with surly porters who expected a healthy
tip in return. The voyagers then strolled onto a leviathan that
was crisscrossed by high-powered arc lamps and ringing with the
sounds of an on-deck orchestra. A reporter assigned to monitor
the comings and goings might step forward and ask a question of
anyone deemed newsworthy enough for tomorrow's papers.

The *Post*'s man on the scene for the *Bremen*'s first midnight
sailing noted that Mayor Walker boarded to say farewell to Albert
Teller of the Ritz-Carlton, Police Commissioner Whalen joined
the party with a squad of thirty policemen, and Sherwood Ander-
son, the celebrated American author, was forced to travel in third
class because no other accommodation could be found.

In the perpetual effort to attract new customers, the shipping
companies encouraged nonpassengers to indulge in the ballroom
dancing, stateroom soirées, and champagne toasts of midnight
sailings. Yet friends and family members weren't the only ones
who paid a small fee and squeezed onto the ship to bid a jaunty
adieu. Instead of listening to the radio or going to the movies,
curiosity seekers would flock to the pier to catch a glimpse of the
glamour. "Visitors pay their dimes, troop through their separate
wickets and board by the visitors' gangplank," wrote a nightlife

reporter. "Once aboard they mix with the crowd, and nobody knows their status." It wasn't unusual for the number of guests to exceed passengers by four to one.

At fifteen minutes before midnight, the ship's horn released a deep-throated bellow, a sonorous warning of impending cast-off that was audible for miles around, a sound that "carried with it the whole history of departure, longing, and loss," wrote E. B. White. Stewards circulated with the iconic shout of "all ashore that's goin' ashore!" Deckhands clamped down hatchways and unfastened towlines. Guests elbowed toward the exit spans while booked passengers fought for positions along the rail, hoping for a good vantage point to hurl streamers, shout promises to write, wave handkerchiefs, and break down in sobs. The captain and his officers kept watch from the bridge, maintaining the sobriety necessary to launch the behemoth upon the waters.

As the *Bremen* prepared to go, many of the departing guests "tottered, rather than walked, down the gangplank, and a rendition of *The Watch on the Rhine* on the upper deck was wobbly in the high spots," wrote the *Post*'s correspondent.

In such a fraught and anarchic atmosphere, a state of suspended animation resonant with the uncertainties of tomorrow, the whole world seemed alive with possibility.

CHAPTER THREE

You've weathered the storms upon the deck,
O, Toilers of the Sea;
You've fallen in the fire-holes
In the days that used to be.
But now the times must change about,
A New Day must appear
When all you Toilers of the Sea,
Begin to see and hear.
—INTERNATIONAL WORKERS OF THE WORLD ANTHEM

BILL BAILEY WAS a strapping fourteen-year-old with a fifth grade education when he talked his way into a job on an undistinguished freighter called the *Lake Gaither*, "a slow ship, a real tramp as the word goes." He would later recall that it was "freezing" when he embarked on his maiden voyage, which likely means that he joined the crew in late 1929 or early 1930, in the first months after the stock market crash sent the world reeling into the Great Depression. He came on board with a single change of clothes and a toothbrush.

On that first trip, Bailey quickly revealed himself as a novice who knew nothing about life at sea. He was shocked to discover that the *Gaither* didn't drop anchor when darkness fell. "How can the ship sail at night?" he wondered. "How can they see?" Assigned to keep watch on the bow—his job was to communicate the position of lights on the horizon by striking a bell in sequence—he fell asleep. "Where the hell is that dumb son of a bitch!?" came the shouts from the bridge. When he took over the wheel for a few minutes of relief duty, he promptly steered the ship off course. "Get the hell back up to the bow," the mate barked, "and don't ever come up here again while I'm here."

The ship unloaded its cargo in Houston, where Bailey was offered his first glimpse of Jim Crow. He was appalled by water fountains marked "whites only" and "colored only," which he called his "awakening to discrimination." During the *Gaither*'s stop in Texas City to pick up loads of raw sulfur, a member of the Industrial Workers of the World (IWW), a Wobbly, visited bearing copies of the union's propaganda sheet, the *Industrial Worker*. Once a formidable radical organization that sought to establish "One Big Union" to seize the means of production and abolish the wage system—i.e., end capitalism—the IWW was now struggling, losing members to the growing influence of the Communist Party. Bailey took a copy of the paper, which contained a reprint of the IWW preamble. "The working class and the employing class have nothing in common," it began. "There can be no peace so long as hunger and want are found among millions of working people and the few, who make up the employing class, have all the good things in life." He wasn't sure what "class" meant—like a class in school?—but he was stirred by the notion that the struggling many could challenge the powerful few.

After returning to New York, he was hired on his second ship, the *El Lago*, bound for New Orleans, where he experienced another milestone in a sailor's life. While sipping an orange soda at a French Quarter bar, a sex worker sidled up and promised a hot time for three dollars. Claiming he only had one dollar, Bailey was allowed upstairs to lose his virginity but forbidden from indulging in what she called "that 'round the world stuff,'" which in practical terms meant he was barred from removing his shirt and shoes. As he ambled back to the ship with weakened knees, he imagined the delectable possibilities of a "round the world" engagement. "I'd have plenty of time to find out," he thought.

"Going to sea in those days was a lonely life," he'd remember. "You had no radios on the ship. You had nothing. You got on ships with 15, 20 men in a room. Didn't even have a porthole. A toilet running all night. Constant noise. Sometimes the decks where you slept were wet. Guys coughing all night long with TB and other diseases. Some guy snoring. Lights going off and on. How the hell could you ever get a night's sleep among these things?

"Sometimes a guy would get up in the middle of the night and pull out a bucket of clap medicine from under his bunk," he continued, referring to the solution of potash that was injected into the penis to treat gonorrhea in the days before penicillin. "The gun would sometimes be laying in the bucket like an old mop. They'd get up. 'Oh, doctor's orders. Here it is two o'clock. I better give myself a shot.' He'd pull up the syringe, put it in his pecker, and clap! And if you woke up and you heard clap, clap, you'd know it was Andy giving himself a dose of the red potash."

Bailey felt immediately at home among the briny characters of the American merchant marine, an obstreperous lot of "thieves, smugglers and users of narcotics, dirty and crummy in person, dirty and revolutionary in speech," as the president of the International Seamen's Union said of them in 1922. "Showboat Quinn, Boxcar Flaherty, Overcoat Duffy, Blackie Myers, Blackie Torch—everyone was either Whitey, Blackie, Heavy," remembered Haskell Wexler, who went to sea as a young man before embarking on a career in Hollywood. "These guys were tremendously resourceful, intelligent, good storytellers. Well read, many of them. But you'd hit a port and they would get stupid-drunk, lose their money, get rolled. Every childish, vulnerable thing that could happen to a human being would happen to sailors." The typical ship included a multinational crew of experienced travelers who, whatever their other qualities, were preternaturally attuned to the political currents roiling the globe. "They were the gypsies of the sea, the last of the romantics, fiercely independent," according to memoirist

Helen Lawrenson, who would later become acquainted with Bailey's crowd. "Jack London termed them 'the alley cats of the world,' and *Fortune* magazine said of them, 'You are dealing, in fact, with the true proletariat of the western world, the homeless, the rootless, and eternally unmoneyed. They are tough, knowing, free.' This was only partially true. Their home was a ship. They spent their money in waterfront bars and shipped out with the slogan 'One turn of the propeller and all debts are paid.' They were true internationalists. They sailed the world; they drank and talked and argued with men of all nations and races; they knew the score."

=====

Following his service on the *El Lago*, Bailey landed on the beach in New York without a job. The maritime industry was suffering just like the rest of the economy and waterfront "crimps," the corrupt boardinghouse operators who served as hiring agents for shipping companies, wouldn't grant him a precious job unless he patronized their establishments. ("There was a famous guy who ran a whole business in Red Hook, Al Gomez, I think it was," Bailey said. "He said, 'Why the hell should I give you a job? You don't lay up with my whores. You don't drink in my gin mill. You don't even eat in my restaurant. I've got a hundred guys who do all this. Why should I give you a job?'") With little else on offer, he snuck aboard a passenger liner bound for Florida, hoping to get a job on an oil tanker sailing out of Tampa. Once the ship was under way, he presented himself to the captain as a stowaway, hoping, in the custom of the sea, to be permitted to work for his passage. Instead, Bailey was handed over to police in Jacksonville and sentenced to thirty days in the city's penal farm for vagrancy. There, he befriended a group of migratory laborers who had been caught up in a sweep on the same charge, part of the bedraggled tribe of hobos and tramps who traveled the railroads in large numbers during the Depression.

Upon release from the penal farm, he joined them on the rails, a big city teenager with a Hell's Kitchen accent stepping into a John Steinbeck novel or Woody Guthrie song. On the "rattlers," he was schooled by wisecracking mentors to decipher the meaning of whistle blasts, avoid decapitation from slamming boxcar doors, wield a needle and thread to mend frayed clothes, comprehend region-specific lingo that described a locomotive as a "pig" in one place and a "hog" in another, and judge the most propitious instant to hop off—such as when the train decreased speed to climb a hill or enter a yard. On foot, he begged meals from farmers and café owners, always offering to work for a little grub. He endured lengthy sermons at Christian-run flophouses in exchange for shelter. He hung out in hobo "jungles," the vagabond encampments with communal stewpots located near every rail hub. He spent many a night among the despised in the local jail, sometimes surrendering himself to the sheriff in hopes of a warm bed for the evening.

At last he reached the port of San Francisco, where he planned to find work on a ship. But the hiring halls were full of unemployed seamen. "Musta been a thousand guys sitting around playing pinochle." He panhandled for spare change, cadged stale bread from bakeries, and joined the long lines at the soup kitchen. Bailey found himself intrigued by the message of a young Communist who stood on a chair in front of one such establishment and preached about the ills of a wealthy society that forced men to line up like "whipped dogs" for a watery bowl of soup. He would never forget how three cops attacked the man, knocking him to the ground and kicking him in the chest for the crime of speaking "a raw truth." In desperation, Bailey came up with the idea of taking the ferry across the bay to Oakland, where he would knock on wealthy families' doors and offer to perform odd jobs for thirty or thirty-five cents an hour. After three or four months, he had twenty dollars in the bank, a veritable fortune.

With little chance of hiring on with a ship, he rode the rails on a three-week journey back to New York, where he was subject to the galling taunts of his stepfather. "This is not your boxcar where you can lay around all day." He sought shelter with a friend who introduced him to homebrew liquor, which he embraced in the family tradition. It wasn't long before he was sleeping on the sidewalk and receiving swift kicks from policemen on their morning rounds. With a pal, Bailey resumed his criminal pastime of extracting resalable metals from empty buildings. Their big score was a five-story warehouse owned by Broadway luminary George M. Cohan, which was full of props, scenery, and costumes from years of productions. Bringing in a third conspirator to help with the heavy lifting, the vandals ripped up walls and floors, removing every trace of lead, brass, and copper they could find. A man tending pigeons on a nearby roof informed the police of suspicious intruders.

Bailey spent six harrowing weeks in the notorious city jail known as the Tombs, where he watched an inmate climb to the top of the tier and leap to his death four stories below. One of Bailey's sisters, Kate, arranged a meeting with Mr. Cohan, the composer of "Give My Regards to Broadway" and "Yankee Doodle Dandy," who agreed to write a letter to the judge asking for leniency. The judge wasn't swayed. Bailey was sentenced to a year in an upstate reform school, where he distinguished himself as a stand-up guy who could take a beating from stick-wielding guards without whine or whimper. His enthusiastic embrace of manual labor—he was quite good at digging ditches—earned him accolades from the administration, which promoted him to plumber's assistant and cellblock trustee. His fellow prisoners appreciated that he was no "stool pigeon," probably the most reviled phrase in his vocabulary. With his sentence winding down, Bailey wrote a letter to the parole board, declaring that he would never again return to such a place. He was revolted by the presence of rapists who set upon elderly women at night and dragged them into dark alleys. "The idea of even being in with them, being near them, made me feel filthy."

Bailey was sixteen or seventeen years old when he was released (with six weeks off for good behavior) into a world that was descending further into the Great Depression. The unemployment rate in the United States had risen to 24 percent by 1932. More than 13 million Americans had lost their jobs in the three years since Bailey signed on with the *Lake Gaither*. The governor of

New York, Franklin Delano Roosevelt, was heading for an easy victory over the unpopular president who was leading the country through the disaster, Herbert Hoover. Bailey was unsettled to learn that his mother had joined the crowds on the bread line. "Everybody is doing it," she told him. "It's the least this bloody country can do for me."

He received permission from his parole officer to hitchhike up to Boston, where he spent a few hungry months trying to hire on with a ship. Eventually, the chief engineer of a battered vessel called the *John Jay* asked him whether he could "fire a boiler."

"Sure can," Bailey responded.

He ventured into the maze of pipes, taps, and valves below the ship's waterline to assume his place as a fireman. It was a bottom-rung (if essential) task typically reserved for the toughest characters on the boat. Steamship firemen were "generally intemperate," according to shipping lore, and they drink "a great deal of spirits." His job was to tend the fires in the boilers that produced the steam to power the turbines, which in turn powered the series of shafts and gears that spun the propellers. He toiled in a chamber of sweat and grime at the very depths of the laboring condition, "working like a dog, eating oil and fumes and stuff like that, filthy all the time, soaked with oil." The quintessential fireman, or stoker, was Yank in Eugene O'Neill's play *The Hairy Ape* (1922), who was portrayed as a barely articulate embodiment of the working class dehumanized by the cruelties of modern society. "Put one of 'em down here for one watch in de stokehole, what'd happen?" Yank says, referring to a passenger in first class. "Dey'd carry him off on a stretcher. Dem boids don't amount to nothin'. Dey're just baggage. Who makes dis old tub run? Ain't it us guys?"

Bailey began to sail into international waters, where he learned that conditions in other parts of the globe were worse than in the United States. During his time as a fireman on the black gang of the *Southern Cross* passenger liner—he was the only native English speaker in a fo'c'sle (crew living quarters) of twenty men— he docked in a number of South American ports. "You'd get off a ship and some little kid would come up and say, 'Hey mister, you want my sister?' I mean they were so hungry they'd do any-thing, ready to sell their souls." In London, he was taken aback at how beggars would leap after cigarette butts, "pushing and el-bowing each other out of the way." On a United States Lines ship, he visited Weimar Germany, where the unemployment rate was 35 percent or higher in 1932, fueling the discontent that turned the Nazi Party into a mass movement. Bailey was inspired by the fighting spirit of the Communist longshoremen (their fist-raising parades, their lung-bursting songs) and outraged by the brutality of Nazi storm troopers, who were "already running all over Ger-many, punching people out, kicking windows in, attacking Jews.

"I was beginning to see the poverty of people no matter where you went, no matter what port," he said. "I was only used to the poverty of Hell's Kitchen, or my own poverty in Hoboken or Jersey City. You don't think the whole world was full of that until you got to visit it and found it no matter where you went. . . . So then you figure, what the hell is going on here? And these are the types of things you wonder about, and you start asking yourself questions."

CHAPTER FOUR

Our flag is fluttering before us,
Our flag is the new age,
And the flag leads us into eternity!
Yes, the flag means more than death!
—HITLER YOUTH MARCHING SONG

F OR THE FIRST three and a half years of the *Bremen*'s existence, which represented the final three and a half years of parliamentary democracy in interwar Germany, the ship was largely insulated from the troubles at home.

The transatlantic passenger trade suffered an inevitable slump with the arrival of the Depression, but the *Bremen* maintained its status as the Queen of the Atlantic. The principal rivals were its sister, the *Europa*, and the pride of Fascist Italy, the *Rex*, which became famous for its vast open-air sunning and swimming areas: the birth of the Lido Deck. Benito Mussolini regarded the *Rex* as "a monument to Italy." Although the British and French began work on new national liners to challenge the Germans' supremacy, both ships were set back by the severity of the economic crisis. Construction was halted on the *Queen Mary*, the majority of its workforce laid off. The *Normandie* sat in its fitting-out dock for nearly three years.

Newspapers avidly recorded the *Bremen*'s latest record-breaking crossings and printed the names of the rich and famous on its passenger lists. On a not-atypical journey to Europe in the spring of 1931, the ship was graced by the starry likes of "Mary Pickford, who is going to France to join her husband, Douglas Fairbanks; Noël Coward, actor and playwright, who this week finished an engagement with the play *Private Lives*; Lillian Gish, stage and screen star; and Edith Fleischer of the Metropolitan Opera Company." By the summer of 1932, the *Bremen* had carried 147,890 passengers, an average of 2,498 for each of its fifty-nine round trips. Articles appeared occasionally about partygoers who failed to heed the "all ashore" warnings during midnight sailings and found themselves headed across the ocean without luggage or passports. In late 1932, when a now-forgotten Broadway superstar named Marilyn Miller became an involuntary stowaway along with a dashing screen actor famous for "Latin lover" roles, the story produced international headlines. Ms. Miller's mother told the wire service that it was "possible that they have been or are going to be married on board the ship." The *Washington Post* put the article on page one.

The papers didn't think to note that the final destination on the celebrity couple's trip—Germany—was so debilitated by political instability that it was practically ungovernable. The country had endured five major elections during the course of 1932, confirming that the National Socialist German Workers' Party—popularly called the Nazi Party—was the largest party in the Weimar system but did not enjoy majority support. In the Reichstag election of November 1932, the Nazis garnered 33.1 percent of the vote, followed by the Social Democrats (20.4), the Communists (16.9), the Catholic Centre (11.9), the conservative German National People's Party (8.3), and the center-right Bavarian People's Party (3.1). With a private army of 400,000 Sturmabteilung (SA) brownshirts and Schutzstaffel (SS) blackshirts under his command, Adolf Hitler spent weeks in backroom negotiations in an attempt to be named chancellor (head of government) by the president (head of state), who was vested with considerable powers over the fraying democracy. On January 30, 1933, President Hindenburg, now age eighty-five, made the tragic decision to appoint Hitler as chancellor over a coalition government of conservative nationalist parties. "It was," wrote Joseph Goebbels in his diary, "like a dream, a fairy-tale."

The new chancellor, who was forty-three years old, persuaded the old president to dissolve the Reichstag and call new elections, which were set for March 5. Hitler was determined to deploy the powers of the state to win a popular mandate for his iron rule. While he crisscrossed the country delivering harangues against the evils of "Marxism and its accompaniments," the National Socialist mob, now an auxiliary police force, was directed to focus its attacks not on the hated Jews but on left-wing opponents, whether they were Jews or not. The Social Democrats and, in particular, the Communists felt the brunt of the onslaught. Rallies were disrupted. Opposition newspapers shuttered. Party officials were attacked, detained, tortured, and occasionally murdered.

On February 27, a fire broke out in the Reichstag, which the Nazis claimed without proof was the first act in a Communist revolution. On the following day, Hindenburg's shaky hand signed the emergency decree that ended freedom of speech, assembly, and press, an essential step on the path to dictatorship. Thousands of leftists—Communists, Socialists, trade unionists, intellectuals—were rounded up and confined in "protective custody." Nearly all of the Communist Party's Reichstag deputies were arrested. On March 3, Ernst Thälmann, the leader of Germany's Communist Party, was seized in his secret headquarters in Berlin. Yet when the returns came in on March 5, the Nazi Party had still been denied a majority, collecting 43.9 percent of the vote. Although Nazi propaganda celebrated a resounding "victory for the national revolution," Hitler was still dependent on the non-Nazi parties in his conservative coalition, which received 8 percent. He would not be able to get rid of "that gang," he muttered on election night, until the old man was dead.

Every public or private institution that survived the initial phase was subject to the Nazi program of *Gleichschaltung* (forcible coordination), which sought to replace all vestiges of degeneracy with a pure National Socialist spirit. Passenger liners were a priority in the nazification campaign. The new government sought to establish a *more* rigid control over shipboard employees than would be possible with citizens within the Reich. Crew members were to be "bearers of the Kultur of National Socialist Germany in foreign countries" and "worthy representatives of National Socialist Germany wherever the German flag waves." The regime wanted model Hitlerites docking in New York: men and women who could withstand the "infamous agitation" about "alleged atrocities" now being broadcast in the media of democratic societies, said Rudolf Hess, Hitler's deputy, in a speech in Hamburg.

Just 11.5 percent of German seamen were loyal to Hitler at the time of his accession, which meant that a cleansing was in order. Within a few years, more than half of the sailors on the tourist vessels had been replaced with enlistees indoctrinated at training academies in German port cities, where they received instruction from Nazi tutors. The management teams of the Hamburg America and North German Lloyd lines were similarly purified. The two companies became fully nazified entities assigned to provide foreign countries with "a picture of the true situation in Germany" and to "deny senseless rumors and lies," according to one of the new executives. All matters relating to personnel were now the purview of the Nazi Party.

On board, the crew of the *Bremen* was divided into cells in accord with job assignments and bunk locations. Each cell had a *Zellenleiter* (cell leader), a graduate of the School of Leaders for Seamen and Germans Abroad in Altona, who was taught "to reply clearly, objectively, and quick-wittedly even to the most stupid question" about the Nazi creed. The school in Altona gave lessons in racial problems, economics, international relations, labor law, and so on, all interpreted through the lens of the National Socialist *Weltanschauung* (worldview). Guidance was provided in the use of weapons. Cell leaders were versed in "duties of control"—to them was left the job of ensuring that every sailor participated in the "intellectual straightening" necessary "for their common work."

The ship was assigned an ideological director, its own *Führer*, who was responsible for overall party discipline. For at least a portion of the prewar years, Erwin Schulwitz held the position. He was an officer of the SA brownshirts who'd been hardened by three years in a Russian POW camp during the Great War. Brash and vain, he maintained direct supervision over the dozens of ideological Nazis who were distributed throughout the ship's departments. Although he wore civilian clothing, he goose-stepped around the public areas with little care for the sensibility of travelers, many of whom were non-German. Schulwitz's hatred of Communists was said to be virulent even by Nazi standards.

Enlightenment was dispensed during propaganda meetings that were held in the crew recreation area far from the passenger decks. *Echo der Heimat*, a quarterly newsreel chronicling the latest progress from Germany, would be screened alongside more artful presentations, such as Leni Riefenstahl's documentaries on the grandeur of Nazism. The "Horst Wessel Lied," the violence-celebrating Nazi Party march, was sung after the traditional "Deutschland über Alles." Special gatherings would be convened on Adolf Hitler's birthday (April 20) and the anniversary of the failed Beer Hall Putsch of 1923 (November 9). Of the lectures on National Socialist themes, shipping line officials assured Berlin that they were "well-attended."

A popular speakers' topic was "The History of the Swastika," which sought to educate the crew on the core icon of the Nazi Party. The motif of four interlocking arms bent at right angles is common to many cultures, known as the *manji* in Japanese, *wan* in Chinese, *tetraskelion* or *tetragammadion* in Greek, *svastika* in Sanskrit, and *Hakenkreuz* (hooked cross) in German. Its design has been found in the artifacts of the Druids, pottery shards from ancient Greece, sand paintings of the Navajo, on the walls of the Christian

catacombs in Rome, and carved into the rock-hewn churches of
Lalibela, Ethiopia. The swastika occupies a revered place in Eastern religions. In Hinduism, the four arms have been interpreted
to stand for the four aims of human existence—righteousness
(*dharma*), wealth (*artha*), love (*kama*), and liberation (*moksha*).
Buddhists believe that the constant motion suggested by the spin-
ning wheel represents the Buddha's never-ceasing compassion
and wisdom, the quintessence of his holiness.

Nazi legend tells us that Hitler first encountered the Hakenkreuz as a schoolboy at the Benedictine monastery in Lambach,
Austria, where he received singing lessons from 1897 to 1899. It
was claimed that the young Führer became transfixed by several
swastikas embedded within the church's architecture, particularly
the prominent one carved in stone in the ornamental gateway.
"The swastika here in our abbey impressed itself upon the child,"
his music instructor claimed decades later, "and the little Hitler
dreamed of it endlessly."

The *Bremen* lecturer would describe how the hooked cross was
the gang sign of a pureblooded race of Nordic supermen known
as the Aryans, who were alleged to have distributed the swastika
throughout the world in the midst of prehistoric conquests. The
myth has its roots in a fin de siècle movement of occultists and
pseudo-scholars with fantastical beliefs about ancient Germanic
glories, cranks like Lanz von Liebenfels, whose supremacist organization, Ordo Novi Templi (Order of the New Templars),
hoisted a swastika flag in 1907 "as a sign of battle and victory of
the Aryan ethnic spirit." During his years as a struggling artist in
Vienna (1905–1913), Hitler was an avid reader of pan-Germanic
publications that promoted the ideas of Guido von List, who
wrote that the swastika was the mark of the Germans' savior, the
"strong one from above," who would be sent to restore the purity
of the Aryan race by preventing mixed marriages with "parasitic"
Jews and launching an "Aryo-German world war" to "regain the
master privileges which were so cunningly taken away from the
master race."

In the period immediately following World War I, Hitler joined the German Workers' Party (DAP)—soon to be renamed the National Socialist German Workers' Party (NSDAP, or Nazi Party)—which evolved out of the Thule Society, an organization of mystical anti-Semites that had as its emblem a dagger superimposed over a swastika. The Nazis' in-house expert on such matters was a dentist named Friedrich Krohn, a Thulean with an extensive library of racist literature. In May 1919, Dr. Krohn wrote a memorandum entitled "Is the swastika suitable as a symbol of the National Socialist Party?" which proposed a prototype of the Nazi flag, but with a left-facing or counterclockwise version of the swastika.

The lectures on the *Bremen* would necessarily include a reading from *Mein Kampf*, which discusses the importance of distinctive symbols to political success. "All those who busy themselves with the tastes of the public will recognize and appreciate the great importance of these apparently petty matters," Hitler had written. "In hundreds of thousands of cases a really striking emblem may be the first cause of awakening interest in a movement." By early 1920, he had become immersed in the process of finding a distinctive identifier for the Nazi Party, at about the time far-right militias, such as the Ehrhardt Brigade (active from 1919 to 1920), were employing the swastika as an adornment. "The question of the new flag, that is its aspect, occupied us very much in those days," Hitler wrote. White was out. "It is suitable for associations of chaste virgins, but not for world-changing movements in a revolutionary epoch." So was black. It wasn't "thrilling enough." White and blue? White and black? Neither combination would "attract attention to the movement." The black, red, and gold of the Weimar Republic (1919–1933), which Hitler regarded as a criminal state of backstabbing "Judeo-Bolsheviks," was "a bed sheet of the most disgraceful prostitution." But the black, red, and white of the Second Reich (1871–1918), under which Hitler had fought as a soldier on the Western Front, created "the most resplendent harmony that exists." This "previous composition," however, couldn't be retained.

Early Nazis were assigned to come up with a prototype that used the imperial colors but was more pleasing to the racist eye and heart. "Yet I had to reject, without exception, the numerous designs that in those days were handed in by the circles of the young movement and that mostly had placed the swastika on the old flag," Hitler wrote. "I myself as the leader did not want to come forth immediately with my own sketch, as it was quite possible that someone else would produce one that was just as good or even better. In fact, a dentist from Starnberg produced a design that was not bad at all, and approached my own design very closely, except it had the one mistake that the swastika was composed in a white circle with curved hooks. Meanwhile, I myself, after innumerable attempts, had put down a final form: a flag with a background of red, with a white circle, and in its center, a black swastika. And this then was kept."

Dr. Krohn of Starnberg claimed that Hitler had flipped his left-facing (counterclockwise) swastika, which he said signified good fortune, into a right-facing (clockwise) swastika, a mark of annihilation in his interpretation. He quit the party in 1921.

Hitler had been giddy with the result. "We ourselves had an almost childlike joy when a faithful woman member had carried out the design for the first time and delivered the flag." The "effect was the same as if we had dropped a bomb." Here was the "best incorporation of the movement's intention," a "sign of conflict in opposition to the Jewish 'Star of David,'" a visual delineation of the Nazi Party program: "In the red we see the social idea of the movement, in the white the national idea, in the swastika the mission of the fight for the victory of Aryan man, and at the same time also the victory of the idea of creative work, which in itself is and will always be anti-Semitic."

Over the period of the Nazis' climb from fringe obscurity to national power, the swastika would become the central feature of the elaborate pageantry that defined the Nazi sensibility. The malign image was held aloft by rows of uniformed men during torchlight parades, mass rallies, street demonstrations, and *völkisch* festivals.

It was affixed to propaganda posters, draped from speakers' podiums, sewn into armbands, imprinted onto helmets. "Millions are looking upon the swastika full of hope," the cadres sang. "The day of freedom and of bread dawns!" Hitler Youth enlistees swore an oath to do their duty "with love and loyalty, for the Führer and our flag." A Nazi bard wrote: "Germany must truly understand / We intend to raise our banner / Over German sea and German land."

The most honored of swastika flags was the Blutfahne (Blood Flag), which was allegedly stained with the blood of Andreas Bauriedl, one of the sixteen Nazis killed during the Beer Hall Putsch in 1923. The artifact was protected by an SS honor guard at the Nazi Party headquarters in Munich and brought out each year for the sinister *Fahnenweihe* (consecration of the flags) ceremony at the Nuremberg Party rally. With an air of solemnity, Hitler walked along columns of uniformed men accompanied by Jakob Grimminger, the SS officer who was the Blood Flag's official bearer. The Führer clutched the tip of the flag in his left hand and applied the accursed fabric to newly commissioned regimental banners, thereby serving as the medium through which the essence of Nazism was transferred.

Swastika flags were to be treated with reverence. They could not be left unattended. They could not be rested against a tree or a building. They were to be prevented from ever touching the ground, a sign of defeat. *"Das Banner Muss Stehn Wenn Der Mann Auch Fällt"* was the message of a propaganda poster showing a collapsing man holding up a pole flying a tattered swastika flag. *The banner must stand even if the man falls.* No Jew or Communist was allowed to even *touch* the symbol of the movement.

The average Nazi Party member, the German writer Hilmar Hoffmann noted, regarded the swastika flag as a proxy for Hitler, "who was, as it were, present in every fold." An attack on the swastika, then, was a strike against the Führer himself.

Hitler often boasted that he would make the swastika the national flag of Germany. But in the aftermath of the election of March 5, 1933, he understood the necessity of maintaining cordial relations with the conservative nationalists represented by the figure of President Hindenburg, who was a living monument to the kaiser years. Hitler wasn't yet in a position to declare that the Nazi Party *was* Germany.

At two p.m. on March 12, the Reich chancellor addressed the German people over the nation's radio airwaves. He began reading the text of Hindenburg's new flag decree, which formally retired the black, red, and gold of the Weimar Republic. In Hitler's voice, Hindenburg announced that "until a definitive ruling on the national colors" the black, red, and white of imperial Germany and the swastika flag of the ruling Nazi Party "would be hoisted in common.

"These flags unite the glorious past of the German Reich and the puissant rebirth of the German nation," he said. "Unitedly they shall embody the power of the state and the imminent interconnection of all the national sections of the German people."

A *definitive ruling on the national colors* would have to wait for the *imminent interconnection* of the German people.

A new order was coming. But it hadn't yet arrived.

On the *Bremen*, according to a decree issued by the Reich minister of the interior, the old black, red, and white tricolor of the kaisers was to be flown from the gaff of the after mast, the elevated rear-ship placement reserved for the flag declaring the vessel's nationality. Hitler's pride, what he called the flaming torch of his crusade, occupied the number two position, flapping from a staff at the bow, the forward-most extremity of the huge liner. The swastika now led Germany's ship of state. It pointed to the future.

CHAPTER FIVE

To trade with Germany is to trade with the enemy of civilization. To travel on a German ship is to travel under the emblem of the swastika, the mark of the beast. To wear a German-made garment is to put on a garment of shame. To buy a German-made toy is to help a government which has flaunted every decent human sentiment, tramped under foot every value sacred to civilization, substituted force for law, terror for justice, blood for brotherhood and war madness for the great peace hope of an harassed humanity.

—EDITORIAL STATEMENT OF THE NON-SECTARIAN
ANTI-NAZI LEAGUE TO CHAMPION HUMAN RIGHTS

T HEN, THEY CAME for the Jews.
In the propaganda-fueled euphoria that followed the March 5 elections, the grass roots of the Nazi Party was allowed to unleash its pent-up rage against the 500,000 Jews of the Reich, who made up less than 1 percent of the population. Uniformed storm troopers who represented the "base" of the party converged on Jewish-owned businesses, which they picketed, vandalized, ransacked, and daubed with swastikas. "Since Monday I have been bombarded by telephone calls and telegrams concerning the boycotting of Jewish stores," said Hermann Goering, the corpulent

World War I flying ace and Nazi stalwart given vast powers in the new government, on March 10. "As Police Commissioner I refuse to let the police be protective troops for Jewish merchants."

Homes of prominent Jewish citizens were searched and looted. Hundreds of Jews were attacked in public places. Synagogue windows were smashed. Headstones in Jewish cemeteries were overturned. Rabbis were insulted, paraded through the streets, and taken into custody. Targeted with particular venom were members of the legal profession, a reviled class in the Nazi imagination with the ability to hinder the systemization of the racial utopia. Jewish judges and lawyers were dragged from courthouses in dozens of locations and told never to return to the administration of justice. The death toll stood at a few dozen by the end of March.

Although editorial pages throughout the United States expressed shock at the "tide of Nazi fury" (the *Poughkeepsie News*), many media outlets were willing to accept that the stories were the product of "exaggeration" and "wild rumors." Ernst Hanfstaengl, the Nazis' foreign press spokesman, told reporters, "The chancellor authorized me to tell you that these reports are every one of them base lies." The American public was more preoccupied with the flurry of economic initiatives introduced by the new administration of President Roosevelt, who declared in his March 4 inaugural address, "The only thing we have to fear is fear itself." The headlines about legislative efforts to repeal Prohibition were set in larger type than those about the actions of the Hitler government. The prevailing attitude toward global affairs was: keep us out of it.

But a dogged minority emerged like the coastal watchmen in the Book of Ezekiel, who were impelled by God to blow the trumpet and warn the people upon first sight of the "sword upon the land." The movement arose from the more combative quarters of the Jewish community and the far left of the political spectrum, a disputatious collection of individuals and organizations with only partially overlapping agendas. These dissenters didn't merely denounce Germany's behavior. They had the countercultural temerity to call for concerted measures to drive the Nazis from power. The international struggle against Hitler's Germany—which would conclude when a "Grand Alliance" of armies and air forces converged upon Berlin in an unimaginable future only twelve years away—began with a nonviolent protest against its artifacts on the world stage. The most prominent targets of the activists' ire were the swastika-flagged seagoing vessels that were recognized as avatars of the German nation. The war started with the *Bremen*.

=====

By the third week of March, 1933, a militant faction in Jewish communities in every part of the globe was calling for a worldwide boycott of German goods, services, and ships, a position opposed by many Jewish leaders as a needless provocation that would endanger Jewish lives in Nazi Germany. The idea was that the pitiful German economy, which was still dependent on foreign trade, couldn't withstand the shock that would result from the precipitous loss of overseas capital. The German people would respond to the obvious failure of the new regime by insisting on a less oppressive form of government. Whatever its merits, here was a real plan to topple the dictator.

On March 23, seven hundred members of the Jewish War Veterans, who represented the vanguard of the boycott effort in the United States, led a march from New York City's Lower East Side to the steps of its City Hall, where a delegation presented Mayor O'Brien with a set of resolutions that included a call for "all citizens" to shun the German shipping lines.

The boycott supporters from the Jewish community—many of them staunch anti-Communists—found themselves in uneasy alliance with left-wing radicals who recognized the existential danger posed by Hitler and didn't hesitate to organize clamorous demonstrations and rallies to urge the public to "Stand Up and Act!"

While the Jewish War Veterans and its allies were marching to City Hall, a group of protesters gathered several blocks to the south, in front of the offices of the North German Lloyd and the Hamburg America shipping lines. The contingent of seamen from the Communist-led Marine Workers Industrial Union carried signs calling for "a struggle against the fascist terror" and distributed a statement that decried the Nazi government's use of "fascist thugs" to purge the *Bremen* and other German liners of left-wing sailors, who "were the strongest sections of the forces fighting Hitlerism."

On the same day, March 23, Hitler took another decisive step in the establishment of a totalitarian dictatorship. With all of the Communist deputies and many of the Social Democrat deputies detained in police custody—some of them in a newly opened "concentration camp" at Dachau—the Nazi Party pushed the Enabling Act through the Reichstag, permitting the Führer to rule Germany without any significant constraint from the legislature or the president. Passage was achieved with the votes of conservative nationalists from the Hindenburg faction and Catholic moderates who hoped to protect the Church from Nazi interference. "You can take away our liberty and our lives, but not our honor," said the chairman of the Social Democrats, Otto Wels, in his speech from the floor. "No enabling law gives you the power to destroy ideas that are eternal and indestructible." The final vote was 441 to 94. All of the no votes were cast by the Social Democrats in attendance, the death rattle of parliamentary democracy in Hitler's Germany.

After the success of the "Law to Remedy the Distress of the People and the Reich," the formal title of the Enabling Act, the Nazi leadership began plotting how to respond to the bad publicity over the anti-Jewish campaign. On March 25, Hermann Goering appeared before a gathering of foreign correspondents and condemned the media reports as "atrocity myths." Some Jewish shops were "temporarily closed" but there had been no instances of looting, he claimed. "Jewish business men in Germany can go about their affairs in peace." Synagogues and Jewish cemeteries have been left untouched. He conceded "sporadic cases" of violence against Jewish individuals and institutions but claimed, ludicrously, that "severe measures" were taken against the offending brownshirts. "If Jewish citizens keep within certain limits," Goering warned, "then nothing will happen to them under the new government."

On the same day, Goering summoned leaders of the German Jewish community and insisted that they contact Jewish groups abroad to deny the stories and urge the cancellation of any form of public protest or boycott. He said he couldn't guarantee the safety of German Jews if his orders were refused. "We unequivocally demand energetic effort to obtain an end to demonstrations hostile to Germany," wrote two prominent German Jewish leaders in a cable to the American Jewish Committee, which, along with the American Jewish Congress and the B'nai B'rith, was one of the "big three" Jewish organizations in the United States. A delegation of German Jews flew to London to deliver the message in person. "We want to emphasize that in all cases known to us," according a statement from a German Jewish federation, "the authorities have proceeded vigorously against excesses wherever this has been possible."

In fact, German Jewish organizations were privately admitting that the anti-Jewish disorders were *worse* than the media was reporting.

On March 26, the US government did its part for the Führer, issuing a statement under Secretary of State Cordell Hull's name that conceded "considerable physical mistreatment of Jews" for a short time but asserted that such unpleasantness "may be considered virtually terminated." Yes, there "was also some picketing of Jewish merchandising stores and instances of professional discrimination," but these "manifestations were viewed with serious concern by the German government," which pledged to maintain law and order. Secretary Hull said he expected the situation "will soon revert to normal."

Let history record that the FDR administration's first statement on Nazi Germany was actually a defense of Hitler's methods.

On March 27, the American Jewish Congress hosted a national day of prayer, fasting, and protest, which explicitly did *not* call for a boycott of Nazi Germany. The centerpiece of the day was a rally at Madison Square Garden. Some twenty thousand spectators packed the arena to hear an ecumenical array of speakers beseech Nazi Germany to end its anti-Jewish activities. Traffic was snarled for blocks around by thirty-five thousand latecomers, who listened to the addresses over loudspeakers set up on flatbed trucks or walked to an impromptu rally a few blocks north, where orators denounced Nazism from a second-story balcony. A million more people in the United States and another million in Europe tuned in on the radio. Similar rallies were held in dozens of cities across the country.

The speakers avoided any mention of an economic war against the Hitler regime. There was no talk of a concerted campaign against representations of Nazism.

The Führer was livid over the protests. He didn't distinguish between those who supported the boycott and those who opposed it, between those who were only interested in raising a protest and those who wanted to materially harm the regime.

In response to "this Jewish international campaign of hatred against Germany," the Nazi government announced its first formal anti-Jewish measures, which were characterized as *defensive* steps against "the intellectual movers and beneficiaries of these treasonable machinations, most of whom are Germans of Jewish origin." The raucous anti-Semitism of the storm troopers was rewarded with the systematic anti-Semitism of official pronouncement. Hitler assured his cabinet that he was replacing the uncontrolled outbursts of the street hooligans with the reasoned actions of a government bureaucracy. First, a committee led by Julius Streicher (a Nazi Party leader from Nuremberg who published the foulest anti-Semitic newspaper in the land, *Der Stürmer*) would organize a centrally coordinated boycott of Jewish stores, bringing "order" to the ongoing process of excluding Jews from the German economy. Second, legislation would be enacted to restrict "the admission of Jews to certain academic professions and public institutions," which would coordinate and supplement a regulatory process ongoing in local and regional areas to drive Jews from the Reich's communal life.

The news that Hitler was reinstating legal discrimination against Germany's Jewish community, which had been granted full civil rights in 1871, appeared above the fold on page one of the *New York Times*. He wanted the world to know he was a hostage-taker who wouldn't hesitate to harm his hostages.

Yet the regime *was* concerned about a movement from abroad that could hinder the country's economic recovery, a necessary prerequisite for Hitler's crackpot ambitions.

Although originally intended to last three days with the option to restart if the bad press from abroad didn't cease, the Berlin-organized boycott of Jewish businesses was just a single day of infamy—April, 1, 1933. The "official" boycott was much like the "unofficial" boycott. Nazis surrounded Jewish shops, carried menacing signs, smashed windows, scrawled swastikas, attacked passersby. But the government was careful not to be too disruptive of market forces. Large Jewish companies with thousands of employees, such as the Ullstein publishing conglomerate and Tietz department stores, were left unmolested by the anti-Semitic gangs. "It was understood tonight," the Associated Press reported on April 1, "that industrial circles were pressing upon the Nazis not to permit resumption" of the boycott.

A week later, the first of the so-called April Laws were passed by the Reichstag, which sought to remove "non-Aryans" from the civil service, judiciary, educational system, and medical administration. Still, exceptions were allowed. Thousands of Jews were able to remain employed, if precariously, due to the personal intervention of the old man. At the urging of President Hindenburg, Hitler agreed to exempt Jews in service since before the World War, "who fought at the Front for the German Reich or its Allies in the World War, or whose fathers or sons fell in the World War," according to the text of the Law for the Restoration of the Professional Civil Service. Jewish doctors were not stripped of their licenses but barred from facilities in the national health insurance system. Instead of expelling all Jewish students from schools and universities, a quota was established to keep their numbers low. The Shoah was as yet in its natal phase.

Even as the decrees and promulgations continued over the following months—disbarring Jewish journalists, academics, creative professionals, farmers, etc.—the Reich chancellor understood the need to keep anti-Semitic agitation from becoming too unruly. It was time to construct the German juggernaut without interference from the forces of moral outrage. "One should not irritate it, when it is not necessary to deal with it," Hitler told district governors, referring to the international conscience. "To reopen the Jewish question would mean to start a worldwide uproar again."

———

His most dedicated adversaries could not be lulled into thinking the worst was over. On the morning of April 14, they were waiting at Pier 4 in Brooklyn when the *Bremen* crossed Ambrose Lightship and steamed into New York Harbor carrying the first Nazi luminary to reach American shores, Hans Luther, the new German ambassador to the United States. A group calling itself the Committee for Action Against Fascism—which included delegates from the Communist Party, the Conference for Progressive Labor Action (led by the radical Christian pacifist A. J. Muste), the Workmen's Sick and Death Benefit Fund, and other left-wing organizations—was hosting an unofficial welcoming party for Hitler's top man in America.

In the customary practice when a dignitary arrived on a steamship, a group of reporters took a cutter down the bay and boarded the ship at the quarantine station in the Narrows. Otto Kiep, the German government's New York–based consul general, docked at about the same time on a tugboat chartered to spirit Ambassador Luther from the *Bremen* and save him the embarrassment of facing the demonstrators at Pier 4.

Short, bald, and bespectacled, Dr. Luther, age fifty-four, was a former president of the Reichsbank who served as finance minister and, briefly, Reich chancellor during the Weimar years. He had been looking forward to his inaugural session with American reporters. Earlier in the morning, he strolled up to the bridge and practiced his lines on a *Bremen* officer, who later described the scene for a reporter from the *New York Herald Tribune*. Of the status of Jews in Germany, Luther planned to say: "What would you do if a group of people came to America from such foreign countries as India or Afghanistan and preached a doctrine of politics not compatible with the principles of American government? What action would you take?"

Consul General Kiep reached Luther's stateroom suite ahead of the reporters and informed the ambassador that Berlin demanded he maintain diplomatic silence.

Once the twenty or so reporters were escorted into the suite, Kiep announced in his thick accent that no questions would be taken.

The reporters vigorously objected, pointing out that other nations' ambassadors had no problem engaging with the press.

Luther, visibly uncomfortable, sought to make small talk. "I hope our relations will always be cordial," he said to the group.

"Yes, we know all that," said the man from the *Times*. "But is it true you are being hurried ashore because there is some fear of a Jewish demonstration?"

Luther turned red with indignation and refused to answer.

"No! No!" Kiep exclaimed. "Herr Luther is in a hurry to get to Washington on important matters."

"The trains leave every hour," a reporter responded.

Kiep then began reading from a prepared statement.

At this, Luther "strode brusquely across the parlor of his suite," the *Chicago Tribune* reported, and snatched the paper from Kiep's hands.

"Please permit me," Luther said. "It is my statement. That you shall not read. If I cannot talk, I shall read this statement, for it is my statement.

"At the moment of my arrival it cannot be my task to make an ample statement on the conditions in Germany," Luther read in part. "I only wish to emphasize that the outward life there is just as normal and orderly as could be desired and was in fact very little upset by the events of the last weeks whilst the inner political life of the nation has undergone a profound change."

With an escort of six agents from US Department of Justice, Luther was loaded onto the tugboat and transported across the water to Jersey City, where he caught the first train to Washington.

During these weeks, the boycott gained its most prominent champion, Samuel Untermyer, a seventy-five-year-old lawyer and civic leader of fabulous wealth and failing health, a gruff eminence of the Democratic Party and leading Jewish organizations who was famous for his relentless interrogations of John D. Rockefeller and J. P. Morgan during bygone legal proceedings. Untermyer was enraged by the news that Henry Morgenthau Sr., one of America's most respected Jews, had boarded the *Bremen* on May 2 and sailed to Europe as President Roosevelt's envoy to a League of Nations conference. During a speech at Symphony Hall in Boston that declared his support for "an effective boycott that will teach the German people that we Jews have not lost our self-respect," Untermyer attacked the FDR administration for the "thoughtless indifference" and "gratuitous affront" of choosing the *Bremen* for official government business.

Untermyer was invited to become the president of a newly formed boycott organization, the American League for the Defense of Jewish Rights, which he soon reorganized into the Non-Sectarian Anti-Nazi League to Champion Human Rights (NSANL). Although many Jewish leaders remained skeptical of his bellicose style, Untermyer enjoyed pushcart-level support from the poor immigrants (or their children) from Eastern Europe and Russia with a collective memory of the pogroms. NSANL's archives bulge with testimonials from neighborhood synagogues, Hadassah chapters, union locals, Young Men's Hebrew Association branches, Yiddish theater troupes. Untermyer was a pillar of the establishment who said he opposed street agitation as "not in keeping with the dignity of the movement" but privately admitted he was supportive of the actions of the more radical wing of the anti-Nazi cause. "Whilst our organization does not and cannot from motives of policy support picketing, and has taken every opportunity of so explaining, between you and me we are glad that it is being done, and hope it will continue," Untermyer wrote in a letter to his son. "It has had very effective results."

At around dawn on May 25, demonstrators began gathering at Pier 4 in Brooklyn to welcome the next prominent Nazi dignitary to sail into New York Harbor, Hans Weidemann, a painter and musician who held a senior post in Joseph Goebbels's Ministry of Public Enlightenment and Propaganda. The *Daily Worker* had called upon the "workers of New York" to "meet this representative of fascism in the proper manner." Over the early morning hours, the crowd grew from a few hundred to upward of a thousand. Among the soapbox orators was a man from the Food Workers Industrial Union, who surely spoke of Hitler's latest act of *Gleichschaltung*, the eradication of all trade unions on May 2. "WEIDEMANN, BLOODY HITLER AGENT, MUST GO," a large banner read. There were shouts of "Get the men who are murdering the Jews!" and "Down with Hitler and the Nazi murderers!" Some in the assembly sang the "Marseillaise," the French revolutionary anthem: "*Contre nous de la tyrannie / L'étendard sanglant est levé*" ("Against us tyranny's / Bloody standard is raised").

The New York Police Department (NYPD) deployed a force that included roughly fifty uniformed cops and fifty plainclothesmen, many of them detectives from the Bureau of Criminal Alien Investigation, the counter-subversion unit popularly known as the Red, or Radical, Squad.

At Quarantine, Weidemann and his bow tie–wearing assistant, Gotthold Schneider, informed the press that they were merely Hitler's emissaries to the Chicago World's Fair. Asked whether he supported "the punitive measures taken against anti-Nazi artists, scientists, writers, and Jews," Weidemann responded: "I wouldn't formulate the matter quite in that fashion, but I certainly approve the program of the Hitler government." The reporters all noted that Weidemann was wearing a swastika pin in the buttonhole of his coat. At 8:10 a.m., the liner docked at Pier 4. After a short conference with NYPD detectives and German consular officials in the captain's quarters, the two Nazis were hustled by city cops to the first-class gangplank, down a winding stairway to the front landing, and into a tugboat, which whisked them off to Manhattan and away from their antagonists. "Weidemann," the *Brooklyn Eagle* reported, "seemed bewildered at what was happening."

The NYPD then ordered the demonstrators to "go back to Second Avenue"; that is, to the Jewish neighborhood of the Lower East Side. When the response was "Down with Hitler!" and "To Hell with the Cops!" the bluecoats launched a vicious assault upon a peaceful protest. Newsreel footage shows policemen on foot and horseback charging into a chaotic melee, throwing punches and swinging clubs at cowering men and women. "A stool pigeon in a grey suit and a well-fed body," one of the protesters wrote of a Red Squad detective who had infiltrated the gathering, "took pride in pointing out workers for arrest and 'indoor' beatings." The anti-Nazis fought back with whatever was close at hand—bricks, bottles, stones, broom handles, fists. Blood flowed freely. "A semblance of order was restored," the Associated Press reported, "after police drew their pistols and leveled them at the rioters."

Seven men and seven women were arrested for charges ranging from felonious assault to disorderly conduct. Two of the righteous troublemakers were not yet out of their teens: They were Flossy Girchgell (17), and Rose Zaretsky (16).

The mainstream press regarded the "Communists," as the protesters were described without differentiation, as responsible for causing the "riot"; and saw the NYPD as merely doing its job in using force to shut down a disreputable gathering. The view taken by the protesters that the cops were "American fascists" using "Hitler tactics" to defend a Nazi whose "hands were dripping with blood" was not shared by the wider society.

Weidemann, who eventually fell out with Joseph Goebbels, would go on to serve with the elite Waffen-SS during World War II. His commanders hailed his "exemplary" work on the Eastern Front, where the Waffen-SS was instrumental in mass killings of the Jewish population of the Soviet Union.

The seamen and longshoremen who participated in the early morning rally were heeding the exhortation to "fight fascism on every dock." They had been hearing stories about port workers in distant cities who refused to unload cargo from German ships unless tyranny's bloody standard was removed from its perch. The trend appears to have started in Antwerp, where delegations of left-wing longshoremen met with German captains and demanded that they "strike the flag" to keep trade flowing. When the master of a German steamer called the *Uganda* refused, "the sailors and dockworkers together went ahead and hauled it down themselves," according to a report in the *Marine Workers Voice*, the organ of the Marine Workers Industrial Union. Reports of similar successes came in from Gdynia, Barcelona, Göteborg, Copenhagen, and Buenos Aires. In Seville, the captain of the German freighter *Klio* made the mistake of replacing the swastika with the banner of the recently deposed Spanish monarchy, which so angered the antifascist longshoremen that police had to be called in to restore order. "The captain has decided not to raise any more flags here," the United Press reported, "even if he never gets his boat unloaded."

By the summer of 1933, the action-now coalition included immigrant Jews distributing petitions calling for a complete cessation of trade with Germany and leftists from a range of factions shouting about Nazism's evils on an endless protest march. In the troughs of the Great Depression, when the average American was preoccupied above all with securing a livelihood, the nuisances were demanding that the wrath of worldwide condemnation be brought to bear on the troubling situation in Hitlerland. But in the language of a US State Department message sent to anyone who expressed concern about the plight of German Jews, "Careful note has been taken of the views embodied in your letter and you may rest assured that this department is most carefully following the situation therein referred to."

The newspapers never failed to quote from the uncompromising message of Samuel Untermyer, who had emerged as the worldwide spokesman of what reporters always called the "Jewish boycott." With his trademark orchid in the lapel of his coat, this "ruthless little man," as an opponent once called him, mounted esteemed platforms to thunder in apocalyptic language about the necessity of waging a crusade against "the evil forces of a reborn, barbaric bigotry and fanaticism of the Middle Ages." Like few other figures in public life, he could see the future, evoking a grim vision of Nazi intentions that was eerie in its prescience. On August 7, after returning from Europe where he was elected president of an international conference of pro-boycott Jewish groups, Untermyer took to the microphones of WABC radio and prophesied that the atrocities of World War I "will pale into significance as compared to this devilishly, deliberately, cold-bloodedly planned and already partially executed campaign for the extermination of a proud, gentle, loyal, law-abiding people."

In many of his speeches, Untermyer reserved especial contempt for those individuals, particularly Jews, who would "travel on German ships flying the swastika flag, which is the emblem of Jewish persecution." He spoke for the select few among the population who were galled by the sight of a floating outpost of the Hitler regime entering American waters with its hateful emblem snapping in the breeze. During an August 27 address at a B'nai B'rith lodge in Youngstown, Ohio, which was broadcast over the airwaves of the Columbia Broadcasting System (CBS), he wondered how such brazenness could be allowed occur "under our very eyes" in "our port of New York."

The transcript reveals that he added the following evocative line: "The black flag of a pirate ship would be more appropriate!"

CHAPTER SIX

═══════════

And as he journeyed, it came to pass that he drew nigh
unto Damascus.

—ACTS 9:3

I N THE LATER months of 1933, Bill Bailey was all of eighteen
years old, a wandering spirit unsettled by the cruelties of the
modern world whose life was about to be transformed by an Indian stowaway.

Bailey was firing the boiler on the *American Farmer*, a freighter
traveling between New York and London on a schedule that allot-
ted ten days for each crossing. A few days into a particularly rough
eastward passage, he learned that a stowaway had been discovered.
In his companionable manner, Bailey befriended the young man.
"A friendly guy," he said. "We gave him blankets, cigarettes, and all
that type of stuff. We took care of him as much as we could." He
was an Indian who had worked for several years as a dishwasher
in New York and wanted desperately to reach Bombay where, as
he had learned via letter, his mother lay dying. The Indian's hope
was that British authorities in London would arrange for him to
continue to the British-controlled subcontinent.

In London, the stowaway was taken into custody by the British
but, lacking proper identification papers, was dumped back on the
Farmer for New York. A few hours into the return journey, Bailey

was shocked to see his Indian friend resting on his haunches in a corner. "The guy is very depressed. He's got tears in his eyes. All sorts of weird things are coming into his mind." The Indian wondered whether the captain would arrange for him to be transferred to a passing ship. "You couldn't get a lifeboat launched the seas were so bad," Bailey said. "You couldn't even go out on deck. We persuaded him it wouldn't work, impossible."

Later in the trip, the stowaway approached Bailey and other crew members and attempted to give away his money and valuables. "Everybody should've got wise to it but nobody did," Bailey said. A few hours later, the young man wrapped himself in as much clothing as he could find, grabbed a life jacket from the ship's supply, and leapt into the raging seas of the North Atlantic.

"I'm down below in the boiler room and all of the sudden the whistle starts blowing," Bailey said. "So the engineer comes running in. 'Pick up steam! Pick up steam! We have to maneuver!' I still didn't know what the hell was going on."

Bailey positioned himself under the natural draft ventilator and heard desperate shouting up on the deck.

"The engineer came in again to make a routine check. I said, 'What the hell is going on?' He said, 'Some dumb sonofabitch jumped over overboard. They think it's that stowaway.'"

The ship spent two hours battling the mountainous swells but the Indian couldn't be found. Bailey was overcome with guilt at his failure to prevent the tragedy. And he and his mates were incensed with the ship's officers and bosun (the senior crewman on the deck) for lacking any compassion toward the poor dishwasher from Bombay. All that mattered to them was the loss of the life jacket.

"Everybody became so demoralized, so disgusted," Bailey said. "We lost a human being. That's the thing that helped set off the trigger in me. A simple thing like making another human being happy, getting him home to his mother, should have been on everybody's mind. They should have done everything possible, but the sonofabitches let a man jump overboard, commit suicide.

That started me off. If I could find a way to right this injustice I would do it."

Landing in New York without a job, Bailey brooded on the fate of the stowaway until, quite by coincidence, he made the acquaintance of John Quigley Robinson, a leprechaun-size seaman from Belfast who became his spirit guide in channeling principled rage into political action. "His profanity was rich and metaphorical; his delivery deadpan," an author wrote of the pipe-smoking Ulsterman who had served with the British Army during World War I. "Robbie" was an organizer with the Marine Workers Industrial Union (MWIU), which had been founded a few years earlier to fight *hard* for the grunts of every "race, creed, or color" in the maritime profession, a stark contrast from the do-nothing unions unwilling to buck the status quo. Although the MWIU was open to any dock or ship worker who wanted to better his lot, its leaders were avowed Communists in thrall to the Soviet Union and keen to establish a revolutionary workers' government in the United States.

Over coffee at a waterfront café, Robinson listened with sympathy to the tale of the Indian stowaway and encouraged Bailey to write an account for the union's monthly newspaper, the *Marine Workers Voice*, which published such stories as "Half Baked Mate Irks *Pennsylvania* Sailors," "Demand Freedom for Scottsboro Boys," "Shore Workers Help Fight Fink System," and "Seamen Live Like Human Beings on Soviet Ships."

Bailey spent two days laboring over the text, which he hand delivered to the MWIU offices on Broad Street in lower Manhattan. Robinson made a few minor changes and published Bailey's first act of activism on page three of the February 1934 edition of the newspaper under the headline "Stowaway Suicides."

"A Hindu stowaway on the *American Farmer* committed suicide at sea rather than return to New York where he had lived for eight years," the unbylined story began. "He stowed away in New York and showed up on deck two days out. They put him to work from four a.m. till 8 p.m. Going over he had two mattresses to sleep on, but coming back they took these away from him."

With a notable racial sensitivity, the piece described how the Indian was treated more harshly than an English stowaway who was caught on a previous voyage.

British officials jailed the Indian and then returned him to the *Farmer* because he lacked identification papers, the article said. "Three days out of London, he told the bosun, 'You'd better lock me up, I'm not going back to New York on the same ship. I'm going to commit suicide.'" The Indian went overboard with twenty dollars that he'd attempted to bequeath to members of the crew. The ship "spent two hours looking for the life preserver and then steamed away. The captain said to the bosun: 'Why didn't you give him a good shellacking before he jumped?'"

"The Farmer," the article concluded, "needs organization in the MWIU."

Bailey was delighted by Robinson's offer to enlist in the union, but he lacked $1.05 needed to pay the membership fee and first month's dues. "I'll have to think about it," he lied. He went outside, panhandled for the necessary funds, and returned to receive his union book, which he revered like a holy medal. "I found myself tapping my pocket on occasion just to feel assured I had not lost it."

He volunteered with the union's Port Organizing Committee, which went among seamen and longshoremen where they dwelled, delivering propaganda, collecting dues, ascending soapboxes, dodging tomatoes, and, on a good day, signing up a new member or two, who were invariably sneered at as "Communist dupes." The job required the fortitude to stand up to the "goon squad" employed by the establishment unions—ex-cons who specialized in pummeling well-meaning activists into the sidewalk. He was teamed with a salty band of colleagues, men with such names as "Whitey" Baxter and "Low Life" McCormack, who had little patience for dialectical theorizing but felt right at home on the hard-knock waterfront.

Among them was "Ding Dong" Bell, a Glaswegian who was assigned to show Bailey the ropes. On that first day, the two tucked bundles of MWIU literature under their coats and snuck aboard a United Fruit Company vessel by posing as longshoremen. They preached to the men about the necessity of joining a real union that would confront shipowners about low wages and pitiful conditions. "If you let it," Bell would say, "the system will make a groveling dog out of you." Bailey found that he was able to sell copies of the *Marine Workers Voice* but had a harder time obtaining signatures for a petition. "You have more sense than that," an oiler told him. "If I put my name to that, somewhere, somehow, sometime, that petition will show up on the boss's desk and wham, I'll be out of a job."

In time, Bailey mounted his first soapbox.

"And you get up there and you look out over a couple hundred faces," he remembered years later. "Nobody's laughing. No expression. No nothing. You don't know if they got a ham sandwich in the hand they're gonna hit you with or what. And you are supposed to razzle-dazzle them. Or stir them. Get them up to where they are screaming bloody *moida*. And you get up there and your mouth is dry. Butterflies in your stomach. You're completely emotional, ready to collapse. And the first thing you say to yourself, 'I wish an earthquake takes place at this very minute.' [Laughs.] But anyway, like anything else, you take a deep breath and you say your first word. And the second one comes out a little easier. And you get 'fellow worker' out of your mouth. Then bit by bit you start warming up."

The apprentice radical was impressed that the most active members of the MWIU were Communists, part of a generation of young people who regarded the Depression as proof that the capitalist system had failed. The "Reds" were out there organizing unemployed councils, hosting antieviction rallies, conducting sit-ins at relief bureaus, demanding antilynching legislation, planning rent strikes, leading hunger marches, and enduring beatings from the "Tammany Cossacks," the nightstick-wielding officers of the mounted New York Police Department (NYPD) units who liked nothing better than to thrash lefty demonstrators. The Communists seemed to be the only ones who were willing to do the hard work to remedy the ills that plagued society. They were ready to take to the barricades to end poverty, injustice, discrimination, joblessness, exploitation, inequality. They weren't afraid to fight.

Bailey was reading as many cheap-press pamphlets as he could lay his hands on. He was learning about "a place called the Soviet Union," a glorious land where the laboring class had thrown off the yoke of the oppressive czar and established a poor people's community with "no oppression, where workers and farmers controlled their own destinies, where unemployment was unheard of and where people referred to each other as comrade," he wrote. The architects of this mythic realm were Lenin and Stalin, who had learned from the sacred texts set down by Marx and Engels. "The heavy or villain in this whole conspiracy to bring havoc and ruin to the new nation, aside from the surrounding bands of capitalists, was a guy named Trotsky," Bailey wrote. "This guy, I read, was forever organizing groups both inside and outside of the Soviet Union who would harm the best interests of the Soviet people."

Within six weeks of enrolling in the MWIU, Bailey went the full route and joined the Communist Party during an initiation ceremony in a West Side tenement presided over by an old-timer who'd lost a hand in a cannery accident.

He was overjoyed. "I pledged to work to bring about a better, more worthwhile life for all of us." He was fortified by the party's demand that he quit "his little nefarious ways": his lying, cheating, drinking, and carousing. "When I got into the Communist Party, all of that stuff went to an end," he said. "There was sort of a new dignity that developed. You felt a certain goodness in you that you were out there struggling for the whole of humanity. Not just a little group anymore. What you did was important. You had to be an example. A light." He was impressed by the willingness of party members to admit their failings and concede that they deserved to be criticized. He was invigorated by their determination in the face of long odds to make "every ship a bastion of socialism," as the slogan had it. And he was delighted by their openness and generosity, their eagerness to offer a bowl of stew when he was hungry, a place to sleep when he was tired. "With such interest and love, was it any wonder that I felt I had found my niche, the right group, the right party to belong to?"

Bailey was assigned to the sea. Robbie Robinson informed him that a job was available as a wiper (responsible for cleaning and maintaining the engine room) on a run-down freighter with the notorious Munson Line. Bailey was instructed to foment a strike at the first port of call. Once aboard, he made the admittedly "unethical" decision to surreptitiously collect all the pulp paperbacks on the ship and hurl them into the ocean, which meant the crew had nothing to read but union literature. By the time the *Mundixie* reached Baltimore, Bailey succeeded in organizing a work stoppage for better conditions but the captain sputtered his contempt and refused to negotiate. The entire crew was fired, pulled off the ship by Baltimore cops, and replaced by scabs. "I felt defeated, humiliated, outmatched, and outclassed."

Bailey joined the MWIU office in Baltimore, where he wrote propaganda leaflets and bulletins for distribution on the waterfront. He watched from afar as thousands of West Coast longshoremen and seamen went on an eighty-three-day strike in mid-1934, a stirring landmark of American labor history that resulted in improvements in the ports from southern California to northern Washington. To take advantage of the organizational energy released by the West Coast strike, Bailey was sent to open up an MWIU office in Norfolk, Virginia. He slept on the floor, earned five dollars a week, and subsisted on little more than beans. But when he signed up a new member of the union, he felt like he was "walking on a cloud."

From Norfolk, Bailey was enrolled in a six-week Communist training course in rural New Jersey, one of a small group of rising stars selected for immersion in Marxian theory and practice. In his autobiography, he writes about how he found it hard to concentrate on the materialist conception of history and the dictatorship of the proletariat in the presence of a fellow student he identifies only as Pele, a beautiful young woman who was an organizer in the Chicago stockyards. "She personified health and beauty and had a brilliant mind." He was blue-eyed, six foot two, and smitten. Soon the two were taking evening strolls in the hills surrounding the school. "It was as if some magic force was at work when, halfway down the mountain, we both stopped," he wrote of one unforgettable night. "Something happened that I had only dreamed of. I looked her squarely in the eyes and we embraced and kissed."

The two young Communists fell in love. They passed notes to each other in class and slipped away for furtive hugs and kisses. Pele penned a letter to her boyfriend back home, announcing that she had fallen for "a big scrawny character." Bill made a formal request to be transferred to the maritime division in the Great Lakes.

The bureaucracy had other plans. In the wake of the West Coast strike, the Party decided that it would no longer build its own radical union but would instead work to radicalize the mainline union. The MWIU ceased operations and its members were instructed to join (or infiltrate) the conservative International Seamen's Union (ISU). Bailey was assigned to secure an ISU union card and sign on with the first ship that would send him away from his true love.

Bailey was disconsolate. He complained to his mentor, Robbie Robinson.

"They feel that if you have no strings tying you down, you'll perform better and be ready for any assignment," Robinson told him. "If you have a girlfriend who keeps urging you to hang around, you'll give up the industry and end up in some tin can factory just so you can rush home every night. If you're unattached, you'll be out on the ships where they think you belong."

Some workers' paradise, Bailey thought. Such a capricious exercise of power, he would come to feel, "bordered on the sinister."

CHAPTER SEVEN

We wish only to be peaceful and happy.

—HITLER IN AN INTERVIEW WITH THE (UK) *DAILY MAIL*, MARCH 17, 1935

T HE *BREMEN* WAS a metaphor for the international community's acquiescence in the Nazi program, stark proof that the Third Reich was seen as a respectable player on the international scene, just another nation dealing with nettlesome internal matters in its own way.

Beginning in early 1934, the great ship abandoned the out-of-the-way Pier 4 in southern Brooklyn and began docking at a glamorous new landing at the foot of West Forty-Sixth Street on the Hudson River in Manhattan. The *Bremen* and its sister ship, the *Europa*, arrived on alternating schedules into Pier 86, which was situated among a group of piers that were being lengthened to accommodate the new French and British superliners. The Italian showpiece, Il Duce's *Rex*, which had seized the Blue Riband from der Führer's *Bremen* in August 1933, anchored just a few quays to the north.

The exclusive stretch of midisland waterfront, which would come to be known as Luxury Liner Row, was much coveted by the shipping lines for obvious reasons. Just a yellow cab ride through the slums of Hell's Kitchen delivered passengers to the hotels of

Times Square and Midtown and the railroad terminals of Penn and Grand Central Stations.

The anti-Nazi boycott was achieving some successes—Saks, Bloomingdale's, Macy's, Gimbel's, Lord and Taylor, and other large department stores agreed to cease carrying German-made goods—but the *Bremen* sailed along without much difficulty. The research department of Samuel Untermyer's Non-Sectarian Anti-Nazi League sent out letters to leading citizens who traveled on the swastika-flagged liners, urging them to refrain from "an expression of sympathy for or, at best, indifference to the deeds of racial and religious persecution for which the Nazi government is responsible." The Jewish press took careful note of Jews who provided succor to Hitlerism by luxuriating in "the Nazi liner." Among those singled out were Joseph Duveen, the prominent art dealer, and James P. Warburg of the distinguished banking family. Even non-Jews were called to account. The British actor George Arliss, known for portraying Jews on stage and screen, issued an apology for taking the *Bremen* from New York to Southampton, claiming he was in a hurry to make a business appointment. Blackface actor Charles Correll, who starred in the radio hit *Amos 'n' Andy*, said he wouldn't "knowingly antagonize" either Jews or Germans. "'Andy' Goes Abroad on 'Verboten' Nazi Liner" read the headline in the *Jewish Daily Bulletin*. "I have a great many Jewish friends as well as numerous German friends," he said when questioned. "The fact of the matter is that I had not the slightest idea what boats I would take, coming or going."

The wider public didn't much care. Claims by boycott supporters that German passenger liners had suffered a "sharp decrease" in passenger traffic were brushed aside by the Hamburg-America and North German Lloyd lines, which had been combined into a single, nazified entity known as Hapag-Lloyd. Although the Depression continued to hamper the transatlantic business in general, the German line boasted of an *increase* in sales since Hitler came to power. The *Bremen* still filled more of its berths than any other competitor on the Atlantic route. Celebrities and other notables didn't rush to cancel bookings. Cole Porter felt no shame in telling a journalist that his favorite things included "brief trips aboard the *Bremen*."

Few people paid much attention when Congressman Samuel Dickstein (D–Lower East Side) convened the first iteration of the House Un-American Activities Committee, which he devised as a forum to call out Nazi sympathizers in the United States. Witnesses before the committee testified that German passenger liners served as conduits between Reich agencies in Germany and Nazi front groups active in German neighborhoods in the United States. Sailors on shore leave were said to convey printed matter, military garb, secret messages, and propaganda films to such entities as the Bund der Freunde des Neuen Deutschland (Friends of the New Germany), which was the principal marching-and-*heiling corps of recent immigrants from the Fatherland. Captain William Drechsel, the New York–based marine superintendent for Hapag-Lloyd, conceded under questioning from Congressman Dickstein that each German liner had "a Nazi leader" whose "purpose is to carry out the dictates and the mandates and the orders of the party."

"But beyond these relatively minor disruptions," declared the *Christian Science Monitor* in an article about "alarmists" attempting to stir up the country over the Hitler threat, "neither Congress nor the Government thinks very much about the intense emotional struggle which Nazism has aroused in Europe and in localized parts of the United States as well."

===

The Nazi story had receded from the front pages by the time a senior Hitler aide sailed into New York Harbor in mid-June 1934, a moment when the country was preoccupied with the banditry of John Dillinger, dust storms in the Great Plains, and the snappy repartee of Clark Gable and Claudette Colbert in *It Happened One Night*. Following its now-standard procedure with arriving Nazi notables, the American state extended every courtesy to ensure that shoreline protesters wouldn't disturb the landfall of the odious Ernst "Putzi" Hanfstaengl.

Hanfstaengl, a hulking man with a lock of slick hair flopped over his forehead, had been a member of the Führer's inner circle since the earliest days of the movement. He was born in Munich to an aristocratic family with artistic pretenses and American connections. His mother was a member of the blue-blooded Sedgwick family of New England. Young Putzi was sent across the Atlantic to attend Harvard, where he rowed crew, became friends with T. S. Eliot, and earned a reputation for his abilities as a pianist. After returning to Munich in the early 1920s, he became Hitler's propagandist, benefactor, and personal piano player, performing selections from Wagner operas to ease the young firebrand's nerves. Hanfstaengl claimed that he gave Hitler the idea for the "Sieg Heil" chant by demonstrating the ecstatic power of Harvard fight songs and cheerleading taunts. Since Hitler's elevation to power, he had served as the regime's foreign press spokesman. "The Jews who already have been ousted were put out because they were morally and politically unfit to safeguard German interests," he said in explaining Hitler's early anti-Jewish measures.

At Quarantine, forty reporters and photographers were marshaled into the main dining salon on the upper promenade deck of the *Bremen*'s sibling, the *Europa*. Sitting at the head of a small table, Hanfstaengl announced that he was not visiting the United States in his official capacity as a Nazi government official. He was merely a Harvard man heading to Cambridge for the twenty-fifth anniversary of the Class of '09. He declined to discuss politics. Asked about the German government's treatment of Jews, he said: "I am sorry I can't answer that. That is a political question. Perhaps at some future date I shall have something to say."

The demonstration at Pier 86 included Socialist student groups and anti-Fascist refugee committees and Communist peace leagues. The New York Police Department (NYPD) force was made up of a hundred uniformed cops, a dozen mounted units, and thirty plainclothes detectives from the Red Squad, who "mingled with the crowd," the papers reported. Pauline Rogers of the Anti-Nazi Federation of New York introduced a series of speakers. Hans Baer, a young escapee from a Nazi concentration camp, described horrors that would grow exponentially worse over the coming eleven years. Robert Minor, a gifted political cartoonist turned Communist leader, roared at the limits of his lung capacity: "While the beast Hanfstaengl is being welcomed by the rotten American bourgeois, the German working class are making ready to rise against their fascist oppressors!"

In his memoirs, Hanfstaengl says he was called up to the bridge and handed a pair of binoculars. "The streets just beyond the dock area were filled with thousands of people shouting only barely discernible slogans," he wrote. "However, they left nothing to chance, as they were carrying banners and streamers with such phrases as 'OUST NAZI HANFSTAENGL!'—'SHIP THE HITLER AGENTS BACK'—'FREE ERNST THÄLMANN.'" The captain informed Hanfstaengl that he wouldn't be able to leave by the main gate. "The problem was, however, solved by the appearance of six extremely natty young gentlemen in brand-new Harvard blazers and ties, the senior of whom introduced himself: 'Good morning, sir, my name is Benjamin Goodman, New York police department, and these are colleagues of mine,'" Hanfstaengl wrote. "He showed me his pass and added: 'President Roosevelt has sent a message to say that he hopes you will have a pleasant visit. We are here to ensure that there will be no incidents.'"

Upon arrival at Pier 86, Hanfstaengl was bundled into a chartered tugboat at the river end of the pier and hurried away from the objectionable scenes on the waterfront, becoming the third Nazi official (along with Ambassador Hans Luther in March 1933 and Goebbels aide Hans Weidemann in May 1933) to be given a taxpayer-supported escape route to avoid the embarrassment of having to face a lawfully assembled protest rally. The insults were instead hurled at a disembarking passenger who had the misfortune to look an awful lot like the lanky Nazi.

"About those little things, those demonstrations," Hanfstaengl told reporters upon reaching Boston, "I think they're just trying to have a bit of fun with me. Really, I had a great time in New York. There's nothing like that in Germany. I can't think of when I've enjoyed myself more."

During commencement week at Harvard, Hanfstaengl was treated as a respected member of the alumni community. "To object to the presence of a Harvard man among other Harvard men in any capacity, on purely political grounds, is an extremely childish thing to do," editorialized the *Harvard Crimson*. He attended a reception given by Harvard president James B. Conant, enjoyed a whirlwind of social gatherings with eminent pals from his college days, lost a few dollars on the horse races at the Country Club in Brookline, and cheered on the Red Sox at Fenway Park. The only trouble came during a brief protest on campus that resulted in the arrests of nine anti-Nazi demonstrators, including "two attractive Irish girls of Cambridge," Sheila Shugrue and Nora Burke, "who handcuffed themselves to the rail in front of their seats in Sever Quadrangle while screaming imprecations against the German envoy," reported a Boston paper.

Hanfstaengl had traveled down to Newport for the wedding of John Jacob Astor III and Ellen Tuck ("Tucky") French when Hitler reclaimed the world's shocked attention by ordering the gangland-style assassinations that eliminated a few hundred figures accused of conspiring against his rule, the infamous Night of the Long Knives of June 30 to July 1, 1934. "I was sitting in the Astor pew, next to the aisle, enjoying the scene and thinking what an enviable life these really rich American families lived, when a rather scruffy fellow tapped me on the elbow," he wrote in his memoirs. "He crept up the church on all fours. 'Can you comment on this doctor?' he asked, handing me a crumpled Associated Press despatch." The Nazi propagandist eventually composed himself well enough to announce to the press that Hitler had resorted to extralegal measures to save "the most precious thing in the world—his providential mission."

He was instructed to return to Germany without delay. A week later, he was back at Pier 86, where he was serenaded with Nazi marches by a forty-piece band from the Friends of the New Germany during the *Europa*'s midnight sailing party. "Hitler has knowledge of everything," he told reporters. "He knows what is going to happen and he takes precisely the steps that are fitting."

Asked again about the fate of German Jewry, he said: "That is a matter that will have to be found out."

The *New York Times* concluded its story with a cryptic comment about how "considerable attention" was attracted "by the ship's swastika, upon which a searchlight was played constantly."

———

Hanfstaengl reached Berlin in time to travel with Hitler to the Prussian estate of the Reich president, Paul von Hindenburg, who was reported by doctors to be near death. After a brief visit that confirmed the old man's frailty, the retinue hurried back to the capital, where the "Law on the Head of State of the German Reich" was drawn up. When Hindenburg died on the following morning, August 2, the powers of the presidency were automatically transferred to Hitler, who retired the title of Reich president and christened himself "Führer and Reich chancellor" over the entire "German empire and people." Later that same day, the German military assembled to swear an oath of unconditional obedience to the person of Adolf Hitler rather than to the constitution as in the previous practice.

After learning of Hindenburg's death, President Roosevelt had his first-ever communication with Hitler, cabling a pro forma condolence note expressing the "sincere sorrow" of the American people at the passing of the Reich president.

Hitler's decision to merge the offices of president and chancellor, a "virtual coup d'état" in the phrase of the Associated Press, was granted retroactive sanction by 89.9 percent of German voters in the plebiscite of August 19, 1934. In his opening proclamation at the annual Nuremberg Rally on September 5, the supreme leader, the possessor of absolute power, declared that Germany would not experience revolution for a thousand years. "If foreigners imagine that the 4 million 'no' voters constituted a dangerous opposition, they are privileged to smile," he said. "Our next attack will demolish the opposition."

Looking upon these events with unabashed admiration was one of America's great thought leaders, William Randolph Hearst, the seventy-one-year-old media mogul then soaking in the mineral baths of a central German resort after a summer of touring the European continent.

In an interview with (yes) Putzi Hanfstaengl that was distributed by the official German news agency, Hearst hailed the German people's "unanimous expression" of support for Hitler, who had the potential to accomplish "a measure of good not only for his own people but for all humanity." In the days following the Nuremberg Rally, Hearst flew to Berlin for a private meeting with Hitler, who lectured him for nearly an hour about the regime's democratic legitimacy and nondiscriminatory aims. When Hitler asked why Nazism didn't have greater support among the American people, Hearst pointed to "a very large and influential and respected element in the United States who are very resentful of the treatment of their fellows in Germany"; in other words, Jews. After the meeting, Hearst was photographed with a group of Nazis that included Alfred Rosenberg, the fanatically anti-Semitic theorist.

Mindful of the bad publicity that was developing in the United States over such "hobnobbing," one of Hearst's New York executives sent a message to "the Chief," urging him to sail home "on a Cunarder, or anything but a German boat." On September 27, Hearst reached New York on his preferred carrier. "He was aboard the Nazi liner *Bremen*," reported a Jewish newspaper. "That in itself is news to the millions of readers, Jewish and non-Jewish, who have decided, for what seemed to them good and sufficient reasons, to withhold all patronage from the Hitler regime."

Hearst, whose newspapers had a combined circulation of 20 million, issued a brief statement upon docking at Pier 86. "Everything was much more peaceful and orderly than in our country," the statement said in part. "There were no riotous strikes, no racketeering, no kidnappings, no gang murders, no organized lawlessness and no violence." He then retreated to his cabin to answer a dozen or so written questions that had been submitted to him by reporters. He didn't emerge from his seclusion for five hours. In this second statement, he predicted that Hitler's policies "will be very much modified, particularly with regard to the Jews." He said he didn't believe Hitler was "a war threat" to Europe. "I do not think he has anything to be a war threat with. I believe he is organizing Germany to prevent disorder and discouragement." Referring to the exhibition drill of fifty-two thousand farm laborers who were shouldering farm implements in the manner of rifles during the recent Nuremberg Rally, Hearst said: "I cannot imagine anyone being mad enough to make war with spades."

Such a credulous view of Nazi Germany's belligerent intentions would be harder to sustain within just a few months, when a series of foreign policy victories inspired Hitler to rhapsodize about "the beginning of a new age."

On January 13, 1935, the mostly German-speaking residents of the Saar Protectorate on the French border voted by a 90.7 margin to be reincorporated into Germany, the first territorial acquisition of the Third Reich. Buoyed by the propaganda coup, Hitler seized upon a pretext (the announcement of British and French military readiness initiatives) to break the news that he was building up an armed force of fighting strength—a blatant repudiation of the postwar treaty dedicated to preventing another Kaiser from menacing the planet. On March 10, Hermann Goering tested international opinion by declaring the existence of his air force, the Luftwaffe, which he (falsely) claimed was already the equal of the United Kingdom's Royal Air Force. With no howls forthcoming from Western capitals, Joseph Goebbels summoned reporters to the Propaganda Ministry on the afternoon of March 16, 1935. In a voice shaking with emotion, he read the "Proclamation of Military Sovereignty," which announced a compulsory military draft with the goal of creating a standing army of thirty-six divisions and 550,000 men. German newspapers printed up special editions: "End of Versailles. Germany Free Again!"

The British, French, and Italian governments issued condemnations and formed a short-lived alliance in opposition to Hitler but failed to take any meaningful action. The League of Nations convened a committee to consider economic sanctions against Nazi Germany. The idea went nowhere.

The US government was silent. Secretary of State Cordell Hull would only say that the administration believed in the sanctity of treaties. President Roosevelt summoned his advisers and conferred with congressional leaders. In the end, he made no public statement. FDR said nothing about the militarization of the Hitler state. *Not one word.*

"What else could I wish for other than calm and peace?" Hitler lied during his infamous "peace speech" in the Reichstag on May 21. "Germany needs peace and desires peace!"

The repudiation of Versailles was soon followed by the British government's surrender in the Anglo-German Naval Agreement, which (in seeking to cap the size of the new Kriegsmarine) condoned the Treaty violations, recognized the legality of vigorous German rearmament, and blessed the construction of a Nazi fleet that would sink 3,500 Allied merchant ships and 175 Allied warships during World War II. The disastrous policy of appeasement—of granting concessions to a despot who had long advocated military aggression to establish racially purified "living space" beyond Germany's borders—was now in place.

"I am a believer in democracy and will have nothing to do with the poisonous European mess," said Senator Homer T. Bone, a Democrat from Washington State, reflecting the prevailing view in the halls of American power. "I believe in being kind to people who have smallpox, such as Mussolini and Hitler, but not in going inside their houses."

Senator Thomas D. Schall, a Minnesota Republican, brayed: "To hell with Europe and the rest of those nations!"

CHAPTER EIGHT

No marked relief in sight.

—WEATHER BUREAU, JULY 14, 1935

B ILL BAILEY OBTAINED his union card with the International
Seamen's Union and, on March 29, 1935, shipped out as an
oiler in the engine room of the *Exchange*, a freighter bound for
several Mediterranean ports roiled by political currents.

The Communist Party had assigned him to "create a base." He
was a few months shy of his twentieth birthday.

In Genoa, he watched as Italian soldiers boarded a transport ship
for East Africa while an officer urged them to shout praise for Mussolini ("Viva Il Duce!"), who was preparing to invade Ethiopia in
what he hoped would be the first conquest of a new Roman Empire.
"Nobody wanted to holler *Viva*," Bailey remembered. "They all know
they're going to die over there. Out in the desert someplace. It was
sad, watching this whole business." In Marseilles, he declined to join
his mates in pursuit of wine and women and instead had a halting
discussion on political matters with a French Communist. In a handful of locales in Spain, Bailey struggled to comprehend the political
disputes that would soon erupt into civil war. "I could feel important
things going on around me but I couldn't put my finger on it." He
promised a group of Socialists that he'd return. He would—via a
mountain pass over the Pyrenees—but that's another story.

Bill Bailey in fascist
Italy. "Nobody wanted
to holler *Viva*."
(Michael Bailey)

Bailey spent every available moment trying to convince his mates to join the Communist Party. "From the time I awoke to go on watch until the time I went to bed, I agitated everyone I met." He was forced to contend with a fireman who said he knew from personal experience that the Soviet Union was a land of arbitrary arrests and food shortages. He had to live down a visit with fellow crew members to a Soviet freighter, which was not a shining example of the glories of socialism but "by far the worst ship I ever had the misfortune to board." Yet Bailey maintained his ideological commitment. He preached about the necessity of transferring power from the wealthy to the oppressed, of creating a planned society "where guns and weapons of destruction would be a thing of the past and the adage of turning swords into plowshares a reality, where men could really call themselves brothers and to allow a person to go hungry would be considered a criminal act." By the time the *Exchange* returned to New York, he had persuaded two shipmates to join the workers' struggle.

In the spring of 1935, Bailey was back on the beach in Manhattan. He continued to exchange letters with his long-distance girlfriend, Pele. "When the hell are you coming to Chicago?" she wrote to him. "Soon I hope." But he was preoccupied with the news from Germany, where the Nazi regime was initiating a new wave of repressive actions against domestic targets. He was angered by the unwillingness of the American people and government to recognize the seriousness of the "menacing reality" of fascism. He joined protesters in front of passenger liners departing for the Reich, handing out faux tourist pamphlets (*Welcome to the New Germany*) that featured a picturesque Rhine castle on the front and jarring concentration camp scenes on the inside. "But Nazism or not, thousands of Americans continued to book passage and pay fares on the many ships that departed weekly for Germany," he remembered.

Nazi storm troopers in the German provinces had launched the second major phase of anti-Semitic persecution since Hitler's rise to power, an upsurge of harassment, property destruction, and mob violence that sought the full removal of the Jewish "threat" from German life. The terror from below was encouraged by state media and condoned by local police, who typically showed up long after an attack to haul the victimized Jews into what was euphemistically known as "protective custody." The Hitler government was only too pleased to distract the public from the unresolved problems of high unemployment and rising food prices. The Jews, after all, were "our misfortune." The more serious incidents brought forth condemnations from senior regime officials, who inveighed against "individual actions" in hopes of maintaining plausible deniability in the eyes of a skeptical middle class and distracted outside world. After a ferocious round of street brawling and window smashing in Munich, the same Nazi chief who organized the disturbances went on the radio to denounce the misdeeds of "irresponsible elements."

The adherents of *Mein Kampf* were not content with ejecting Jews from public and administrative life, which was only partially achieved by the April Laws of 1933 and the array of anti-Semitic ordinances and codes adopted by municipalities with every passing day. The Nazi Party was founded upon the mock-scientific obscenity that Jews were a disease that had to be flushed from the bloodstream of humanity. The true believers were lobbying Hitler to fulfill his vow to protect the Fatherland from a *biological* hazard. They wanted a genocidal delusion—Jews as pestilence—to be adopted into national policy.

It was the season of Julius Streicher, publisher of *Der Stürmer*, the only periodical that Hitler read with relish from the first vile cartoon to the last. A stocky philanderer in brown uniform and high boots with a cue ball–bald head and toothbrush mustache, Streicher was in the midst of a speaking tour of German cities, where he fulminated in quasi-pornographic language about the necessity of "the cleansing of our foul, dishonored fatherland of deadly vermin." He spun lurid tales about the ongoing assault on the nation's purity by the lustful aggression of Jewish males. Just a "single cohabitation of a Jew with an Aryan woman," he informed his audiences, "is sufficient to poison her blood forever." He claimed that every year 100,000 young German girls were "ruined" while working as servants in Jewish homes.

During these months, mixed couples were named in local newspaper stories, surrounded in their homes by angry crowds, dragged through the streets in what were known as processions of shame, and taken to jail for "racial disgrace of a character dangerous to public safety and order," as the Gestapo in Breslau announced after arresting six couples. In towns and villages throughout the country, registry clerks took it upon themselves to refuse marriage licenses to "race defilers," a decision that was upheld in Bad Sulza, near Weimar, by a magistrate who refused to sanction a union "adulterating Aryan blood and rendering it useless for all time from the national point of view."

The anti-Jewish onslaught was occurring at the same time as a drive against the Catholic Church, the confessional home to one third of the German population. Although the Hitler state had negotiated the Reichskonkordat with the Vatican in July 1933, permitting Catholic clergy to continue worship practices as long as they stayed out of politics, the Nazis were deeply suspicious of a foreign-led institution that didn't regard Adolf Hitler as the one true god. During the spring and summer of 1935, the regime placed strictures on Catholic lay organizations and institutions, ransacked church properties, suppressed or censored Catholic newspapers, and harassed Catholic youth organizations, which were regarded as competition to the Hitler Youth. A Catholic school principal in Opladen was "taken into protective custody for his own safety" after forbidding his pupils from attending a Nazi mass meeting. A gang of Hitler Youth stormed a meeting in Duisburg hosted by a Catholic priest who preached against the forced sterilization law, which had just been strengthened to sanction compulsory abortion up to and including the sixth month of pregnancy for women who were deemed "hereditarily ill."

In an effort to show ordinary Catholics that the Church was immoral and corrupt, the Nazi government rounded up dozens of Catholic monks and nuns, who were seized from monasteries and convents and charged with smuggling church funds out of the country in violation of the Reich's byzantine currency laws. "Many of the nuns arrested, Catholic sources said, had been in solitary retreat for more than five years, scarcely knew who Adolf Hitler was and 'most certainly never heard of the foreign exchange laws,'" the Associated Press reported after a series of raids in late April. Sister Neophytia, the mother superior of the Augustinian Sisters, was sentenced to five years' penal servitude for secreting 100,000 reichsmarks into Belgium. Under questioning, she broke down and admitted that she carried sealed envelopes containing from 5,000 to 10,000 marks concealed in her nun's garb. During another trial, Sister Wernera, secretary of the Order of St. Vincent, admitted that she arranged for 252,000 reichsmarks to be taken into Holland. She also received five years' penal servitude. The prosecutor called her "worse than a Galician Jew."

While the regime was conducting its crusade against a range of internal "enemies," a native of Seattle named Lawrence Simpson sailed into the waters of the Reich.

Simpson was an able-bodied seaman, one of five hundred crew members on the SS *Manhattan*, a passenger ship of the United States Lines that plied between New York and Hamburg. Like Bailey, he was a Communist and a veteran of the Marine Workers Industrial Union who had come under the sway of the diminutive waterfront organizer John Quigley "Robbie" Robinson. Simpson, age thirty-five, had been recruited by Robinson to be one of a group of couriers delivering anti-Nazi propaganda into Germany. In the locker under his bunk, Simpson had a duffel bag full of propaganda in the German language and a flimsy delivery contraption with three fuse-equipped balloons, which was designed to float over the countryside and release printed subversion upon the populace. Thousands of stickers in his possession bore the slogan *"Der Faschismus muss sterben wenn die Arbeiterschaft leben soll"* ("Fascism must die if the working class is to live").

On June 28, the *Manhattan* reached the quarantine station at Cuxhaven at the mouth of the Elbe. "I was working on the afterdeck with several of my shipmates, getting the lines ready to tie up the ship when she reached her dock, when the second boatswain came aft and said, 'Simpson, the mate wants to see you right away,'" he later wrote in his account of the episode. "I went to the mate's room. As I came in, a German was questioning the mate about 'Simpson.' No sooner did I enter then a second German who had been standing behind the door, grabbed hold of my arm and told me in German that I was under arrest. I replied that they could not arrest me, since a ship, according to international law, is considered to be the territory of the country under whose flag she sails, and I was an American citizen aboard an American ship." The two Germans, who Simpson identified as members of the Gestapo, ignored his protestations.

"They took me down to my bunk and started to search through my locker," Simpson continued. "There they found, among my other possessions, anti-Fascist literature. Against my protests, they forced me to go along with them to shore. As I was being rushed off the ship, the captain (who is also commodore of the United

States Lines) came down from the bridge and shouted with warm consideration: 'Take him and give him fifty years!' I didn't know it then, but I later learned that the United States vice-consul stationed at Hamburg was aboard the ship at the time, and had readily given the Gestapo men permission to take me off."

Simpson was thrown into solitary confinement at the Fuhlsbuettel concentration camp outside of Hamburg.

In the days after the Fourth of July holiday, the newspapers in New York began using the phrase *heat wave* to describe the weather. Without the cooling winds of air conditioners, which would not become widely available until after World War II, even two or three rainless days in the upper 80s could become unbearable. Desperate New Yorkers sought any opportunity to escape their stifling apartments. They sat in shirtsleeves or housedresses on front stoops, slept on fire escapes and tenement roofs, rode elevated trains and trollies for hours on end to catch a tepid breeze. Poor kids didn't hesitate to leap into the rank waters of the Hudson and East Rivers. "As for Coney Island on the weekends," recalled the playwright Arthur Miller, "block after block of beach was so jammed with people that it was barely possible to find space to sit or to put down your book or your hot dog."

On Thursday, July 11, the temperature reached 90 degrees, the hottest day of the year so far. Even though it was a weekday, throngs of people jammed public transportation bound for the Atlantic beaches on the city's southern coast. The papers kept grim tabulations of the "dead," "drowned," and "overcome." At the Rockaway peninsula, lifeguards rescued more than fifty people. On Friday, July 12, the thermometer hit 91.4 degrees, which led to five deaths, eight "prostrations," nine drownings, and one suicide. An Upper West Side doctor leapt from the window of his fifth-floor apartment because, his wife said, he had been depressed for several days over the infernal conditions. On Sunday, July 14, with the temperature cresting 89 degrees, it was estimated that 2 million people streamed to Coney Island and the Rockaways. "The Coney crowd, in a way, took care of itself," a reporter noted.

"There were so many in the water that it was almost impossible for anyone to find room enough to drown, with the result that the day passed without casualties."

The Weather Bureau issued its prediction: "No marked relief in sight."

Bill Bailey was sleeping on the benches of the International Workers Order hall on Union Square, just another out-of-work laborer in the sweltering city. Joining him on the hardwood was his good friend Arthur "Mac" Blair, a Liverpool-born Irishman who went to work on the barges when he was twelve years old and immigrated to New York as a teenager, where he found himself drawn to the revolutionists on the docks. Like Bailey, Mac Blair was a merchant seaman with engine room experience who had graduated from the Marine Workers Industrial Union to the Communist Party. He would later be described by a friend, poet Thomas McGrath, as "Mac with his mournful face" who "comes round the corner / (New York) up from the blazing waterfront, preaching/His strikes."

The two were livid over the fate of Lawrence Simpson, whose full story was related by sailors who had just arrived back at the West Side piers on the SS *Manhattan*.

"I felt terrible," Bailey wrote. "I was more than emotionally involved. Simpson was a seaman. He was one of us."

Margaret Weaver took pity on the two itinerants. She was a Stanford University graduate from a wealthy family, a twenty-five-year-old organizer in a bobbed haircut who had the arduous task of visiting the docks each day and trying to convince longshoremen to join the Communist Party. According to a contemporary, she was a "powerhouse" with the courage to face down the ruffians of the International Longshoreman's Union, which controlled the waterfront in a smash-mouth manner that occasionally deposited corpses in the waters off Red Hook. Although she may have already had her eye on Mac Blair, Weaver later admitted that the romance was yet in a fledgling phase.

She invited Bailey and Blair to stay at her Greenwich Village apartment while she went to New England for two weeks to build roads with a progressive organization.

On July 15, 1935, the anti-Semitic violence in Germany reached the most fashionable thoroughfare in the capital, the Kurfürsten-damm, the neon-illuminated boulevard in the West End of Berlin. The Ku'damm, as it is known to Berliners, was long seen by Nazi ideology as a hive of crass commercialism, gutter art, cabaret decadence, shiftless bohemianism, and, in keeping with the obsession of the moment, "race defilement"—the sexual coupling of Jewish males with German females. In the late afternoon of the fifteenth, the personal scandal sheet of Joseph Goebbels, *Der Angriff*, published a front-page screed about an incident that allegedly occurred in one of the cinemas along the strip. "Jews Have the Insolence to Demonstrate Against an Anti-Jewish Film." Goebbels's hacks described how a group of Jewish moviegoers hissed and jeered during the showing of a Swedish film called *Pettersson and Bendel*, which tells the story of a Christian peasant (Pettersson) who is preyed upon by a Jewish con man (Bendel). Such unacceptable behavior, the propaganda minister's rag declared, must not be condoned.

With a timeliness that was clearly orchestrated from above, hundreds of young hooligans in civilian clothes, reinforced by truckloads of uniformed Nazis, swarmed Germany's version of Broadway, stopping traffic, invading businesses, shouting curses, throwing punches, overturning tables, hurling chairs, smashing plate-glass windows. "All along the Kurfürstendamm, the crowd raised the shout 'Jude!' whenever any one sighted a Jew," wrote Varian Fry, a New York journalist on a study tour of European conditions, whose account was distributed by the Associated Press and printed in newspapers across the world on the following day. "The cry sent the crowd converging on the poor victim, who was asked for his identification papers. If he could not prove himself a good 'Aryan' he was insulted, spat upon, roughly handled, and sometimes knocked down, kicked and beaten."

The police prevented damage to Nazi-favored establishments, while approved targets such as the Bristol, Dobrin, and Kranzler cafés were sacked without obstruction. "The café of the famous Hotel Bristol was wrecked," according to a wire service report.

"Its tables were overturned and the plate glass window smashed. Foreign tourists, quietly seated there, fled into the lobby and to their rooms." A Polish Jew named Moritz Kleinfeld was dragged from the Café Hessler and trampled by a gang of thirty men. He later died. Women were not spared, especially if they could be singled out as "Aryan" consorts of Jewish partners. A mixed couple accosted on a side street was "severely kicked," the wife "called vile names and berated for marrying a Jew," according to a witness. "Heil Streicher!" shouted a portion of the rioters, who went from café to café, brandishing large placards of *Der Stürmer's* notoriously grotesque caricatures of Jews. Average citizens joined in, swept up by the festive atmosphere on the balmy evening. "In fact, one German youth said to me, 'This a holiday for us,'" Fry wrote. "Old men and young men, boys, storm troops, police, young girls of the domestic servant type, well-bred women, some even in the forties and over—all seemed to be having a good time."

At around midnight, a large Nazi stood atop a car and announced that the gaiety was to conclude. "The demonstration ceased as if by magic and the streets were cleared rapidly," reported the United Press. Dozens were left bloodied and battered.

The presence of so many foreign witnesses—a few hundred American midshipmen visiting from ships docked in Copenhagen, a contingent of British war veterans on a friendship mission, and a delegation of athletic officials preparing for the Olympic games scheduled for Berlin in 1936—guaranteed that the story would receive extensive coverage in the West. The "Berlin Riots," which continued on a lesser scale for a few more nights, were widely regarded as the most consequential anti-Jewish outburst in the short history of the Third Reich, sobering confirmation that Hitler was not moderating his extremism. The *New York Herald Tribune,* the voice of mainstream Republicanism in the United States, was appalled that the "inspiration of these disgraceful scenes was undoubtedly official, emanating from Adolf Hitler's intimate circle."

The regime responded in typical fashion, saying the Jews (who "feel themselves again at home") got what was coming to them but blamed any too-rowdy behavior on agents provocateurs seeking to bring the cause into disfavor. As such, the conservative police chief of Berlin was fired and replaced by a staunch Nazi who pledged to continue the purge but in a more orderly manner. The Reich interior minister announced that comprehensive legislation was being drawn up to safeguard German blood from Jewish contamination.

"It is primarily necessary that the public conscience be aroused to realize that there is a Jewish problem, so that laws that sooner or later must be enacted, may take root in the public conscience," said Julius Streicher in an interview. "Only when everyone understands that the racial fate of the nation is at stake will the ground be prepared for further serious work."

On July 15, the first day of the Kurfürstendamm disturbances, the Vatican published a protest against Nazi infringements on Catholic liberties, arguing that hindering Catholic youth organizations, closing Church newspapers, and forcing Catholics to abide by the sterilization laws were violations of the Concordat. Hermann Goering was so incensed by the papal effrontery that he issued an edict on July 18, which directed "the authorities to employ all their legal weapons against members of the Catholic clergy who falsely employ the authority of their spiritual position for political purposes." He attacked the Church for conducting elaborate pageants and festivals, which "imitate" the Nazi "formulas." He ordered the suppression of Catholic youth organizations if "a complete reform does not take place." He demanded that priests "not only refrain from a negative attitude toward National Socialism" but "positively support" the Hitler state. Goering's pronouncement garnered bold-type headlines larger even than those inspired by the Berlin Riots.

Within hours of Goering's announcement, reports were broadcast about additional anti-Jewish actions. Storm troopers in Berlin launched attacks on Jewish-owned ice-cream parlors, which were attracting considerable business in the summertime heat. Elsewhere in Germany, towns and villages were announcing bans on Jews from swimming pools, health resorts, and public beaches to "prevent provocative behavior toward fair-haired Aryan women and girls," according to the language of one injunction.

In Washington, DC, the US government made its first substantive comment on the Lawrence Simpson case. It released a statement declaring that the German authorities were "clearly within their rights" in seizing Lawrence Simpson from the SS *Manhattan*. A spokesman explained that international law allows such arrests to be made within a 3-mile limit of German territory.

The outrages had achieved convergence. Bill Bailey regarded the campaign against Jews as the equivalent of an attack on his own family. "There was nothing in my soul that was more devastating than to see the Nazis laughing—bastards!—laughing while they dragged some poor Jewish woman naked across the street through spit and manure and everything else and threw her on the sidewalk by the back of the neck," he remembered. "Write 'Jew' all over the windows. All this type of stuff. I mean, because I saw . . . that was my family that they were doing it to. If they could do it to Jews, they could do it to my mother. And no sonofabitch was going to do it." Although the Catholic Church had been a villain of his childhood, he knew that curbing the free exercise of religion violated basic tenets of justice, which perhaps goes to show how long he would last under the state atheism of the Soviet Union. "Hitler was telling the Catholics, 'Look, we'll proscribe the rite, we'll proscribe what you read off to your constituents on a Sunday morning at Mass. We'll tell you what the letter, what the Sunday letter should be.' So it was getting that bad." The kidnapping of Lawrence Simpson—who was taken by German agents from an American-flagged ship with the apparent approval of an American consular official—was "an affront and an insult that had to be challenged.

"We decided between all the combination of things—the anti-Semitic business, Hitler and fascism in general, Lawrence Simpson, and the Catholic issue—that it was time now to do something to wake this goddamn United States up . . . ," Bailey said. "So we passed the word to some of our Party people. 'Hey, look, we're getting a little tired of nothing being done, goddamn it. It's time we organize something big here.'"

On July 19, the *Bremen* departed Nazi Germany and headed toward New York City.

CHAPTER NINE

Intensification of campaign against Jews and Roman Catholics, the former characterized by mob violence in Berlin, and the widespread suppression of the Stahlhelm have come as a climax to several months of agitation by Nazi Party extremists. The public is perplexed and uneasy, fear being expressed lest the checks hitherto supposed to be more or less effective against subversive tendencies latent in National Socialism should no longer be functioning.

—WILLIAM DODD, US AMBASSADOR TO GERMANY,
IN A TELEGRAM TO WASHINGTON, JULY 23, 1935

THE SUMMERTIME ASSAULT against what Adolf Hitler called the "pigmy remnants" of anti-Nazi resistance seemed to be gaining in intensity with every passing hour.

The hammer fell on the Stahlhelm (Steel Helmets), the extreme-right paramilitary corps of ex-front fighters from the Great War, dedicated supporters of the Führer who made the mistake of retaining non-Nazi uniforms and flags. The organization was tarred as a "reactionary" hive of "state enemies," its leaders arrested and sent to concentration camps. The last of the Masonic lodges, whose rituals relied upon what the Nazis called "Semitic sources," were forced to close, their premises vandalized and artifacts confiscated. The international organization representing vaudeville artists, nightclub entertainers, and circus performers was abolished for "toleration of activities that threaten security," which meant it failed to prevent members from making fun of prominent persons. In Magdeburg, a man of no particular affiliation was arrested for making "improper" remarks about the regime to his colleagues. In Upper Franconia, six men were sent to a concentration camp for "shirking work."

On Sunday, July 21, 1935, after an evening during which thousands of New Yorkers abandoned their apartments to sleep on the sands of the Atlantic beaches, the newspapers in New York blared the news about a decree from the Reich minister of justice that ordered Germany's state attorneys to proceed with "calm determination and emphatic vigor" against "political Catholicism" for "disintegrating the state and disrupting popular unity." The decree was widely interpreted to mean that Nazi agents would be monitoring Sunday sermons and preparing to arrest any priest who questioned the divinity of Adolf Hitler. "Quick proof of misdeeds," it said, "must be followed by even quicker punishment." The newsboys shouted the commonplace prediction that priests were about to be rounded up en masse in Nazi Germany. "Priests Who Assail Nazi 'Purge' Today Will Be Arrested," was the page-one headline in the *New York Times*.

On the same morning, Communist canvassers fanned out to Catholic churches in New York to distribute a mimeographed handout ("Protest Nazi Terror! Unite Against Fascism!") that quickly found its way into the hands of the New York Police Department (NYPD). "While you are at mass today, the Hitler fascist government is launching the most brutal attack on religious liberty in modern history," the sheet declared, which is a lot more than the cardinal archbishop on Fifth Avenue was willing to say. "Political police thugs are attending all churches ready to imprison worshippers and priests. Worse may happen if the Hitler government doesn't feel the weight of aroused opinion quickly!" The cops discovered that Communists were planning a rally that would not be held in the quiet of the *Bremen*'s arrival on Thursday afternoon but during the hubbub of the ship's Friday evening fare-well. The handout asked Catholics to join Jews, Communists, and anti-Fascists "on Pier 86 (46th Street and West Street) between 11 p.m. and midnight on Friday, July 26, on the occasion of the sailing of the S.S. *Bremen.*

"We urge you to flood the pier with anti-fascist workers and others as an immediate showing of strength to the Hitler govern-ment!" it read. "A large and successful meeting on the pier will help your brother Catholics in Germany.

"ALL VICTIMS OF FASCISM MUST UNITE TO WIN CIVIL AND RELI-GIOUS LIBERTY!"

The departure festivities of the *Bremen*, as a story in the *Daily Worker* noted prior to the rally, would provide a perfect opportu-nity to confront the scourge of Nazism:

"Every ship sailing is the occasion of a pro-Nazi demonstra-tion," the writer explained. "On the pier itself, at 46th Street, on sailing nights bands play the anthem of the Nazi pimp saint, Horst Wessel. In front of the pier stands a degenerate-looking 'Aryan,' selling papers. He is surrounded by a bodyguard. He hawks the 'Stuermer,' the chief anti-Semitic organ in Germany. The United States government, which frequently bars labor literature, cannot find anything 'immoral' or 'indecent' in this swill sheet."

On about the same day, July 21, Bill Bailey learned from Rob-bie Robinson that the district leadership had devised an auda-cious act that would target the focal point of the evening's revelry: the spotlight-illuminated swastika flag at the *Bremen*'s forward tip, which would flutter above the protesters gathered in front of the ship on the open pier.

The idea was that a few dozen activists from the Communist Party, women and men, would dress up in evening wear and board the *Bremen* with the boozy multitudes of *bons voyageurs*. In the final minutes before the decks were cleared of anyone not holding a ticket for Europe, a few of the women would create a diversion by handcuffing themselves to the mast and chanting about conditions in Germany. The rest of the infiltrators would form a locked-arm cordon leading to the bow. A few of the seamen who had come aboard with the activists would march down the corridor, climb several steps up the bowsprit, seize the swastika while precariously balanced in illuminated view of the entire tableau, march back off the boat, emerge in front of the rally, and make a presentation to the party chairman, who would be narrating in a shout from his spot below the bow. The prize would then be doused in kerosene and set on fire to the roar of the crowd.

Bailey understood at once the importance of such an operation. He was brought up in the Irish tradition that celebrated the farsighted few who mounted audacious risings to bestir the unenlightened many. He felt in his soul that it was past time to challenge the mainstream insistence that Germany was somebody else's problem, which only emboldened Hitler into greater ruthlessness. "And it came down to the fact," as he said, "that the *Bremen* was an ideal object lesson." But he was aghast at the orderly scenario thought up by the uptown commissars. Did they know nothing of life on a ship? "What was the crew supposed to do, sit there and watch you lock arms?" he said. "We thought we might even be beaten to death." Had they never heard of the Red Squad? Did they imagine that the NYPD, which rarely hesitated to crack heads on the picket lines, wouldn't continue its innovative efforts to defend the privileges of a most favored nation?

"Sometimes, I don't know how the Christ we get things done, how things get done at all," he told an interviewer. "But you have to figure what would happen if this had been an American ship and some Nazis came aboard your ship, to take the American flag off. I mean, you'd be in a state, ready to tear their eyeballs out. That's exactly what's going to happen here. To us seamen, the few of us, we said these people, the 'planners,' are out of their minds. We'd never get to within five feet of the bow. It's impossible. They're crazy. It's not going to work. Absolutely not going to work."

The papers on Monday morning, July 22, revealed that Catholic priests in Germany had been cowed into silence by the regime's threats. No arrests were reported. "Today's Nazi press takes the view that General Goering was merely issuing a 'last warning' to Catholics to toe the line and that action against them would come later," the *Times* reported. The Reich interior minister announced a new measure forbidding all Christian youth organizations, Catholic or Protestant, from marching in closed formation, wearing distinctive garb, or displaying unapproved insignia, part of the nearly completed plan to eliminate all competition to the Hitler Youth. The actions of non-Nazi youth groups, the interior minister said, "brought about a general danger to public security and order."

The Catholic issue received greater play in the papers than the continuing campaign against Jews. Foreign correspondents filled out their dispatches by reprinting items from the German press about the latest repressions. "No Jew or Jewess is permitted to move into Osann," according to the text of a resolution approved by a town council in western Germany. "No Jew can rent or buy a house or land in Osann. No craftsman, merchant, or any other citizen can get work or orders in the town if he has had anything to do with a Jew. Purchases from Jews mean treason against the people and the nation." A Jewish man was incarcerated in the Esterwegen concentration camp for engaging in intimate relations with twelve "Aryan" women. "Out with the Jews" and other anti-Semitic slogans were scrawled on the stately synagogue on Prinzregentenstrasse in western Berlin.

On the following day, the twenty-third, Mayor Fiorello LaGuardia released the text of a letter outlining his controversial decision to deny a masseur license to a German national living in New York, his clumsy attempt to lodge his own protest against the Führer. The "Little Flower" argued that Nazi actions against Americans living in Germany represented a violation of a 1925 commercial treaty between the two countries. Since "American citizens of the Jewish faith have been discriminated against in Germany," he wrote, the city of New York had every right to discriminate against German citizens in the United States. The State Department declined to comment, but unnamed sources told reporters "no specific cases of discrimination against Americans in Germany were before the department to substantiate the mayor's charges." German residents of New York were furious. "We might go down to City Hall and give the mayor a piece of our mind," said Joseph Schuster, of the Friends of the New Germany, during a rally attended by one thousand Nazi supporters in Brooklyn. "He is supposed to be the mayor for all people, not for the Jews only."

In the late morning, the blunt-speaking Samuel Untermyer, who led the Non-Sectarian Anti-Nazi League, told reporters that he hoped Catholics, Protestants, and Jews would join together in a "united boycott drive" that would "accomplish the economic disaster of the Hitler regime within 90 days.

"The boycott is the only effective weapon," he said before boarding the Italian liner *Conte di Savoia* for a month of convalescence in Europe. "If the Catholics of the world will join in this boycott as a body, they can destroy this unholy pagan reversion to the dark ages almost over night."

Untermyer, who was seventy-seven years old and in ill health, told the reporter from the *New York Post*: "Don't say I am a sick man. Just say that I feel fairly good but need a rest. I have trouble sleeping."

The Associated Press reported that hundreds of Jewish children were informed by social welfare workers that they were not welcome on a popular Berlin playground. In the spa town of Waren in northern Germany, a prominent hotel nailed up a sign that was increasingly seen on approach roads and town squares in every corner of the Reich: "Jews Not Wanted Here." In Cologne, a Jewish man identified as Joseph Herz was arrested "because of habitual sexual intercourse with Aryan women."

The State Department was receiving a flood of telegrams, letters, and resolutions from individuals and organizations urging the FDR administration to take some kind of a stand against Hitler. Impassioned messages were received from the Assembly of Hebrew Orthodox Rabbis of the United States and Canada; Rose Kaprove of Hartford, Connecticut; Local 42 of the Painters' Union in Hazel Park, Michigan; Harry Pryweller, proprietor of the New York Fur Shop of South Bend, Indiana; Local 10 of the Amalgamated Ladies Garment Cutters Union in New York; and the Eastside Democratic Epic Club of Los Angeles. "JEWS IN GERMANY THREATENED WITH WHOLESALE ATTACKS STOP," read the telegram from the Jewish National Workers Alliance of Saint Louis. "SITUATION VERY GRAVE STOP BELIEVE AMERICAN GOVERN-MENT SHOULD EXPRESS ITS OFFICIAL CONDEMNATION OF NAZI GOV-ERNMENT'S TERRORISM STOP."

On July 24, Senator William King, a Democrat from Utah, made headlines by delivering a speech in the US Senate, calling for a congressional inquiry into the "barbarous religious perse-cution" with an eye toward severing diplomatic relations with the Hitler regime. The proposal was so far outside the Washington consensus that even he conceded it was dead on arrival. "I don't want it to go on record that not a single person in this nation pro-tested," he said. According to a memo in the State Department files, Senator King approached Undersecretary of State William Phillips at a dinner and apologized for any embarrassment his public comments may have caused the FDR administration. "He referred to his resolution and explained to me that he assumed, of course, I understood that it was only meant as an expression of the feeling of many people with regard to conditions in Germany at this time; that he, naturally, did not expect to push his resolution, and that if I had an opportunity to tell the president that that was his idea, he would be glad to have me do so," wrote Phillips of Senator King's mea culpa.

On Thursday, July 25, the heat wave in New York entered its twenty-first day. Dr. James H. Kimball, a senior meteorologist with the United States Weather Bureau, said he could not recall such a sustained period of high humidity in all his years of service. Even the great heat wave of July 1901, which he remembered well from his days as a junior member of the bureau, was not nearly as un-comfortable as the torrid spell from July 4 to July 25, 1935.

It was estimated that 250,000 people were now sleeping on the sands of the Rockaways.

On the morning of the twenty-fifth, Congressman Samuel Dickstein, the Tammany Democrat from the Lower East Side, rose in the House of Representatives in Washington and delivered a long denunciation of the "idiotic tyranny" of the Nazi state. Hitler has "stooped to coldblooded murder in his self-appointed task of enforcing upon the people of Germany his absolute control of the affairs of state, of religion, and of matters pertaining to foreign trade." In the course of his jeremiad, Dickstein described Hitler as "the madman of Germany," a breach of decorum that caused Congressman Thomas Blanton to leap to his feet and embody the voice of the people with his Texas accent: "There is plenty here at home for him to look after, if he would protect our home folks and would attend to his own business, and let foreign governments attend to their own business!"

At just after noon, the most honored possession of the Nazi state made its 111th entrance into New York Harbor.

A handful of reporters were waiting at Quarantine. The *Bremen* "came in with 904 passengers, a heavy load this way at this season," wrote James Street, the ship news columnist for the *New York American*, the lead paper of the Hearst chain. The liner had left Germany six days earlier, stopping as was customary at Southampton and Cherbourg and traveling at an average speed of 26.58 knots. Street was able to score an interview with the senior man on board. "Commodore L. Ziegenbein, the genial skipper, said he had eight hours of fog and was delayed a whit."

Mr. Street wanted to ask Ziegenbein about the new French superliner, the *Normandie*, which had earned the Blue Riband during its maiden voyage two months earlier. The ship was widely regarded as the most impressive transatlantic steamer now afloat, a five-star Parisian hotel on the water, just as lauded for its fine cuisine, opulent interiors, and brusque waiters as the Ritz back on place Vendôme.

Ziegenbein insisted that he "will never try to beat *Normandie*'s record," Street wrote. "He's content to keep his express schedule."

The men from the *New York Times* and *Herald Tribune* boarded to speak with the young American who had provided the world with an eyewitness account of the Berlin Riots of ten days earlier. Varian Fry, the journalist in horn-rimmed spectacles, was

The *Bremen* at Pier 86.
(Acme Newspictures)

traveling in third class, which put him in a multiberth cabin among strangers down on the C or D deck.

The *American*'s James Street saw no reason to interrogate the "serious-faced soldier of pen and ink," whose "narrations had too much blood and thunder for our timid soul."

For the two gentlemen from the serious broadsheets, Fry recounted his harrowing experience on the Kurfürstendamm, adding the detail that he heard the pogromists chant: "*Wenn's Judenblut vom Messer spritzt / Dann geht's nochmal so gut*" ("When Jew blood squirts from the knife / Then everything will be fine again"). He told the reporters about a visit he made on the morning after the riot to the office of none other than Ernst "Putzi" Hanfstaengl. Both were Harvard men—Fry was a member of the class of '30—and they spoke (in English) as two members of a select community. During the course of the talk, Hanfstaengl unburdened himself of a revelation. He told Fry that a segment of the Nazi leadership wanted to solve the Jewish question *with the physical extermination of the Jews.*

"I only half believed him," Fry would write in 1942. "It was not much more than a year after the Blood Bath of June 30, 1934; yet even then I could not believe that there were men in positions of power and authority in western Europe in the twentieth century who could seriously entertain such a monstrous idea."

During these hours, Maggie Weaver returned to her Greenwich Village apartment after completing a two-week trip to New

England. She found Bill Bailey, Mac Blair, and a few other seamen "having a little meeting and they all had Catholic rosaries around their necks and they were refreshing themselves on the Hail Mary," she remembered. The men, cradle Catholics who had long since abandoned the faith, decided to impersonate devout followers of Christ who were roused to attack the *Bremen* swastika solely because of the Hitler government's drive against the Church.

"If we get arrested, we can't say we're Communists," Bailey explained. "No percentage in that. 'Tell you what, let's say we're Catholics.' But in order to do that we had to revert back a little to our childhood. We had to go out and buy rosaries and put them around our neck. We had to buy some medals with the Virgin Mother and wear that. And we had to go around, checking our language a little bit. Relearn the 'Hail Mary' and the 'Our Father.' It was quite a little job. There's nothing worse than a Catholic parish cop in New York who is getting ready to beat your brains out and he's waiting for you to make one mistake. 'You're a Catholic boy are you? Say the Act of Contrition to me!' Man, you had to know it. And if you don't know what the hell you're saying, you're in big trouble."

In the early afternoon, in the hour or two after the *Bremen* reached its berth at Pier 86, the skies opened up. The downpour lasted for hours. The Weather Bureau predicted that the rains would be accompanied by a cool wind from the north. At long last, the mercury was dropping.

CHAPTER TEN

Hear it, boys, hear it? Hell, listen to me! Coast to coast!
HELLO AMERICA!

—CLIFFORD ODETS, *WAITING FOR LEFTY*

S EVEN MILLION NEW Yorkers, few of them in possession of
the luxury item known as an electric fan, woke up to the best
news in three weeks on Friday, July 26, 1935. During the overnight hours, the humidity plunged by 33 points. By sunrise, the
temperate air from Canada had completed its work. The heat
wave was over.

"Humidity Goes Into Tailspin," the *New York Post* exulted. "Rain
Ushers in Cool Spell," declared the *Brooklyn Eagle*.

The *New York Times* and *Herald Tribune* didn't make much of a
fuss that morning over Varian Fry's revelations about his conversation with Ernst Hanfstaengl. "Reich Divided on Way to Treat Jews,
Says Fry," was the cautious headline on page eleven of the *Tribune*.
One faction of the Nazi Party, the paper went on in summary of
Hanfstaengl's comments to Fry, "were the radicals, who wanted
to settle the matter by blood." The other, "the self-styled moderate group," wanted to "segregate the Jews and settle the question
by legal methods." The *Times* ran its version on page eight and
devoted most of the article to Fry's retelling of the Berlin Riots.
"There were literally hundreds of policemen standing around but

I did not see them do anything but protect certain cafés which I was told were owned by Nazis," Fry was quoted as saying. The paper saved its preview of the Holocaust for the ninth of eleven paragraphs. The nation's newspaper of record didn't see the value in highlighting the disclosure that "the radical section" of Hitler's regime "desired to solve the Jewish question with bloodshed."

Reached for comment in Berlin, Hanfstaengl called Fry's account "fictions and lies from start to finish."

The morning papers carried the news that Jewish athletes would not be represented on Germany's Olympic team. Nazi officials claimed that Jews were eliminated from competition because they lacked the requisite ability to compete with "Aryans." The announcement led to immediate calls for the United States to boycott the Summer Games scheduled for Berlin in 1936. Avery Brundage, the president of the American Olympic Committee, found merit in the Nazi argument about Jewish inferiority. "The fact that no Jews have been named so far to compete for Germany doesn't necessarily mean that they have been discriminated against." Brundage said he saw "no racial or religious reasons" why the US team shouldn't attend the Berlin Olympics. Organized amateur sport "cannot, with good grace or propriety, interfere with the internal political, religious, or racial affairs of any country or group."

In Washington, DC, on the same morning, a delegation that included representatives of the American Jewish Committee, the American Jewish Congress, the B'nai B'rith, and the Jewish Labor Committee was granted a meeting with Undersecretary of State William Phillips. (Secretary of State Cordell Hull was on vacation.) The group handed Phillips a letter protesting the Nazi "reign of terror," which targeted Jews with particular severity but was "beginning to affect the lives of numberless Catholics and Protestants and liberals of every description." The administration was urged to "take all steps consistent with international practice to inform the German government of the outraged sentiments of the American people." Phillips was cordial but promised nothing.

At noon in New York, the thermometer registered a glorious 76 degrees.

Bill Bailey and Mac Blair were preparing for the evening's undertaking with Pat Gavin, an Irishman with a rich brogue who was reputed to have served, as a young teenager, with the Irish Republican Army during Ireland's War of Independence. Blue-eyed and ruddy-faced, Gavin was a native of Currane, a remote village in County Mayo on the west coast of Ireland. He stood just over six foot one and weighed 190 pounds. "Since his first days in the States he allied himself with the revolutionary struggle of the people," Bailey wrote of Gavin. "He was always a good man to have at your side in the event of trouble."

The Communist Party leadership had decided that the privilege of hauling down the swastika would fall to the oldest and most accomplished of the dozen or so mariners who were to board the *Bremen*. Edward Drolette (pronounced Dro-LETT) was thirty-six years old. The son of an English father and an Irish mother, he had risen from a Dickensian childhood in Manhattan without resorting to crime. At age sixteen, he began working in the engine rooms of oceangoing vessels. "I have been to sea since 1915," he later said, continuing, "I traveled in a fire room with a banjo, a shovel, stoking six-day fires." In November 1917, he enlisted in the American Expeditionary Force and went to France to fight in the World War. After his discharge in 1919, Drolette labored to become the youngest chief engineer licensed in the US merchant marine. By the summer of 1935, he was an outspoken and eloquent labor activist praised in the pages of the *Daily Worker* for his "long and splendid record of working class activity."

But Eddie Drolette, for all his dedication to the cause, was utterly unsuited for participation in a covert conspiracy. For the truth was, he couldn't keep his mouth shut.

Drolette had been "talking to everybody" about the *Bremen* plan "for several days," according to Maggie Weaver, who called him "Mr. Talk Too Much."

It was hardly a surprise that word reached the New York Police Department (NYPD) about a Communist plot, purportedly led by Drolette, to cause some kind of disruption aboard the *Bremen* during the sailing party.

By 3:30 p.m. on the appointed day, two detectives from the Red Squad began conducting a surveillance of Mr. Talk Too Much, who seemed to be chatting with everyone hanging around the lower blocks of South Street, the district on the East River waterfront filled with thousands of unemployed marine workers.

Harold F. Moore was a kind of supercop, a shoot-'em-up specialist most famous for ambushing a gangster named Edward "Fats" McCarthy at a hideout outside Albany in 1932. Moore had been wounded sixteen times in three separate incidents over the previous decade. "I've been pretty lucky," he once quipped to reporters. He seemed to go to work each day in hopes of discharging the revolver strapped under his jacket. Matthew Solomon was a pioneering Jewish member of the force. He, too, was a "hero cop." One night in 1926, he left a benefit dinner for the Shomrim Society, the fraternal association of Jewish officers, and chased down a cocaine-addled stickup artist, suffering a gunshot wound to the chest in the process of detaining the frenzied suspect. Solomon was a model for his people now placed in the morally vexed position of safeguarding the prerogatives of Adolf Hitler.

Moore and Solomon parked themselves in the office of a trucking company near the corner of Broad and Front Streets, located on a shabby block not far from two mammoth men's shelters, the Seaman's Church Institute at Twenty-Five South Street and the Municipal Lodging House at the foot of Whitehall Street. The plainclothesmen watched as Drolette entered 111 Broad Street, which included a radical bookstore in its basement level. For an hour and a half, they waited for him to emerge. The clatter of the elevated train over Front Street provided an intermittent soundtrack.

At four p.m. in Washington, President Franklin Roosevelt was asked during a press conference to "outline" how he would keep the United States out of foreign entanglements.

"I could do it in an hour and a half," he responded. "It is a very big subject. Of course, there are two main, salient facts: The first is the Good Neighbor policy to keep us friendly with nations, and the other is every effort, through diplomatic agencies, to keep us from getting involved in specific cases that do not concern us. I do not think I can go any further than those two general statements."

He was asked about Ethiopia, which was bracing for an invasion from Fascist Italy. "Do you consider Ethiopia a specific case that does not concern us?"

"I should say yes," the president responded.

At 5:30 p.m., Drolette, who was five foot seven with a slight build, emerged from 111 Broad Street. The cops recorded that he was wearing a brown coat, brown trousers, white shirt, and no hat.

Over the next three hours, as late afternoon transformed into early evening, the detectives watched Drolette's blithe wanderings around the immediate vicinity, making careful note of his every movement.

In the meantime, the commanding officer of the NYPD's Red Squad rushed up to Pier 86 for a conference with Hapag-Lloyd officials. Lieutenant James A. Pyke urged the German shipping line to take precautionary measures to keep "unauthorized persons" from coming on board to commit "the contemplated disturbance." But the Germans were hesitant to adopt any suggestion that would make it burdensome for visitors to flock to the festival of conviviality that was featured in all the advertisements. The passenger list included well more than a thousand names, which, coupled with the perfect weather conditions, meant that a few thousand walk-ons would get a promotional glimpse of the comforts on offer. Each was a potential contributor to a German economy that was struggling for self-sufficiency in the face of what Nazi invective described as a "Jewish international campaign of hatred."

The marine superintendent of the German shipping line, William Drechsel, asked the NYPD to maintain security in and around the pier. The crew "would be sufficient and thoroughly able" to protect the territory of the *Bremen* from a handful of bumbling deadbeats, he said.

The sun set at 8:19 p.m.

At about 8:30 p.m., Drolette and an unknown man walked to the South Ferry subway station, pushed through the turnstiles, and walked up to the platform for the Ninth Avenue elevated line.

Detectives Moore and Solomon followed close behind.

Drolette and his companion allowed a few trains to pass through the station before boarding. Moore and Solomon hopped in a few cars back.

The train rumbled along the elevated tracks past the Battery and north through Greenwich Village and Chelsea. At the Fifti- eth Street stop, in the heart of Hell's Kitchen, the suspects disem- barked. Moore and Solomon trailed behind as the two walked up to a union headquarters on Eighth Avenue between Fifty-Fourth and Fifty-Fifth Streets.

Drolette and the unknown man entered the building at about 9:15 p.m.

The detectives staked out across the street.

The fifty individuals chosen to occupy the liner—the dozen or so seamen assigned to the flag extraction and the two dozen or so who would provide support—had been directed to attend a stag- ing meeting for final preparations.

"We dressed in our best clothes, as per instructions," wrote Bai- ley. "I looked good in my new suit and Panama hat which I had purchased two weeks earlier."

Once the plotters were inside the building, an official from party headquarters went over the ill-considered scheme to remove the flag, which depended for its success on the blinkered belief that the *Bremen* sailors would experience an epiphany, decide the time was right to rise against Hitler, and *join* the offensive against the swastika.

The intended occupiers of the ship were instructed to act cau- tiously and pretend to be seeing off friends or relatives bound for Europe. Before a skeptical question could be asked, a comrade with a bag of coins was circulating and handing out the ten-cent admission fee.

On the way to the pier, Bailey, Blair, and Gavin dumped out most of the contents of a half pint of whiskey and swayed through the streets like happy drunks on the prowl for a nightcap. "We never touched a drop," insisted Bailey. Their pockets had been cleared of incriminating identification and filled with crucifixes, prayer beads, and holy cards. "They bought red roses to put into the lapels of their suits," recalled Maggie Weaver. On the chance that he got close to the swastika, Bailey carried an uncovered Gem razorblade, which, unknown to him, was already cutting a hole in the lining of his pants. Mindful of the vast superiority of the opposing forces, the seamen took care to equip themselves with makeshift weapons for self-preservation. Paddy Gavin found an old spike. Mac Blair procured a fountain pen.

Without the knowledge of the others, Eddie "Mr. Talk Too Much" Drolette carried a pair of metal knuckles, which were illegal to possess in New York State.

"Had we known that, we would've said, 'Hey, dump them sonofabitches,'" said Bailey. "It's as bad as carrying a gun or a big long shiv. We didn't come here to murder people. We just come here to get a flag."

Drolette left the building at 10:15 p.m. He was alone.

The detectives followed as Drolette walked south on Eighth Avenue and turned west on West Forty-Sixth Street. He traveled for three long blocks until reaching Eleventh Avenue, where the NYPD had established one of a handful of checkpoints. Automobile and pedestrian traffic was increasing. The theaters in Times Square were beginning to let out. At the Belasco Theatre on Forty-Fourth Street and Broadway, the curtain was coming down on a double-bill of *Awake and Sing!* and *Waiting for Lefty*, Clifford Odets's pair of agitprop masterpieces. "Hear it, boys, hear it?" a character cries during the stirring final scene of *Lefty*. "Hell, listen to me! Coast to coast! HELLO AMERICA! HELLO. WE'RE STORMBIRDS OF THE WORKING CLASS, WORKERS OF THE WORLD . . . OUR BONES AND BLOOD! And when we die they'll know what we did to make a new world! Christ, cut us up to little pieces. We'll die for what is right! Put fruit trees where our ashes are!"

Told by the patrolmen to approach from another direction, Drolette continued south on Eleventh Avenue, turned right on West Forty-Fifth Street, and reached the police checkpoint at Twelfth Avenue (also known as West Street), which ran parallel to the Hudson River underneath the West Side Elevated Highway. He was now a block south of the ship.

New York's Finest had been instructed to "not interfere with the persons coming onto the pier" or to disrupt "the regular routine business of the line." Like everyone else on this night, Drolette was waved through.

Moore and Solomon were right behind him.

They came upon a wondrous spectacle. The *Bremen* was surrounded by a circus of humanity worthy of a neorealist film. Souvenir peddlers sold postcards, buttons, and other knickknacks on German themes. Florists did a brisk business in orchid corsages, a required accessory of midnight sailings. Newsboys hawked the late city editions: "Reich Jews 'Eliminated' from Olympics!" Taxis, limos, and private cars dropped off bejeweled women in glittering gowns accompanied by tuxedoed men in opera hats and white gloves. Neighborhood strollers gazed up at the tiers of shipboard lights and listened to the muffled sounds of the on-deck bands. Stevedores loaded freight on swinging hampers. Porters manhandled baggage carts. Pickpockets trolled for victims.

"We went down to see the *Bremen* off the other evening and you might have thought you were caught up in a sort of formally dressed commuters' rush," wrote high-society columnist Lucius Beebe of a recent midnight sailing. "There were mobs of people, avalanches of baggage whirling up out of the glare of the arc lamps, whole tide-rips of orchid corsages flowing, paradoxically, up the gangways, a hundred shrieking stevedore's whistles and a general air of hysterical and frenzied leave-taking reminiscent of the boom years. Wine corks popped, stewards maneuvered like steamers breasting rapids, the cargo hoists clattered and snarled and two or three bands played cheerful Teutonic music, sawing and tooting and whanging for all they were worth."

Elissa Landi, one of the stars of MGM's recent hit *The Count of Monte Cristo*, arrived with her mother, Countess Caroline Zanardi Landi, who claimed, dubiously, to be the illegitimate daughter of Empress Elisabeth of Austria. Henry S. Morgan, the son of J. P. Morgan, was traveling with his wife, three of his children,

and a Russian governess. He was about to co-found a business
called Morgan Stanley. Arthur Robinson had just been defeated
for reelection as US senator from Indiana. A number of Disciples
of Christ clergymen were sailing to the denomination's international convention in Leicester, England. Geraldine Rockefeller
Dodge was the youngest daughter of William Rockefeller Jr., who
had founded the Standard Oil Company with his brother John
D. Rockefeller. James Forrestal was recorded on the manifest as
a banker but he would eventually become FDR's secretary of the
navy. There was a London hairdresser; a handful of Japanese dip-
lomats; Frederic and Elnora Boda, a Christian missionary couple
bound for East Africa; a journalist or two; numerous business executives; Humberto Fombona-Blanco, a Honduran nobleman;
and Charles H. Swift, a Chicago food-processing magnate, who
the poet Ezra Pound once described as the "porkpacker." Perhaps
the most precious cargo aboard was William Donner Roosevelt,
the two-year-old grandson of the president of the United States,
whose mother was taking him on an extended vacation abroad so
he wouldn't be kidnapped like the Lindbergh baby. The flagship
of Nazi Germany's merchant marine, then, was entrusted with the
safe passage of a little prince of the American republic.

The photographer on assignment for the Associated Press
aimed his Speed Graphic at tuxedo-clad Anthony J. Drexel Biddle,
the new US ambassador to Norway, who was shaking hands with
a grinning well-wisher, Governor George H. Earle III of Pennsylvania. The two men, Philadelphia socialites who had contributed
handsomely to FDR's election campaign, had arrived at the ship
after attending a farewell dinner at the Starlight Roof of the Wal-
dorf Astoria.

Drolette passed in front of the *Bremen* and slipped into the two-
story terminal along its north (port) side. He took the stairs or
elevator to the second level and followed the German/English
signs to the gangplank reserved for nonpassengers, thus avoiding
the scrum of activity around passport control. Paying his dime to
the Seaman's Fund, Drolette joined the stream crossing over to a
spot on the B (bow) deck about 150 feet from the flag. With the

shore-facing section of the B deck closed off to guests, the crowd was directed up a narrow staircase to an open portion of the A deck just below the bridge, joining an elbow-to-elbow bacchanal under the starry sky of a cool, clear Manhattan night.

Upon entering the terminal, Detectives Moore and Solomon met the Red Squad's commanding officer, Lieutenant James Pyke, who, in an indication of the seriousness of the situation, was now coordinating the response with two deputy chief inspectors. With no apparent hesitation, Lieutenant Pyke allowed the detectives to continue tracking Edward Drolette onto Nazi government property, which revealed that the NYPD was willing to go *beyond* the German shipping line's own wishes in defending Hitler's territory. Pyke assigned an additional detective, Edward F. Murphy, to accompany Moore and Solomon onto the vessel.

Shipping line employees, then, were unaware that reinforcements had arrived in the form of three clandestine agents wearing civilian attire and concealing firearms. Nor did they have any idea that one of the allies, Detective Matthew Solomon, was a member of a race that Nazi propaganda identified by physical description as the enemy of German interests.

The time was now about 10:30 p.m.

Following their own route to the pier, Bill Bailey, Mac Blair, and Paddy Gavin had no trouble advancing through police lines and coming within sight of the liner.

"The *Bremen* stood motionless alongside the pier," Bailey later wrote. "Her bow jutted up, looming over the street. Large, powerful floodlights in various parts of the ship directed their beams to one spot: the jackstaff which held the Nazi swastika. It fluttered brazenly in the summer breeze. It seemed as if all New York could look out their windows and see this flag lit up like a house on fire."

Paddy Gavin, whose Irish accent was as thick as the fog over the Cliffs of Moher, purchased a swastika badge from a vendor. He was instructed to keep his mouth shut. Bailey and Blair each bought a pennant emblazoned with a Rhine castle and the word

Vaterland. After a "fast lookin' over" from the harried monitors at the gangplank, the three proceeded to the B deck and then up the stairs to the A deck, occasionally barking out a spirited "*Sieg Heil*" for appearance's sake. They were surrounded by so many champagne guzzlers, tray-balancing stewards, curiosity seekers, Western Union messenger boys, and forlorn lovers that it was difficult to move.

"This is the first time we've been aboard the ship," Bailey told an interviewer. "Man, we had to survey everything. I mean, you know, your life depended on it."

Bailey looked back toward the front of the ship.

"The bow and the swastika seemed miles away."

By 10:45, the protesters could be heard parading up from downtown, carrying banners, shouting slogans, and singing the nineteenth-century socialist anthem, "The Internationale":

> *Arise, you prisoners of starvation!*
> *Arise, you wretched of the earth!*
> *For justice thunders condemnation:*
> *A better world's in birth!*
> *No more tradition's chains shall bind us*
> *Arise, you slaves, no more in thrall;*
> *The earth shall rise on new foundations*
> *We have been naught we shall be all.*

Onward marched an assortment of left-wingers from lightest pink to deepest red. The largest sign read "FREE THÄLMANN!" referring to the leader of Germany's Communist Party who would never make it out of Buchenwald. "NAZISM BREEDS WAR," proclaimed another. The men could be seen in dark slacks and button-down shirts, some in suit jackets and/or ties, many donning fedoras or straw boaters. The women, who were said to represent the majority, were in summer dresses or skirts with a midcalf hemline. A few wore a close-fitting beret or cloche hat. The chairwoman of the demonstration was a Russian-born feminist named

June Croll, who was married to the African-American author and journalist Eugene Gordon.

Julius Rosenberg was there, the seventeen-year-old militant with the Young Communist League at City College who would be executed eighteen years later along with his wife, Ethel, convicted at the height of the McCarthy era of stealing atomic secrets for the Soviet Union. He would boast to his brother-in-law that it was *he*, Julius, who led the raid on the *Bremen*. Also present was Dorothy Day, the thirty-seven-year-old former socialist and cofounder of the Catholic Worker movement, which promoted Christ-centered pacifism through its newspaper, houses of hospitality for the poor, and farming communes. An ardent supporter of the boycott of German goods and services, Day was skeptical of the Kremlin's sincerity in calling for popular or united fronts of "fellow travelers" to come together against the threat from Nazism, a policy shift just now in the midst of formal promulgation during the Seventh World Congress of the Communist International in Moscow.

"It was eleven at night when we started out, going up to the *Bremen* demonstration, called by the Communists, but at which we had decided to distribute literature and leaflets," she wrote. "Songs succeeded speeches, there was a succession of chants— RED FRONT . . . RED FRONT . . . RED FRONT. It is not a United Front, as they admit always when demonstrations get underway, but a Red Front."

"Catholics and Jews! Protest the religious persecution in Germany!" read the circular she distributed with the other Catholic Workers. "The Friends of Catholic Germany is an organization formed to protest against the brutal technique of Germany's one-man government and to combat fascism in the United States. . . . We invite all lovers of freedom to join with us in boycotting German products so long as the German Government persists in this disgraceful and un-Christian practice."

A few thousand liberals and radicals assembled directly opposite the ship, swarming across Twelfth Avenue and into the side streets. They jostled to get a good look at the figures leading the exhortations from atop a large piece of squared timber in the shadow of the hull. All attention was directed toward the flag that glowed from a perch about 50 feet above the makeshift platform.

According to the newspapers, the police "sensed trouble." Backups were requested, which pushed the size of the contingent to about 350 officers, including a hundred undercover detectives and a few dozen mounted units. A private security firm hired by the German shipping line deployed fifty uniformed and five plainclothesmen. The demonstrators were opposed by a group of pro-Nazi German-Americans, members of the Friends of the New Germany, who were handing out flyers denouncing Mayor LaGuardia's attempt to protest Nazi excesses by denying a masseur license to a German national named Paul Kress. The Friends may have found a receptive audience among the patriotic *Volk* from immigrant enclaves who were known to come out to *Bremen* sailings to experience a little taste of home.

Several hundred unaffiliated bystanders, at the very least, were assembled along the waterfront to catch a glimpse of the pageantry, a cheap diversion at a moment in the Great Depression when about one fifth of the city's population was on some form of public assistance.

"Many have made the ocean voyage, more hope to, all long to do so," a writer noted of the spectators who came out to see a previous visit of the *Bremen*. "Home ties and duties, adverse economic circumstances, one thing or another compels them to remain ashore but . . . down they go to watch the great floating palace begin or end its journey, conjuring up thoughts of distant places, reminiscences of past voyages or anticipation of travel joys still to be realized."

At 11:15 p.m., the NYPD informed the German shipping line that the security of the liner had been breached. The message was that "some of the Communists" were slipping aboard "accompanied by well dressed women." After receiving the news up on the bridge, Commodore Leopold Ziegenbein, the mustachioed eminence who had helmed the vessel since its inauguration in 1929, issued an order seeking the removal of all visitors, which was easier said than done. Police estimated that *4,800 people* had

joined a shipboard celebration that was notorious for lasting until the last stragglers were dragged out of the swimming pool on
the G deck. The manifest listed 1,260 passengers and 943 crew
members, which put the number of people on the ship at roughly
7,000.

Amid the crush of merrymakers on the A deck, Bailey knew
that the well-laid plan of his party leaders was destined to fail. The
women assigned to shackle themselves to the mast approached
and admitted they were having trouble with the handcuffs. "We
got our own problems," he told them. The route to the flag was
impeded by mooring winches, anchor chains, cargo hatches, sea
breakers, a 6-foot-high gunwale, and a large number of well-fed
crew members, who had come up to the forward deck to get a look
at the noisy demonstration on the pier. "Jesus Christ, it seemed
like a lost cause," he remembered. "Here we have a chance to
really do something and it's all screwed up because of this dumb,
idiotic planning."

"Well, we've got to do something," said Mac Blair.

The seamen conferred among themselves and came up with an
alternative plan. It was decided that a group led by Eddie Drolette
would rush to the starboard side, which would draw the attention
of the sailors who were congregated on the forward deck to get a
better view of the rally. A group led by Bailey would then make a
dash for the flag from the port side.

In his nervousness, Bailey kept reaching in his pocket to check
on the razorblade, opening up little cuts in his fingers.

The Red Squad detectives (Moore, Solomon, and Murphy)
watched as Edward Drolette moved through the A deck and con-
versed with his fellow conspirators, which permitted the policemen to make a visual identification of each participant. They were
able to lean in close enough to catch snippets of the conversations.

At 11:45 p.m., the signal went off.

The *Bremen*'s whistle released the eardrum-shattering blast that
was understood by all as the fifteen-minute warning, the bitter-
sweet herald of midnight that had the power to unsettle emotions.
The sound hung in the air for several long seconds, calling a brief

halt to the evening's frenzy like a summons from another dimension. Before the echo bounced back from the Jersey side, stewards were clearing their throat and delivering the iconic cry that spelled the end of the high-toned socializing.

"The demonstration was going on and then we heard 'all ashore that's goin' ashore,'" remembered Maggie Weaver, "and we thought, 'Well, the flag wasn't going to come down.'"

The twelve seamen squeezed into the mob moving toward the stairs that led from the A deck to the B deck.

Detective Solomon was closest to Drolette. Lagging behind were Detectives Moore and Murphy.

At the foot of the fifteen- or twenty-step descent, *Bremen* crew members were directing everyone onto the gangplank that led back to the terminal.

The first to refuse was Vincent "Low Life" McCormack, a diminutive scrapper who, like the rest, was a former member of the Marine Workers Industrial Union who had joined the Communist Party. ("A wonderful guy," said Bailey.) McCormack walked toward the restricted portion of the B deck, which earned him a rebuke from a *Bremen* officer. With barely a hesitation, McCormack lobbed a haymaker that knocked the man flat on his back.

Passengers shrieked. Orders were shouted in German from the bridge.

The three detectives were shoved *away* from the action.

At the bottom of the stairs, Drolette led his small unit up toward the starboard side.

Bailey, Blair, and Gavin followed the agreed-upon course up the port side, slipping past the (unfair) fight developing around "Low Life" McCormack.

Pat Gavin was next to play blocking back.

He intercepted an angry band of antagonists with a flurry of lefts and rights.

Bailey and Blair couldn't afford to look back.

They rushed toward the bow, maneuvering over and around the on-deck obstacles.

Then, Blair had his turn.

He jabbed the fountain pen into the face of a sailor who caught him by the neck.

Bailey hesitated, eager to help out the stalwart buddy who would become a lifelong friend.

"Keep going! Keep going!" Blair shouted. "Get up there! Get up there!"

With a boost of adrenaline that came to him "just unconsciously," Bailey leaped onto the elevated gunwale that ringed the lip of the bow. He grabbed the "very cringy little ladder" attached to the bowsprit and ascended to the top, a five- or six-rung climb.

Backlit by the klieg light from the bridge, Bailey's large frame was now in silhouetted view of the spectators on the shore.

A roar went up. "A roar of triumph," wrote Dorothy Day.

The police troops surrounding the assemblage reached for their nightsticks.

"Watch that flag!" someone shouted.

Feeling "almost stage fright," Bailey took a moment to glance down. Without a rail to brace himself, he understood that the slightest misstep would put him in the drink.

He tugged at the swastika, which ripped along the top seam.

He pulled again and again. And a few more times. But the bottom half would not give.

"I was in an open area, almost like a stage," Bailey said. "Everybody on the dock is now watching. All eyes are focused on the bow. I'm standing up there like an idiot, pulling."

He reached into his pocket. Instead of a razorblade, he found a hole.

Panic was setting in.

"So I turned around. It's like knowing there's something in back of you, looking. And I thought . . . and I had that feeling that something was going on next to me, within inches of me, and sure enough, when I turned around, right on the deck, practically at my heels, was a hand going up. And I thought, 'Oh, God! Another inch and he's got me and he's going to yank me off, and I'll never get this rotten dirty flag off the ship.' So sure enough, I gave another look, and it was a guy named Duffy, a seaman. And he had worked his way up the ladder, too. Now he didn't even have to go up to the top where I was. He just said, 'Pull the flag still! Pull it still! Give me the rope! Hold it still!' And he took out a switchblade knife, and I heard 'click, click' and he let it go, on that part of the halyard, and the flag is now home free."

Bill Bailey hurled Hitler's treasure into the Hudson River.

The swastika "came sliding down, disappeared a moment, ballooned up and went skimming through the air dropping neatly into the water below," according to one account.

"What a beautiful sight that was, to see the flag in the spotlight go down in the river," remembered Maggie Weaver.

Adrian Duffy, short and wiry with "a sort of slightly crooked eye," vanished as quickly as he appeared.

"And it was . . . believe me, it was a moment worth everything that happened afterwards just to see that sonofabitch in the water," said Bailey, "and the Germans going stark mad! Absolutely stark mad! And the crowd on the dock stark mad with delight."

CHAPTER ELEVEN

The shot that wounded Edward Drolette rang around the world.

—*LABOR DEFENDER* MAGAZINE

BILL BAILEY WOULD invariably call what happened next "the hard part" of the story.

After heaving the swastika flag into the brackish slime of the Hudson River, he turned to jump down from the bowsprit.

"No matter where you look, guys are getting tumbled."

Several *Bremen* crew members were waiting for him, "figuring this bastard's got to come down sometime."

He landed on the deck and fell to his knees.

The Germans lifted him to his feet and threw a barrage of punches that somehow failed to land.

Bailey struggled past.

A German sailor advanced toward him.

"I could swear to this day I could read in his eyes that he wanted to say, 'Comrade, well done,'" Bailey remembered. "I felt he was anti-Nazi. Our side was always believing that the whole world was just waiting for us to do something. If he's one of us and he's trying to tell us we're doing a good job, the bridge is watching what's going on, so I have to make it look good."

A French newspaper's fanciful illustration of the strike
against the swastika. (Pèlerin)

Bailey protected the man's standing by pounding him hard across the face.

At about the midway point between the bow and the gangplank, Bailey was caught and thrown to the deck. A polished shoe with a sharp toe, probably worn by a waiter, administered a series of kicks about his forehead, jaw, and solar plexus.

Bailey slipped from consciousness.

Matthew Solomon was the first of the three detectives to push through the crowd around the gangplank and reach the forward deck. He came upon a pitched brawl between radical seamen disguised to look like respectable sailing party attendees and German crew members dressed in dark sailor uniforms and black-and-white berets with the words "Nordd. Lloyd Bremen" across the headband.

The actions of the next several minutes would become the most hotly disputed of the evening.

Solomon claimed he witnessed a Communist—the unknown man who had ridden the subway uptown with Drolette earlier in the evening—strike a *Bremen* seaman. Solomon identified him-self as a police officer and attempted to arrest the man, who re-sponded by punching him in the face. Solomon pulled out his pocket billy club (or blackjack) and struck the man with a single blow to the head. The unknown Communist was knocked to the deck. Solomon was then surrounded by a group of noncombatant protesters who began chanting a political slogan. He said he drew his revolver and identified himself as a police officer.

Then, he was attacked.

"Drolette and the others ganged me, knocking me down," he would say in his first comments after the incident. "They took my badge and weapons, shouting, 'Let's throw him overboard.'"

At this point, Detective Harold Moore was rushing toward the melee.

"I decided something must be done," Moore later boasted to reporters. "I fired at Drolette, one shot. He fell to the deck and that part of the riot was over in the twinkling of an eye."

Hit in the groin, Drolette slumped to the deck. He was badly injured but still conscious.

Drolette had a different version of the events that led up to his shooting. He said that Solomon, who was dressed in a green suit with two-toned tan wing tip shoes, was attacked by Nazi-indoctrinated German sailors who saw the detective as just an-other Jew Communist with hostile intentions toward Hitler. It was the *Germans* who were trying to throw Solomon overboard, a story confirmed by a *Herald Tribune* report that "some members of the crew" carried a man "to the rail" and "women screamed hysteri-cally, crying that if the man were thrown overboard he would be killed." Drolette and the others leapt into the scrum to *protect* the plainclothesman from harm. They were responding to Solomon's plight in keeping with the purpose of the evening, which was to agitate on behalf of threatened communities in the Third Reich.

In the midst of the fighting, Drolette saw Detective Moore point his revolver at him. "The man who shot me had the bullet aimed at my heart," Drolette said later. "The gun was less than a foot away from me, when I grabbed it and deflected the shot downward." The bullet cut through his groin and came out the side of his leg.

Whatever the precise circumstances, Detective Moore's gunshot represented the night's second great act of historical resonance: The reactionary response to the revolutionary gesture.

Eddie Drolette was the first casualty in the Allied confrontation with Nazi Germany.

Detective Murphy followed closely behind Moore. He fired a second shot, but no one was hit.

The gunfire was loud enough to be heard out on Twelfth Avenue, which was now the site of an open battle between charging policemen and cowering protesters. "Ashore modishly gowned women and their top-hatted escorts stampeded to shelter behind parked cars as Communists used their placards as clubs in hand-to-hand combat with cops," reported the *Daily News*. The *New York Times* estimated that it took the police "a half hour or more" to put the demonstrators "to route."

An angry horde of detectives and patrolmen stormed across the gangplank and onto the B deck, where they joined with *Bremen* sailors in inflicting a savage beating on the now-cornered Communists. The brutality lasted for several minutes near the port side railing, readily viewable to shocked witnesses at the waterside.

"The crowds stood motionless, fascinated and horrified by the untiring rhythm of blackjacks on faces and heads now indistinguishable except as a mass of red blood and torn flesh," wrote one witness, who went on, "Now many could not remain silent and from all along the pier came cries of 'Stop it!' 'You're killing them.' But the Nazi thugs and police had no intention of stopping. Brown shirts and red-spattered shirts, the blackjacks continued to swing, up, DOWN, up, DOWN, up, DOWN."

A *Bremen* lifeboat was lowered and sent out into the river to retrieve the swastika, which had been carried seaward by the tide. Either the sopping original or a dry replacement was hastily run up the bowsprit. The papers reported that *Bremen* crew members belted out the "Horst Wessel Lied" in desperate semblance of Nazi ceremony.

"*Die Fahne hoch!*" they began. "*Die Reihen fest geschlossen!*" ("The flag on high! The ranks tightly closed!")

In the minutes after the shots were fired, a Red Squad detective boarded the ship and turned over Drolette's prone body.

The detective said he discovered metal knuckles "semi-clutched" in Drolette's right hand.

"I hate to say this about our guys but he was just dumb," said Bailey of Drolette. "He had the brass knuckles. He's conscious. And he could've wiggled them off, push them away, an inch, two inches. But he didn't. He held onto them."

After a period of insensibility that may have lasted as long as ten minutes, Bill Bailey was startled awake by police officers dragging him to the gangplank. "Open up!" they shouted at irate passengers who loathed nothing so much as a travel delay. "Open up!"

"Then they took me through this mob of people," Bailey remembered. "You had to bump open the line to let me through. I'm sure if there were no cops there and they had a rope—the look on their faces was so sickening that they would've gladly hung me."

In his bleariness, Bailey was appalled to overhear the first evidence of miscomprehension.

"One woman said, 'It must be a bunch of college punks,'" he said. "I felt such a waste—here we took a beating, ripped the flag off, and this was the social significance—'college punks.'"

He was dumped into a third-class ticket booth in the terminal, joined by the rest of the banged-up characters whose names were about to be printed in newspapers across the globe. The police apprehended Vincent "Low Life" McCormack, who was nursing a battered right ear. William Howe and George Blackwell were there, two of the seamen from Eddie Drolette's decoy squad that drew attackers to the starboard side. Arthur "Mac" Blair was thrashed so soundly that he was bound for Bellevue Hospital, which was a long ambulance ride away on the far distant East Side. He would be joined at Bellevue by Drolette, who was doubled over with a gunshot wound that caused "a swelling of penis and laceration of left thigh," according to the police report.

Bailey didn't recognize the seventh man in the room. "There was a guy laying out there absolutely covered with blood, from the head all the way down," he said. "I mean, blood all over." Detective Matthew Solomon was barely able to speak. He was whisked to Polyclinic Hospital, which was located just a few blocks away.

The third member of the port-side team, Paddy Gavin, was nowhere to be seen. He had deployed his shamrock-rich brogue to convince cops that he was just another Irish detective responding to the trouble. He was gone.

As was Adrian Duffy and the talismanic switchblade that ripped the swastika free.

"Every few minutes cops sauntered over to the booth to look in on us with scowls of hatred on their faces," Bailey wrote. "One thing was certain, the way I saw the picture: We were going to get worked over.

"So the next thing was takin' names," he said. "What's your name? Bailey? Where do you come from? Oh, West Side. Okay, next, McCormack, where do you come from? West Side? Next one, Blackwell, Howe, Blair. There's not a Jew among any of these guys. They're all goddamn Irishmen! That hurt them because they expected us to be all Jews and Communists. And especially when they searched our pockets and out come prayer beads and all that. We were sittin' there, half of us, running prayer beads up and down, you know, dangling the crucifix. And the Irish cops could not understand what's going on. They wanted to physically destroy you, see, and they keep saying, 'Why'd you do this lad? What's this all about?' We'd say, 'Well, look at what that butcher is doing to our people over in Germany. Our fathers can't even say a word in church.' Some way, the cops wanted to do the right thing. He wants to belt you, but would it be right? So, anyhow, just contradictions going on. We knew we confused them."

At 12:40 a.m. on Saturday morning, the *Bremen* pulled out into the Hudson with none of the celebratory fanfare of usual. No streamers were launched. No handkerchiefs were waved. "The cheers and jeers as the giant liner started down the river were about evenly divided, although groups were seen making menacing motions and faces in the direction of all derogatory sounds," said the *Herald Tribune.* The ship was escorted by three New York Police Department (NYPD) launches. Forty officers remained on board until Quarantine in the Narrows to ensure that all trespassers had been ejected. (They had.)

Although it is hard to know the extent of the injuries on the German side, a postwar account described how a *Bremen* deck seaman had his front teeth knocked out.

Reporters were given the chance to speak with Commodore Ziegenbein, who alone seemed to understand the significance of the event that transpired under his nose.

"We don't know what the future has in store for us," he said, cryptically. "We don't know what is going to happen next."

The authorities succeeded in forcibly clearing the pier of all but a few fistfights, leaving scores of leftists bloodied up enough to require medical attention. With word circulating about the capture of the seamen, the protesters regrouped and marched to night court on West Fifty-Fourth Street. When it was learned that the seamen were headed instead to the Eighteenth Precinct, the processional turned south for the old yellow-brick station house on West Forty-Seventh Street. The streets along the route were crowded with people spilling out of dance halls, tenement houses, and corner bars.

"Free the Arrested Seamen!" the protesters chanted. "Down with Hitler!"

Among the marchers was an activist attorney, a member of the International Labor Defense, a Communist-affiliated legal society that specialized in representing the marginalized, downtrodden, and politically immoderate in high-profile cases. Abraham Unger may have been tipped off to the flag operation so he could get a head start in representing the indigent perpetrators who expected to be arrested. Unger was probably already plotting defense strategy and deciding whom to bring in as cocounsel.

Bailey, Blackwell, Howe, and McCormack were thrown into the back of a patrol wagon bound for the precinct.

"It was a big relief that we didn't get our brains beat out," said Bailey.

Escorted by a large contingent of police cars and motorcycles, the patrol wagon traveled a block north and three blocks east until reaching the vicinity of the station house.

Dorothy Day, who participated in the march from the pier to the precinct, watched as a man in civilian clothes appeared on the steps and ordered the cops to "get in there and clean up."

"Thus prompted those thugs in uniform, always present at these affairs, proceeded to do the cleaning up," she wrote. "They beat the Communists down the street with their clubs, and one of the Catholic Workers saw two plainclothesmen drag one of the demonstrators up into a dark hallway and one holding him, the other beat his face in while the victim screamed and crumpled underneath the blows. There was fifteen minutes of carnage, and the rioting was all on one side. The three Catholic Workers were in the thick of it, and aside from the shouting and jeering of the Communists, they saw no other but verbal violence from that side."

Infuriated by the actions of the NYPD, Maggie Weaver admitted that she went beyond verbal violence and "pounded one of the policemen on the back."

"You really should not do that," she conceded. "The cop came after me to arrest me and this Portuguese fellow came over to rescue me and he got arrested."

Several newspaper photographers were struck down by police, their cameras seized and smashed to the sidewalk, which is likely the reason no photographs have ever surfaced of the moment when Bill Bailey threw the swastika into the Hudson.

"Householders arrayed in nightshirts and pajamas appeared at windows above the surging, scuffling crowd, and added to the confusion by raining showers of missiles on the combatants," according to a newspaper report. "Brushes, boots, and buckets of water were flung down on their heads."

The patrol wagon traveled slowly down West Forty-Seventh Street.

"The people are beating on the wagon, 'Free them! Free them!'" said Bailey. "Here they are yelling, 'Okay, comrades, good job!' and we're trying to act as Catholics."

The scene in front of the precinct on West Forty-Seventh Street. (International News Photos)

Maggie Weaver remembered when Bailey emerged from the vehicle. "I saw him and said, 'Bravo!'—something silly—as they took him into the police station," she said.

The four seamen were taken upstairs, where they were surrounded by a group of detectives. "Low Life" McCormack was selected for interrogation.

"The last guy they should've picked out," Bailey said. "They want McCormack to admit that this was all a conspiracy. Big Communist conspiracy."

McCormack insisted he was a Catholic motivated only by his love of the Church.

After absorbing punches and kicks from the detectives, he was thrown back into the room with the others.

"So poor McCormack comes back, sits down, all red in the face, shaken up," said Bailey. "A detective comes over and looks like he is ready to pick another victim. Then they gave up on us. That's it."

At 3:07 a.m., each of the six seamen—four in the precinct and two in the hospital—were booked for "felonious assault" in the gang attack on Detective Solomon, who was listed as the arresting officer even though he was in Polyclinic Hospital. The "Bremen Six," as the men would come to be known, had not yet been charged in the violence against the swastika.

A few hours later, the four from the precinct (Bailey, Blackwell, Howe, and McCormack) were taken for arraignment at night court on West Fifty-Fourth Street, arriving in time to be the last case on the docket for Magistrate Michael A. Ford. The press photographers, perched behind Ford, snapped photographs of the young troublemakers, who were still disguised as sailing party revelers. Bailey, who stood taller than the others, was wearing a thin, striped tie and dark jacket. McCormack's right ear was haphazardly bandaged. His tie was the only one askew.

"There isn't the slightest reason in the world why any one of these defendants should be held on the charge that they have here," insisted the seamen's lawyer, Abraham Unger, according to the transcript. "The only reason why there were arrests made in this case is because the Nazis on board the *Bremen* are annoyed because of the fact there is opposition in the city of New York to the existence of Nazis and swastika and Hitler. That is the whole point."

He said the seamen were the victims of a "concerted attack on them that I saw personally."

"How did you happen to be there?" asked Magistrate Ford.

"I happened to be there the same way that 10,000 or so other people were there," Unger said. "There were 1,000 people on the dock. There was a crowd to see various persons off and the dock was crowded, showing what was going on at the time."

Magistrate Ford asked why he went to see the ship. "Do you know that anything was going to happen there?"

Unger said he did not.

Ford was shocked that "a member of the bar" should be present during the commission of felonies. "You are treading on very dangerous grounds," he said. "The Appellate Division may be interested in knowing something about that."

Unger shot back: "You had as much right to be on the pier as I did. There were thousands of human beings on the pier, thousands on the pier, many of whom might have been attorneys. What took place in front of the police station at the time I happened to be there and I saw. Do you want me to say that I did not see it? Do you want me to withhold a fact which I know to be true? Do you want me to mislead you? Do you want me to act as an attorney, a person who wants to tell the truth and be an honest officer of the court?"

"Please do not shout, counselor," Ford said. "I hear you."

The assistant district attorney suggested that bail be set at $2,500 for each of the six seamen.

"Bail is fixed at $2,500 for each defendant," responded Ford.

"Is there any reason, because the District Attorney says $2,500, the Magistrate has to repeat $2,500?" demanded Unger.

"Now, I have disposed of the case," Ford said. "I have heard the arguments. I have ruled and made my decision."

The case was adjourned until Monday.

At about the same moment in Washington, DC, Wilbur J. Carr, a State Department official, rushed before the press to express the FDR administration's regret over the *Bremen* incident even though the Nazi government hadn't yet lodged an official protest.

"Of course it is unfortunate," he said, "that two or three persons should mistreat the flag of any nation with which the United States is at peace."

CHAPTER TWELVE

As an American citizen I demand full and immediate apology to the German government for the disgraceful cowardly depredation committed on the liner Bremen in New York by Jewish and Communist gangsters. I also demand that this government make full payment for damages to property and for loss of time in the sailing of this vessel.

—A RESIDENT OF WASHINGTON, DC,
IN A TELEGRAM TO THE STATE DEPARTMENT, JULY 29, 1935, 9:30 A.M.

THE GRAND ACT of political theater variously described as the Bremen Flag Incident, Bremen Riot, or Bremen Affair made headlines throughout the world: "U.S. Mob Raids the Bremen"—the *Observer* (London). "Communists Rip German Flag from Bremen's Bow in New York"—the *China Press* (Shanghai). The *Globe*, Canada's national newspaper, attacked the "disgusting performance of a crowd of Jewish sympathizers in tearing the swastika ensign from the liner *Bremen* on Friday night." The disturbance on the ship, Jerusalem's *Palestine Post* declared, "culminated the wave of resentment which passed over the United States as a result of the renewed excesses against the Jews in Berlin."

The state-controlled newspapers in Nazi Germany howled. "Bolshevism is able to perpetrate such deeds only in countries where the state authority is too weak," stated the *Boersen Zeitung*. According to the *Allgemeine Zeitung*, the problem had been caused by "daily publication of alarmist reports from Germany." Mayor LaGuardia incited the flag attack with his "support of the propaganda of international Jewry against Germany," said *Der Angriff*. "This insult to the German colors must have a diplomatic sequel," declared the *Hamburger Fremdenblatt*. "It must be expected that American officials will excuse themselves for this incident."

The mainstream American press found nothing to celebrate in the foul deed at Pier 86. "Germany has good reason to protest the invasion of its territory by a gang of hoodlums bent on desecrating its national emblem," the *Hartford Courant* reported. "Wars have been fought on less provocation." The Nazi government "doesn't endear itself to the American public," editorialized the *Los Angeles Times*, "but its flag should not be insulted." The *Washington Post* harrumphed about "a gross and irresponsible violation of international etiquette." The radical newspapers swooned. "Bremen Fight Spurs Drive on Terror" read the banner across the top of the *Daily Worker*. "I saw the ripples from that swastika hurled into the Hudson River spreading to the oceans and the deep seas," wrote a *Worker* columnist named Alice Evans. "I knew that the shot which pinned Seaman Drolette to the dangerous No-Man's-Land between life and death would be answered around the world, wherever workers rose with new hope against their oppressors."

The Anti-Nazi Federation of New York, which helped organize the dockside rally, announced that further demonstrations were planned for sailing nights of German liners, which would "serve to highlight the fact that prominent American citizens are patronizing the Nazi shipping lines." The action on the *Bremen*, the group said, was not a riot but a "magnificent example of the courageous will of the American people to combat the barbarism of the Hitler regime."

Foreign policy commentators in the United States were hopeful that the State Department's voluntary statement of regret, delivered by Wilbur J. Carr while the flag was practically still wet, would put an end to the episode. Many took heart in the fact that the swastika was seen as the banner of Germany's ruling Nazi Party. The black, white, and red tricolor of the Second Reich, which Hitler had restored to prominence after assuming power, had been left unmolested on the stern staff at the rear of the ship. A diplomatic contretemps of far-reaching significance had been avoided, it was thought.

On Sunday, July 28, Joseph Goebbels sent a wireless message to the *Bremen*, which was still making its passage across the Atlantic. "Heartiest greetings to the crew for their brave attitude against the impudent attack of Communists who, as usual, appeared in superior numbers." Commodore Ziegenbein, who surely knew that he would be forced into retirement, telegraphed back: "The crew thanks you for your friendly greetings and promises to observe duty to protect flag anywhere any time." Privately, Hitler and Goebbels believed Nazi newspapers weren't apoplectic enough over the incident, which gives a hint at the level of rage in the senior levels of Reich leadership. Goebbels wrote in his diary: "Communists attacked the '*Bremen*' in New York City and tear down flag. The German press made almost nothing of it. I intervened. Now, the barrage really gets underway. The Führer also complained about this lax attitude. We have an information but no combat press. I will bring order to it."

Upon arrival in Bremerhaven, two of the *Bremen*'s officers were imprisoned for dereliction of duty.

Bailey had emerged as the spokesman for the Bremen Six. In brief comments to the press, he maintained the story that nobody bought anymore: He was a faithful servant of the Catholic Church who boarded the ship to urge passengers to cancel their bookings. Even though he was twenty years old, Bailey maintained the fiction that he was twenty-five. His address was listed as 505 West Twenty-Second Street in Manhattan. Vincent "Low Life" McCormack, who said he was twenty-eight, also provided a West Side address. He said he worked as a "painter." Like Bailey, McCormack had a criminal record, serving three months in the workhouse for attempted grand larceny. George Blackwell, twenty-four, was a "printer" with a residence on West Fourteenth Street. The authorities didn't seem to realize that William Howe—who was identified as a twenty-seven-year-old resident of a Bowery flop-house—was really William Jamieson. Howe/Jamieson later told the State Department that he changed his name when he shipped out as a young man "not wanting his parents to locate him as they were endeavoring to do" and "having once used that alias he found it necessary to continue to use it when subsequently signing on ships." The newspapers said that Howe had once been arrested for trespass in Charleston, South Carolina.

In the prison ward at Bellevue Hospital, Arthur "Mac" Blair, thirty, claimed he was born in Ireland. (He was a British national of Irish descent who had been born in Liverpool.) "I had one beer aboard the ship, but I didn't do a thing," he told the press. "I didn't start any riot." Maggie Weaver, who was in the midst of fall-ing in love with Blair, visited him a number of times at the hospital. "And he told me he was getting fan mail from all over the country on it," she said. "And also he looked healthier than I had ever seen him because he had been beaten up. His face was full. It was swollen up from the beating and made him look much healthier. Oh, he was very thin. In fact, he had a terrible cough. I'm sure he had TB at that time. But anyway he really looked wonderful after this beating up." In an adjacent bed was Edward Drolette who, like Blair, said he resided at the Seamen's Church Institute, the shelter for marine workers on South Street on the East River waterfront. Some newspapers described Drolette as homeless, which was the basic circumstance of many merchant seamen in the middle of the Depression. Suffering from a gunshot wound to his groin, he was initially given a fifty-fifty chance to live, but his condition was steadily improving.

At ten o'clock on Monday morning, the four nonhospitalized members of the Bremen Six returned to the courthouse on West Fifty-Fourth Street, transported uptown from the Tombs, the city jail where Bill Bailey had served a six-week stint as a juvenile. The assistant district attorney, Morris Brody, requested an adjourn-ment in light of Detective Solomon's continued confinement at Polyclinic Hospital.

Detective Solomon had gained widespread notice as the Jewish cop who defended Hitler's swastika, "an ironical twist of circumstances," the *New York Post* noted. "Solomon was forced to choose between his duty as a policeman and his own sympathies as a Jew," reported *Forverts* (Forward), the Yiddish-language daily. "He decided to fulfill his police duties." In interviews from his hospital room, Solomon said he was merely doing his job. "As a man, I don't like Hitler," he was quoted as saying. "But as a citizen and a police officer, I must protect his property here and keep law and order." He added: "I'd do the same thing over again." The papers noted that Solomon lived at 30 Buchanan Place in a Jewish section of the West Bronx with his wife, Mildred, and three-year-old son, Herbert Ira. His departmental record was described as excellent.

Abraham Unger, the International Labor Defense lawyer who represented the seamen on the morning after the incident, again appeared on their behalf. He made a request for bail to be reduced, alleging that "Nazi seamen" on the *Bremen* and not his clients were responsible for the attack on the Jewish detective.

Magistrate Burke permitted the defense attorney and the prosecutor to argue the point before declaring that the bail would remain at $2,500 for each of the six seamen.

———

Just before noon on the same day, Rudolf Leitner, the chargé d'affaires of the German Embassy in Washington, marched to the State Department and delivered a protest note to Undersecretary of State William Phillips.

The German ambassador to the United States, Hans Luther, wasn't available for the task. He was vacationing in Germany. The secretary of state, Cordell Hull, was still relaxing in the hot springs of Bath County, Virginia.

"Late in the evening of July 26, shortly before the departure of the German steamship Bremen from New York harbor, the German flag flying from the bow of the steamship was violently torn off by demonstrators," the note read. "I am instructed to make the most emphatic protest against this serious insult to the German national emblem, and I venture to express the expectation that everything will be done on the part of the American authorities charged with the prosecution of criminal offenses in order that the guilty persons may be duly punished."

The Nazi government, then, was not requesting an apology. It was asking the FDR administration to ensure that the desecration of the foul rag be avenged by the US legal system. The Hitler regime had noticed that the Bremen Six had thus far only been charged with assaulting Detective Solomon.

An hour later, the State Department released the text of the letter that was sent to the delegation of Jewish leaders who met with Undersecretary Phillips on the day of the *Bremen* incident. The letter said the "American people are always sympathetic to the maintenance" of "religious freedom and liberty of conscience" in "the United States as well as other nations," which is precisely as far as the US government was willing to go in criticizing the Hitler regime. President Franklin Roosevelt had still not yet uttered a word in condemnation of Nazi Germany's policies.

On that afternoon in the capital, Mayor Fiorello LaGuardia left the White House after a meeting on a New Deal program. "Everything possible has been done and will be done," he said when queried by the press about the case against the Bremen Six. "Of course, they are all being prosecuted, absolutely. And another thing: the flag was protected by an American citizen, Patrolman Morris Solomon," mangling the name of Matthew Solomon.

Mayor LaGuardia took the opportunity to blame German shipping line officials for failing to heed the advice of the New York Police Department (NYPD), delivered in the hours before the flag was attacked, to prevent all nonpassengers from boarding the ship during the sailing party.

In response, the German shipping line released a statement that praised the NYPD for its "efficiency" and noted the "impossibility of cross-examining each and every person applying for permission to go on board at sailing time."

"The average passenger will have from three to four relatives and friends wishing to see him off, and to exclude them would invite the severest criticism," the statement read. "Every precaution was taken to confine the visitors on the *Bremen* to the friends and relatives of the departing passengers but, in spite of this, some Communists succeeded, by subterfuge, in getting on board. The same would have happened if ten times the number of police had been on guard."

On the following day, July 30, the State Department asked city and state officials in New York to prepare a report on the *Bremen* matter, which would serve as the basis for a formal response to Hitler. Undersecretary Phillips urged New York governor Herbert Lehman to "take such steps as you may deem appropriate to expedite the report." When Mayor LaGuardia learned that the State Department had sought the NYPD's cooperation without first notifying him, he fired off a letter to Secretary Hull: "May I suggest that in the future whenever information of this kind is desired, the request come directly from you to me, following the regular established custom," LaGuardia wrote.

On that night in the German neighborhood of Yorkville on the Upper East Side of Manhattan, more than five thousand Hitler supporters attended two separate rallies to excoriate the Jews who traduced the symbol of Nazism. "Jewry is giving the signal for a general offensive against Germany," declared one speaker. Every mention of the slashing of the swastika inspired catcalls, hisses, and boos from Nazism's New York affiliates.

On July 31, during a bail hearing in New York Supreme Court, defense attorney Abraham Unger delivered another impassioned defense of the Bremen Six. "That flag doesn't represent the German people," he insisted. "It doesn't represent Germany. It is the flag of a party in Germany that is obnoxious to a great many people in this country." Justice Edgar J. Lauer agreed to lower bail for each of the six from $2,500 to $1,000. After Maggie Weaver put up the money—"I got it mostly from my sisters, both of whom had good jobs then," she said—Bailey, Howe, Blackwell, and

McCormack were released. Blair and Drolette remained in Bellevue Hospital.

Separately in Magistrates' Court on West Fifty-Fourth Street, the case against the six was adjourned until August 7 to permit Detective Solomon to continue his recovery at Polyclinic Hospital.

In the evening of the same day, Acting Secretary Phillips spoke over the phone with President Roosevelt, who surely was aware that his grandson was on the *Bremen* when the trouble broke out. Phillips and Roosevelt discussed the language that would be used in the official reply that the administration was eager to relay to Berlin. On the following morning, August 1, Phillips sent a draft copy over to the White House. "Referring to our telephone conversation of last night with respect to our note on the *Bremen* flag incident, I should be exceedingly grateful if you would give me the benefit of your opinion in regard to the enclosed draft," Phillips wrote to FDR. "It seems important that we should send our reply this afternoon."

Within hours, the US government delivered a packet of materials to the German Embassy, which included a five-paragraph statement under the signature of Undersecretary Phillips and an extensive NYPD narrative of the night of July 26, 1935.

The statement outlined the heroic actions taken by the American state on behalf of Hitler, even in the face of resistance from the *Bremen*'s representatives. The NYPD had "suggested measures to prevent persons other than the passengers and other duly authorized visitors from boarding the vessel" but the "officers of the steamship line did not deem it necessary to adopt such measures." When unauthorized persons boarded the vessel and "started a demonstration," the police took "immediate and efficient action with a view to clearing the ship of all unauthorized persons." The statement then singled out the Jewish detective by name, emphasizing that "Detective Matthew Solomon, in attempting to apprehend the ringleaders, was set upon, knocked down, and sustained serious injury."

After assuring the Nazis that "the persons implicated in this disorder have been apprehended and are being held for trial," the

FDR administration offered what amounted to its second apology in the swastika incident: "It is unfortunate that, in spite of the sincere efforts of the police to prevent any disorder whatever, the German national emblem should, during the disturbance which took place, not receive that respect to which it is entitled."

It is hard to imagine a lower moment in American diplomatic annals.

But worse was yet to come.

═══════

The Nazi government did not issue an official response to the US government's statement but three days later, on August 4, Joseph Goebbels rose before a gathering of Nazi district leaders in Essen and sneered at the "civilized" ways of the United States.

"Let me observe that in our ports the merchant flags of friendly nations are not stripped from their mastheads," he said.

The propaganda minister, who had just returned from an invigorating holiday at a Baltic seaside resort, was in the midst of a violent speech that targeted an array of regime enemies. He assailed the paramilitaries of the Stahlhelm. "We shall have no pardon for saboteurs from the Right more than from the Left." He condemned the Catholic press ("superfluous"), Catholic youth organizations ("German youth belong to us"), and Catholic clergy accused of money smuggling ("If Christ came to Germany he would scourge them out of his temple"). But the address was most noteworthy for its ferocious anti-Semitism. Goebbels called Jews "the jackals of German economic life." He announced that the Nazi state would "no longer tolerate" marriage between "Aryans" and Jews. "We have been patient with them, but it is they who have provoked us," he said. "We shall treat them in the same manner they have treated us." He warned "the next few weeks will show what we are going to do to them."

"No foreign protest will prevent Germany from annihilating the Jew, who is the enemy of the German state!" he ranted.

The Jewish Telegraphic Agency (JTA) reported that the speech, which was described as the most "vitriolic and inciting anti-Jewish

harangue" ever delivered by Goebbels, inspired a "pogrom atmosphere" in Berlin. Busloads of uniformed storm troopers arrived
in the Kurfürstendamm and marched up and down the boulevard, shouting anti-Jewish slogans. "So frightened were the Jewish
patrons in the cafés at the time that they fled terror-stricken from
the section," the JTA wrote. "The cafés on the Kurfürstendamm
were emptied of Jews within a few minutes." On the following day,
the Jewish citizens of Berlin kept away from public places.

The US government's statement of apology—with its promise
of a criminal prosecution of "the persons implicated in this disorder"—led to justifiable worries among Bremen Six supporters
that the seamen were about to be given stiff prison sentences
to curry favor with the Führer. A "Provisional Committee for
the Defense of the Bremen Demonstrators" was formed to raise
money for a legal defense. "Winning freedom for these men will
give a tremendous impetus to the world anti-Nazi struggle," the
committee said in a statement. "It will help to stem the Nazi terror." The Anti-Nazi Federation of New York sent delegations to
meet with officials at City Hall and the State Department, organized pickets in front of the German consulate in lower Manhattan, and planned a mass meeting for Madison Square Garden.
The International Labor Defense, which was adding lawyers to
its Bremen Six defense team, urged all "New York workers and
anti-Fascists" to attend the courtroom sessions "to demonstrate
against the Nazi pogroms, race and religious persecutions in
Germany" and "for the freedom of the Bremen demonstrators
and for the release of Lawrence Simpson," the SS *Manhattan*
sailor who remained incarcerated in a concentration camp outside Hamburg.

At ten a.m. on August 7, Assistant District Attorney Morris
Brody opened the next hearing with the startling announcement
that new charges would be lodged against the six. In addition to
felonious assault in the attack on Detective Solomon, each of the
seamen were accused of unlawful assembly with "intent to commit an act tending to breach the peace and particularly to tear
the ship's emblem from its staff," which meant, in accordance

with the Nazi government's wishes, the defilement of the swastika would be subject to judicial review. The pronouncement sparked an uproar among the *four* defense attorneys from the International Labor Defense (ILD) and the scores of sympathizers jammed in the spectators' section.

The shouts and jeers from the gallery continued for several minutes until Thomas A. Aurelio, the latest in a revolving cast of magistrates to hear the case, succeeded in restoring order with repeated hammer blows of his gavel.

"This is nothing more than a conspiracy on the part of the police to victimize these defendants and keep them in jail!" insisted one of the new defense attorneys, Joseph Tauber. "The original complaints were drawn two weeks ago. Why have they waited two weeks to think up the charge?"

Tauber continued his tirade against "conspiracy and oppression by the police" until Magistrate Aurelio threatened to have him ejected from the courtroom.

"I know you will threaten to order me out of the court but that doesn't scare me a bit," Tauber said.

The papers differ on whether Tauber was actually escorted into the hallway by court officers or whether he merely retreated from the railed enclosure in front of the bench.

"I protest against your honor's vicious decision!" bellowed the ILD's Roy H. Ellison. "Up to now we have not yet had a court in this country compared to Nazi Germany or Fascist Italy. I want to make my protest against your order, and you can order me out of the courtroom, too, if you desire."

"The spectators cheered wildly, whistled and stamped their feet," the *Times* reported. "The patrolmen having cases in court loosed their weapons and prepared for trouble. A hurried call to the West 47th Street station brought several radio cars and additional patrolmen, but the crowd blew off all its steam vocally and finally sat down."

Joseph Tauber, who either returned to the courtroom or never left it, entered not guilty pleas on behalf of the six seamen on the unlawful assembly charge.

Magistrate Aurelio didn't set bail on the new charges. The case was once again adjourned.

On the following evening, August 8, more than twenty thousand people packed Madison Square Garden for the Anti-Nazi Federation rally, which was open to "Jews, Catholics, Protestants, non-religionists, Socialists, Communists, Republicans, Democrats—all who oppose fascism." Chaired by Roger Baldwin, the executive director of the American Civil Liberties Union, the meeting passed a resolution urging the United States to boycott the Olympic Games slated for Berlin in 1936, sent protest cables to Adolf Hitler and Secretary of State Cordell Hull, and listened to a procession of speeches from such left-wingers as Kurt Rosenfeld, the exiled former minister of justice for Prussia; Herman Resig, a Protestant clergyman from Brooklyn; Moissaye J. Olgin, editor of the radical Yiddish daily *Morgn Frayhayt* (Morning Freedom); and author and journalist James Waterman Wise, who famously said that when fascism comes to the United States, it will be "wrapped up in the American flag and heralded as a plea for liberty and preservation of the Constitution."

Five of the Bremen Six at Madison Square Garden. From left,
Howe, Blair, Bailey, McCormack, and Blackwell. Edward Drolette
was still in the hospital. (Michael Bailey)

Congressman Vito Marcantonio, the former assistant US attorney who represented the poverty-stricken district of East Harlem, was prevented from delivering his speech because of official business in Washington, DC. He sent a telegram of regret, expressing his desire "to participate in united front against Nazi atrocities" and wishing "more power to" the *Bremen* demonstrators.

The ILD attorneys were probably already speaking to him about joining the defense team as lead counsel.

Then, the Bremen Six were introduced. Roger Baldwin urged three cheers for the roughhewn champions of justice. The raucous applause lasted for a full ten minutes.

Bill Bailey stepped to the microphone.

"I am a Roman Catholic and that is one reason why I participated in the demonstration against religious persecution in Germany," he said. "The other reason was to protest against the arrest of the American sailor Lawrence Simpson of the liner *Manhattan* by the Nazi government in Hamburg."

The audience cheered wildly.

After thanking the crowd for its support, Bailey urged the entire assemblage to "pack the courtroom to see that we seamen receive our justice."

CHAPTER THIRTEEN

The spirit of the Boston Tea Party lived again in those who hauled down the flag of reaction and tossed it into New York Harbor.

—WINTHROP STERLING, LETTER TO THE EDITOR OF THE *NEW YORK POST*

MOST OBSERVERS ASSUMED the so-called Trial of the Bremen Six would be nothing more than a perfunctory recounting of the facts followed by the quick imposition of sentences. The FDR administration was content in the belief that an unpleasant diplomatic episode had all but concluded. Few paid much attention when the case was assigned to the next magistrate on the rotation, Louis B. Brodsky. He seemed to be just another Tammany Democrat who held the conventional view that the seamen were radical scofflaws undeserving of polite consideration. But Brodsky was scandalized by the casual respect accorded to the Hitler regime by the enlightened peoples of the world. He was ready for his turn on the stage of history.

Brodsky, age fifty-two, was one of the great characters of Depression-era New York. He was born in czarist Russia in 1883. "We were the 'wheat Brodskys,'" he once told a reporter while chomping on a cigar. "There were two other branches of the family—the 'sugar Brodskys' and the 'banking Brodskys.'" He escaped the pogroms, arriving in New York City with his mother, father,

Judge Brodsky. "I hope
this court will always
be regarded as a poor
man's court."
(Acme Newspictures)

and seven sisters when he was just two years old. "I went to public
school in New York and then was tutored privately for a time and
received my LL.D. from New York University in 1900," he said.
He built up a lucrative practice as a trial attorney specializing in
commercial law. In 1924, he accepted an appointment as a city
magistrate in the depths of the court system, taking a considerable
pay cut to enter public service. He was reappointed in 1929 to a
ten-year term.

Brodsky made headlines by delivering unorthodox verdicts
that recognized the mortal condition of the petty criminals who
slumped before him each day. To a newsboy who spent a night
in jail for the crime of selling papers in the subway, he offered
a heartfelt apology. "Governor [Al] Smith was once a newsboy
and other men of high standing have sold papers," he said. "They
might easily have been arrested under similar circumstances." He
lauded an elderly woman who was accused of feeding pigeons in
defiance of a city ordinance. "Madam, you are doing noble work,"

he said. "Discharged." When a young Salvador Dalí was booked for malicious mischief after smashing a Bonwit Teller window display that he'd designed, because the store management had altered it without his permission, Brodsky suspended sentence: "These are some of the privileges that an artist with temperament seems to enjoy." He defended the rights of striking fur workers ("who are entitled to every protection in their desire to better their conditions"), burlesque dancers ("nudity is no longer considered indecent in uptown nightclubs and theaters"), and litterateurs (dismissing a complaint against the Gotham Book Mart for selling risqué foreign literature, noting that courts should not "exercise a censorship over literary production"). He was proud of the leniency he showed toward sex workers, expressing contempt for any judge who "puts a woman outside the pale of decent society to make a record for himself." Louis Brodsky had a flair for ensuring that the letter of municipal code didn't conflict with an ethical framework of higher standing.

"He wears a pince-nez; his brows are upraised, his forehead triple-arched in deep frowns as he concentrates on the case before him," wrote a journalist. "His manner is that of a physician, concerning, interested, tentative, probing, balancing. His sentence is his diagnosis and treatment. He doesn't seem to care what kind of figure he cuts, whether he is duly impressive; he doesn't mind changing his mind or retracting an order if some cogent reason strikes him. He has no dread of declaring a mistrial should the complainants wish it. If they'd like another judge better, let them go to it. He is human, decent, has a sense of humor, a level pleasing manner of speech. He is not sentimental but has a power born of intuition or long experience which smacks of second sight. Court workers who have watched him for years comment on it. It is a trait common to great diagnosticians in the medical profession."

In 1930, he was the Tammany nominee for the congressional seat in his Upper West Side district, losing by 651 votes to the Republican incumbent, Ruth Pratt. The Socialist candidate in the race, newspaper columnist Heywood Broun, noted that Brodsky barely made any appearances on the stump. "I offer to him gratis the following slogan for his congressional campaign: 'Keep an honest judge on the bench,'" said Broun, who placed a distant third. In the following year, Brodsky's honesty was called into question when he was investigated over his real estate and stock market speculations during an inquiry into (the endemic) corruption in the city's Magistrate Courts. He was known around town as New York's "wealthiest magistrate." When a five-justice appellate panel cleared him of wrongdoing, Brodsky broke down in tears and embraced his nineteen-year-old daughter. The court's decision described him as an "industrious, intelligent, and satisfactory magistrate."

Brodsky had a deep connection to his Jewish roots. He seemed to devote every free hour to Jewish causes—he was a director and trustee of various Jewish hospitals, orphanages, and welfare societies. He marched at the head of the parade through the Lower East Side to celebrate the opening of the Home of Old Israel on Jefferson Street. He was the toastmaster for fund-raising dinners for the Hebrew Orphan Home and the Israel Zion Hospital. And he was an outspoken backer of the anti-Nazi boycott campaign headed by Samuel Untermyer of the Non-Sectarian Anti-Nazi League (NSANL). Brodsky was one of the sponsors of a testimonial dinner in honor of Untermyer in late 1933. According to a document in the NSANL archives, Brodsky described himself as a supporter of "the peerless leadership of the originator of a militant Jewish policy." After spending three months traveling throughout Nazi Germany and Austria in mid-1934, he returned to New York and gave a talk on behalf of the league over the airwaves of WEVD. The title was the "True Face of Hitlerism." Brodsky "urged the widest application of a world wide boycott against Germany as the only means of effectively fighting the Nazi menace," according to a newspaper summary.

The resistance, then, had a sleeper in the Magistrates' Courts.

═══════

Following two additional adjournments, the trial—actually a series of three hearings to determine whether there was enough evidence to proceed to trial—began on August 23, 1935. The setting was a second-floor courtroom in the West Side courthouse on Fifty-Fourth Street, an improbable location for a legal drama of worldwide resonance. Reporters, cops, and anti-Nazi protesters climbed the winding marble stairs and entered Judge Brodsky's unpretentious domain, which was "long, high-ceilinged, utterly without proper ventilation," according to a contemporary report. The usual cast of pickpockets, barroom brawlers, hawkers, public urinators, wife beaters, hucksters, streetwalkers, and muggers would have to wait for their cases to be called. Among the lucky ones to find a seat in the gallery was Maggie Weaver, whose apartment in the West Village had served as a headquarters for the conspiracy.

Mac Blair and Ed Drolette were now out of Bellevue Hospital. "It was worth getting shot a thousand times to hear the cheer from the demonstrators when the Nazi flag hit the water," said Drolette, who, according to a reporter, was "still weak from the loss of three quarts of blood." All six of the seamen sat at the defense table with three attorneys from the International Labor Defense— Joseph Tauber, Abraham Unger, and Edward Kuntz. Congressman Vito Marcantonio, the young radical who had joined the team as lead counsel, was stuck in Washington, DC, waiting to vote on a package of legislation that included the first Neutrality Act, which sought to ensure that United States could not be pulled into another European war. (Marcantonio would vote aye.)

Representing the People of the State of New York was Irving J. Tell, a sharp-tongued assistant district attorney who had been wounded during World War I. He presented a simple case: The seamen were not inspired servants of the people warning the world about the evil designs of the Third Reich. They were lawless provocateurs so lacking in idealistic intent that they committed a vicious physical assault against one of New York's Finest. They were thugs who deserved to be targets of police gunfire.

Detective Solomon, now discharged from Polyclinic Hospital, was ready to appear as the first witness.

After the proceedings were called to order, Joseph Tauber asked for an adjournment to allow Congressman Marcantonio to return from Washington.

"The district attorney may say, 'Well, this is an ordinary assault case,' but I think he is mistaken," Tauber said, according to the transcript. "In my opinion," he continued, "in a sense, the People of the United States are on trial, and I am mindful—I recall the Boston Tea Party and other things like that that were taught in the public schools."

"We are ready to proceed," Tell said. "The witnesses are here."

Following a lengthy debate that touched upon Detective Solomon's impending vacation, Magistrate Brodsky agreed with the prosecution.

Brodsky's refusal to delay the hearing for forty-eight hours was further proof that the "six heroic seamen" were "being railroaded into long prison sentences," the *Daily Worker* would write.

"Now take the stand, Officer Solomon," Brodsky said.

In emotionless, matter-of-fact tones, Solomon described the bluecoat version of the raid on the *Bremen*, disclosing that he and Detective Harold Moore had been following Edward Drolette from early in the afternoon of July 26, nearly ten hours prior to the scheduled sailing of the ship. He would not reveal the name of the informant who tipped off the Red Squad to the planned disturbance on the *Bremen*. "That is confidential," he said.

"I saw this defendant, Edward Drolette, go on board the boat," Solomon explained. "I saw him in the company of a man who is not a prisoner in this case. I saw them walk about the boat, on the deck above where this assault took place. I saw them walking around, the unknown man following Drolette, the defendant. I saw Drolette engage other people in conversation. I saw him whisper to a number of people on the *Bremen*. When the whistle blew, apparently for the people to leave the ship, which was about 11:45 p.m., your Honor, I saw Drolette go down a staircase on board the *Bremen* to the lower deck, where the assault took place. I followed Drolette as closely as I could, your Honor, but owing to the large number of people who got between us—there was a small, narrow staircase—I lost sight of him."

Solomon said nothing about the attack on the swastika, which was occurring at the same time he was struggling through the crowd to reach the forward deck.

"Then I was proceeding toward the bow of the boat, your Honor, and I saw this unknown man strike a person who was in a seamen's . . . clothing," he said. "He then ran in my direction, and as I was about to apprehend him he struck me in the face."

Solomon described having taken a blackjack from his right rear pocket—a "pocket billy" he called it—and swinging it at the unknown man. "I struck him and knocked him down," Solomon testified.

Like a Greek chorus sent to make a declaratory comment on the drama, a group of men and women had then surrounded Solomon. "People started to call out, 'We are citizens,' and they began to circle around me," he said of the surrealistic interlude. "I assumed they were going to attack me." He said the phrase was repeated "four or five" times.

The defense later suggested the group had chanted "We are citizens" so as to ward off any potential attacks.

"I took my shield from my hands—from my pocket—and placed it in my left hand," Solomon continued. "I took my revolver from my pocket and placed that in my right hand, and I called out six or eight times, 'I am a policeman,' holding the shield in my hand, and I warned the crowd to stand back. During this procedure someone from behind grabbed hold of my revolver and held on to it. At that time, Drolette stepped out from the crowd and struck me in the right eye."

"Drolette struck you in the eye?" asked Assistant District Attorney Tell.

"Yes, sir."

"Did you see what he had in his hand?"

"He wore metal knuckles."

Solomon said he had lost control of his gun and fell to the deck.

"Then some unknown persons proceeded to beat me around the face, head, and legs," he continued. "Then I heard some people call out, 'Throw him overboard.' I clung to something. I don't remember what it was. The next I remember I was being tossed off the *Bremen* gangplank by some unknown persons into the arms of acting Lieutenant Pyke."

"I ask that these knuckles be marked in evidence at this time, your Honor," said Tell.

The knuckles were identified as People's Exhibit #1.

In the lengthy dispute that flared over the admission of the knuckles, Joseph Tauber accused the prosecutor of trying the case for "a certain part of the press."

"I think, your Honor, counsel's statements are more for the press than are mine," Tell responded. "I have not brought up the Boston Tea Party or the Revolutionary War in this case. I am trying this case on the facts."

"Your Honor, the Boston Tea Party is a historic fact, even if the district attorney has long since forgotten about it," Tauber countered.

"We will adjourn for something like a tea party, which I will call by another name," said Magistrate Brodsky. "We will adjourn for lunch."

After the break, the International Labor Defense (ILD) law-yers launched into a relentless cross-examination of Detective Solomon, who refused to concede that he was acting as a col-laborationist with the Nazi regime. He didn't seem pleased to be delivering the isolationist version of the just-following-orders defense to be made infamous by the postwar Nuremberg trials.

"Were you going out to protect anything at the bow of the boat?" asked Edward Kuntz, referring to the swastika gleaming in the spotlight.

"No, sir," Solomon responded.

After a few additional questions about Solomon's movements, Kuntz asked: "Now, I ask you: Did you go out to protect anything at the bow?"

"No."

Kuntz kept browbeating Solomon in an attempt to get the Jew-ish detective to admit he was protecting the anti-Jewish symbol.

But Solomon refused to concede that he even *saw* the brightly lit flag at the bow of the ship.

Kuntz then turned to the alleged metal knuckles attack, seeking to cast doubt on Solomon's ability to identify his assailant as Drolette. During questioning, Solomon admitted that he was singularly focused on retaining possession of his revolver when he was hit suddenly in the right eye. After Kuntz concluded, Joseph Tauber took over the cross-examination, deploying a brilliant strategy to force Solomon to admit that he didn't see the metal punch coming.

"I am asking you, before you received the blow, did you bring up your hand to protect yourself?" Tauber asked.

"No, sir," Solomon said.

"As a matter of fact, you didn't expect the blow, did you, because if you did expect it you would have brought up your hand to ward it off?"

"That particular blow I did not expect," Solomon said.

That particular blow I did not expect.

If Solomon didn't see the punch coming, then he couldn't identify who threw it. Solomon had just about acknowledged that it wasn't possible for him to name Drolette as his attacker.

Under further questioning, Solomon conceded German shipping line officials had no idea he, a plainclothes officer, was on board the ship. He admitted that *Bremen* crew members were part of the crowd of about two hundred people that surrounded him when he was struck in the eye. After objections from the prosecution, he acknowledged that he was a member of a minority group loathed by the official ideology of the German state. "I am of Jewish extraction," Solomon said.

The defense later described Solomon as a "quiet, soft-spoken man of middle age" who looked more like "an intellectual or a professional" than a detective. "This, together with his Hebraic features, would expose him to grave danger in any group that includes people who uphold the tenets of the Hitler-Streicher 'Aryan' call to annihilate the Jew."

"For all you know, these people who hoisted you up to fling you into the water may have been the seamen hoisting you?" asked Tauber, referring to *Bremen* crew members.

"I couldn't tell you," said Solomon, making a stunning admission.

The hotheaded Tauber concluded his cross-examination by asserting that the allegation against Drolette was a blatant fabrication intended to protect the reputation of the New York Police Department (NYPD).

"And isn't it a fact that the reason this charge is made against Drolette is to cover up Detective Moore, who fired a bullet into the body of Drolette?"

"No, sir," Solomon said. "That is not the reason."

"That is all," said Tauber.

=====

Detective Harold Moore exhibited none of his partner's reticence when he took the witness stand for the second act of the trial on August 28. He was boastful, expansive, and contemptuous, a departmental legend who wasn't at all conflicted to be working on behalf of an oppressive foreign government. Moore "has been in several pistol duels," the papers noted. He was celebrated for gunning down Edward "Fats" McCarthy, an underworld henchman once associated with gangster Dutch Schultz, but the story of the upstate ambush seemed to vary with each telling. His exalted reputation didn't extend to Harlem, where he first made his violent reputation. There was the time he fired twice into the chest of an African American elevator operator named George Jackson in what seemed an awful lot like target practice.

Detective Moore was pitted against the newly arrived lead counsel for the defense.

At age thirty-two, Congressman Marcantonio was the dashing young star of leftist politics, a protégé of Mayor LaGuardia who had just been elected to represent the poor Italians and Puerto Ricans of East Harlem. His constituents paid little heed to his sympathy for Communism just as long as he addressed their day-to-day

Rep. Vito Marcantonio, *right*, with his mentor, Mayor Fiorello LaGuardia.
(New York City Municipal Archives)

concerns, which he did in the manner of an Old World *padrone*.
He was known to his Italian constituents as "the Honorable Fritto
Misto" (Mixed Fry), a reference to his eclectic collection of asso-
ciates. His closest friends were Luigi Albarelli, a local barber, and
W. E. B. DuBois, the civil rights giant. "Marc" could be seen in the
company of mobsters at Cinciotti's Café or on the picket line with
striking garment workers. He was short, dark, and handsome, a
snappy dresser in beige fedora and pinstriped suits who delivered
impassioned speeches "in the reasonably clear and precise accents
of a New Yorker who has tried hard to cultivate a good speaking
voice," wrote a journalist.

The congressman well understood the geopolitical potential of
the case. But he felt that the action against the swastika couldn't
achieve full expression without the vindicating triumph of acquit-
tals. He would deploy the methodical techniques he had learned
during his time as a federal prosecutor to *prove* that the Bremen
Six were acting out of high moral purpose that could serve as an
example to the world.

"In one of our court appearances I saw a short guy take over the whole defense," remembered Bill Bailey. "Nicely dressed in a white suit, he stood before the judge and words flowed smoothly out. His demure tone of voice shocked me. 'Who the hell is this guy?' I asked."

On this day, Bailey was wearing a gray shirt and red tie. He sat next to Mac Blair, who was outfitted in a dark suit.

"The courtroom was crowded with sympathizers of the defendants," reported the *New York Times*. "Twenty-five policemen were on hand but no disturbances occurred."

Marcantonio walked Detective Moore through the surveillance of Drolette and the unknown man, which began in the South Street district in lower Manhattan on the late afternoon of July 26. Moore described how Drolette carried on a running conversation with a group of men huddled on a street corner and went about preparing for what appeared to be a dapper night on the town. He entered a large-windowed tailor shop and had his pants pressed. He descended into a bookstore and came up with his face washed and hair combed. "At one time, when Drolette was having his shoes shined, I was standing within eight or ten feet of him," said Detective Moore. "He was sitting on the shoe shine stand against the building and I was at the corner reading a paper."

Moore said he and Solomon followed Drolette and the unknown man—at first on the subway and then on foot—to a union headquarters in midtown Manhattan. After Drolette emerged from the building alone, the two detectives trailed as he walked through the traffic of Hell's Kitchen and then onto the *Bremen*. With permission from Lieutenant Pyke, who was waiting at Pier 86, Moore and Solomon boarded the ship accompanied by Detective Edward F. Murphy.

Detective Moore said he watched as Drolette and the unknown man, who had rejoined Drolette, moved through the A deck and conferred with groups of fellow conspirators.

"I should say about seven or eight groups, in different parts of the upper deck, that is, the deck above the bow deck," Moore said. "In one conversation that Drolette had with Bailey and Blair on the left side, that is, the dock side of the upper deck, that was as follows. Bailey said something about a woman, would she be there. In answer to Bailey's question about the woman, Drolette said, 'Well no, you know you're in love with the woman. She will be there at 11:45 sharp. Now, remember 11:45 sharp. She won't be there before then.'"

After the 11:45 whistle blew, Detectives Moore and Murphy were caught in the crowd surging toward the staircase leading down to the B deck. "There was a jam," said Moore. "We lost sight of the defendants mentioned and Detective Solomon."

Moore said nothing about the attack on the swastika that was in progress while he was pinned back by the throng.

He claimed it took "possibly four minutes" to reach the top of the staircase.

He looked toward the bow. "Drolette pushed somebody aside and struck Solomon with something he held in his hand," he said.

Moore said that Solomon remained standing, which conflicted with Solomon's statement that he immediately fell to the deck.

Then "Low Life" McCormack "punched Solomon," a detail that Solomon never mentioned in his testimony.

Moore testified that about twenty people were in the vicinity of Solomon, significantly less than Solomon's estimate of two hundred. Moore said he was viewing the incident from "maybe 50 feet, 75 feet" away but noted that "the bow was very brightly illuminated—drop lights and all."

The defense would allege that Moore was "never in a position to have a clear view of the incident."

"Then you ran toward this crowd or did you walk?" Marcantonio asked.

"Hardly," said Moore. "I ran as fast as I could. With as much opposition as we had, it took us a little time."

"Did you have your gun out?" Marcantonio said.

"I did."

"Drolette ran toward me," said Moore. "I shouted I was a police officer and showed my shield on my coat. At that time he had brass knuckles in his right hand. He did not stop and I shot him. He fell and I kept going into the group." Detective Murphy then fired a shot at McCormack, which missed. "There was a general free-for-all then and we placed—we placed them under arrest," said Moore.

In Moore's bizarre telling, he and Murphy dashed toward the group with guns drawn while Drolette, in defiance of logic, *ran in the direction of the weapon-wielding cops.*

"Just how far away was Drolette from you when you shot him?" Marcantonio asked.

"I don't know," Moore said. "I didn't count. He was running toward me."

Marcantonio asked several follow-up questions in an attempt to determine the precise distance between the two men when the shot was fired.

At first, Moore said the distance "could have been more than ten feet." A few questions later, he thought "maybe ten, 15" feet. After another few questions, he revised his estimate: "Yes, 15, 20 feet, maybe a little more." Eventually he landed on a final answer. "Maybe 20 feet, 25 feet, maybe less," he said. "I don't know."

Moore denied that he rushed up to the brawl, pointed his revolver at Drolette's heart from less a foot away, and fired just as Drolette threw out his hand, causing the bullet to travel in a downward trajectory through his groin and out the side of his leg, which was Drolette's version of the story.

Over the course of an hour and half, Marcantonio's masterly cross-examination exposed the contradictions and inconsistencies in the state's case. Detective Moore couldn't help but sputter his contempt for the left-wing congressman. "You are putting words into my mouth," he snapped. "Don't rush me counsel," he growled at one point. At another, "Don't misquote me!"

"He covered every conceivable point," Judge Brodsky would say of Marcantonio's performance. "He carried the witness to and from the scene of the occurrence as brilliantly as I ever saw an examination before me."

After Marcantonio concluded his inquiry, Joseph Tauber stepped to the podium and asked Detective Moore a simple and direct question.

"How many people have you shot in the course of your service?" Tauber asked.

"I object to that," said prosecutor Tell.

Tauber told Judge Brodsky that Moore was guilty of shooting "ten or 11 people" in his career, which made him a police officer "who shoots readily, quickly, and, as in this instance, without seeming provocation."

"I move to strike that from the record," said Tell.

"May I put a few more questions to this witness?" asked Tauber.

"The witness is ordered from the witness stand," said Brodsky.

———

The final day of testimony featured Lieutenant James A. Pyke of the Red Squad, the brusque commanding officer responsible for organizing the defense of the *Bremen*. He had ignored the wishes of German shipping line officials and directed Detectives Solomon, Moore, and Murphy to follow Edward Drolette onto the ship. A veteran of World War I who reputedly served as a chauffeur for General John J. Pershing, he had been garlanded with commendations and citations during his police career. The Italian government honored him with the Order of the Crown of Italy in recognition of his service "during the visit of General Italo Balbo and the transatlantic Italian aerial fleet to New York" in 1933.

Pyke was called to the stand on September 4. The defense was eager to have him answer for a national policy of slavish deference toward the Third Reich.

Marcantonio opened his questioning by asking about the NYPD report on the *Bremen* incident that was included with the State Department apology delivered to the Nazi government on August 2. The NYPD report, which was published in newspapers across the country, described the assault on Detective Solomon but did not identify Edward Drolette as the attacker. The culprit was "one of the Communists." The author of the report was identified as Lieutenant Pyke.

The defense regarded the NYPD report as clear evidence that the charge against Drolette was concocted after the fact to provide some semblance of justification for Detective Moore's use of deadly force.

If the NYPD had identified Drolette as the attacker, why wasn't he named in the report delivered to the nation's newspapers, the State Department, and the Nazi government?

In response to Marcantonio's questions, Lieutenant Pyke claimed that the report he filed with the NYPD's chief inspector was *not* the public report that appeared under his name. He claimed he filed another report—an original report—that *did* identify Drolette as the attacker of Solomon. But he was unwilling to answer any further questions about the content of the original report, which was "confidential," "privileged," and "not to be discussed in open court."

Over the course of a mind-numbing day of testimony, Pyke stonewalled even in the most minor of attempts to establish basic facts. The interrogation slowed to a standstill.

"You are here in a case affecting the liberty of several defendants and still you quibble about a simple question as to whether you made the report or the stenographer made the report?" Marcantonio said.

Pyke barely concealed his disregard for Vito Marcantonio and the ILD lawyers. The defense was apoplectic. Marcantonio protested to Judge Brodsky that Pyke "has practically refused to give us any information at all." Joseph Tauber jumped to his feet and lambasted Pyke for his "continuous smile" and "supreme degree of contempt for all concerned."

The proceeding devolved into an open attack on the integrity of the NYPD, which was accused of falsifying testimony and suppressing evidence.

Judge Brodsky didn't provide any help. He defended Pyke's refusal to engage in a substantive discussion of either the (alleged) original report or the public report. Brodsky denied every attempt by the defense to obtain internal NYPD documents or summon high officials, such as Police Commissioner Lewis Valentine, to the witness stand, noting that such actions wouldn't "make the slightest difference in this case."

Brodsky was criticized in the left-wing press for his "zeal to shield the police," as one publication put it. The *Daily Worker* said the magistrate was engaging in "a desperate effort to close the hearings on the Bremen Six."

Lieutenant Pyke left the stand with his self-satisfaction intact, having resisted the defense's attempt to cast him as the senior figure in what Bill Bailey called a "frame-up."

After requesting a brief recess, Marcantonio returned to his chair and delivered a forceful closing argument. He asserted that "not a single iota of evidence" was presented to implicate William Bailey, Arthur Blair, William Howe, or George Blackwell in the violent assault on Detective Solomon. Marcantonio pointed out that Detective Moore's account of the attack on Detective Solomon—which Moore said he viewed from 50 to 75 feet away in the midst of a chaotic scene—differed from Solomon's account on several key points. Marcantonio noted that Moore provided the only evidence against Vincent "Low Life" McCormack, who Moore (and not Solomon) claimed assaulted a still-standing Solomon. Marcantonio went on to outline how "highly improbable" it was that Solomon "could have seen or could have been in the position so as to be able to identify the person who assaulted him."

Of the charge that Drolette possessed a deadly weapon—the metal knuckles—Marcantonio asserted (less persuasively) that "the evidence points conclusively to the fact that no brass knuckles were seen on the defendant Drolette on the night of the incident."

Regarding the unlawful assembly charge, Marcantonio said that "not a single iota of evidence" was submitted to prove that the assembly—the conspiratorial conversations between the six defendants on the A deck prior to the 11:45 p.m. whistle—led to "an act tending to breach the peace and particularly to tear the ship's emblem from its staff," in the words of the indictment. In fact, not one of the police officers testified to witnessing Bill Bailey throw the swastika flag into the Hudson River.

But Marcantonio deployed his most impassioned rhetoric in a brief hastily filed with the court. The case would be worth little "if it results merely in a discharge of the defendants because the

People failed to make out a prima facie case," he argued. "For the court to discharge them and leave the implication that their act was inherently improper, but fell short of being illegal, is to do both the court and the defendants a grave injustice. The right to assemble and to protest against injustice, whether such injustice occurs in our land or elsewhere, is too precious to be befogged by technicalities or ambiguous dismissal." The Bremen Six were among the honored few who refuse "to remain silent while culture is degraded, nay more, when civilization itself is threatened by a vicious depraved band which is a menace not alone to its own people but internationally."

Marcantonio urged the judge to go *beyond* declaring the seamen were not guilty of the charges lodged by the state.

It isn't enough to rule that "these men are not guilty of the comparatively minor offense of unlawful assembly," he asserted, building to his conclusion. The court must proclaim that they acted in "the best tradition of American freedom, comparable to the action of our brave forefathers when they lodged their memorable protest against oppression and persecution in the never-to-be-forgotten Boston Tea Party."

After the arguments concluded on that Wednesday afternoon, Magistrate Brodsky announced that he would render his decisions in two days' time at another venue, Traffic Court in downtown Manhattan, which, a careful observer might note, was located not far from the newspaper offices on Park Row.

"Very well, gentlemen," he said. "It is adjourned to twelve o'clock Friday at 300 Mulberry Street."

CHAPTER FOURTEEN

CASSANDRA: These walls breathe out a death that drips with blood.

LEADER: Not so. It is only the smell of the sacrifice.

CASSANDRA: It is like the breath out of a charnel-house.

LEADER: You think our palace burns odd incense then!

—FROM AESCHYLUS'S *AGAMEMNON*

I N THE MIDST of the legal battles in Magistrates' Court, Bill Bailey received a surprise visit from his long-distance girlfriend, the young Communist organizer from the Chicago stockyards whom he identified as "Pele" in his autobiography. The two had maintained contact even after Communist leadership denied Bailey's request to be transferred to the Great Lakes region. Now she was on her way to Moscow, where she would be an American delegate to a Communist youth conference. The romance was renewed. They decided to wed.

The Communist sweethearts spent every available moment together during the week Pele was in New York attending orientation sessions for the Moscow event. The plan was that Bill would procure a marriage license while she was abroad. The wedding would be held the instant she returned to the United States.

"We drove to the pier of the Cunard liner that would take her to Europe," he wrote many years later. "I left the cab a block earlier and kissed her goodbye. I felt elated. I walked on air. Everything was beginning to jell in the right direction."

Bailey was in the flush of a love affair when he entered Traffic Court on September 6, 1935.

"Will the defendants please rise?"

The Bremen Six rose to their feet.

"We stood motionless as Judge Brodsky adjusted his glasses," remembered Bailey.

Irving J. Tell was the lone representative for the People of the State of New York. Congressman Vito Marcantonio stood for the defense, joined by his three cocounsels from the International Labor Defense: Joseph Tauber, Edward Kuntz, and Abraham Unger.

"As on other occasions a heavy police guard was on duty to prevent any untoward demonstration," reported the *World-Telegram*.

With his pince-nez successfully affixed to his nose, Louis B. Brodsky began reading from a fourteen-page statement, which, in its own way, was one of the great denunciations of foreign tyranny ever issued from an American judicial tribunal, in this case the Seventh District of the City Magistrates' Courts, Borough of Manhattan.

He began by outlining the charges against the Bremen Six. Then, he recited the passages that would be reprinted in newspapers throughout the world.

"It may well be, perhaps, as was forcibly urged upon me in the attempted exculpation of the tearing down of the standard bearing the swastika from the masthead of the *Bremen*, that the flying of this emblem in New York Harbor was, rightly or wrongly, regarded by these defendants and others of our citizenry as a gratuitously brazen flaunting of an emblem, which symbolizes all that is antithetical to American ideals of the God-given and inalienable rights of all peoples to life, liberty and the pursuit of happiness; that in their minds this emblem of the Nazi regime stands for and represents war on religious freedom; the disenfranchisement of nationals solely on religious or ethnological grounds; the debasement of the learned professions; the deprivation of the right to education and the earning of a livelihood, the enslavement of women and workers, the imprisonment of sweet Sisters of Charity on flimsy pretexts, the suppression of the blessed trinity of free speech, freedom of the press, and lawful assembly; the degradation of culture, an international menace threatening freedom; a revolt against civilization—in brief, if I may borrow a biological concept, an atavistic throwback to the pre-medieval, if not barbaric, social and political conditions.

"Nor, am I unmindful of the fact that to these defendants, again rightly or wrongly, the prominent display of this emblem even carried with it the same sinister implications as a pirate ship sailing defiantly into the harbor of a nation, one of whose ships it had just scuttled, with the black flag of piracy proudly flying aloft.

"In a large sense, indeed, it might seem as though whatever disturbances attended the sailing of the *Bremen* were provoked by this flaunting of an emblem to those who regarded it as a defiant challenge to society."

Brodsky's winking avowals of impartiality ("may well be," "rightly or wrongly," "might seem") couldn't disguise that he had taken a stand on an essential issue before the court. He had lent his nonradical authority to the supposition that the worsening crisis in Germany required the attention of all right-thinking people. And he used provocative language to guarantee that his message would be heard far and wide: The most esteemed creation of the German state was a "pirate ship." The swastika flapping from its forward-most position was "the black flag of piracy."

But he wouldn't hesitate to convict the six defendants, he stressed, if they were shown to be guilty of the charge of unlawful assembly, which was a part of the opinion that wouldn't be broadcast as far and wide.

"Nevertheless, if it had been proven that there had been a concerted attempt on the part of citizens, whose sensibilities had been outraged by this emblem, to protest against it, not verbally but by the symbolic action of tearing it down, as technically to bring such act under the strict definition of an unlawful assembly, it would have been my sworn duty to ignore this *argumentum ad hominem* and to have held those who had committed such a palpable violation of the statute governing unlawful assembly, no matter how strongly persuasive the provocation may have seemed."

The *Bremen* incident, he made a point of noting, was not like the Boston Tea Party, at least as a legal matter.

"In this connection it may not be amiss to remind those of counsel for the defense who so eloquently argued upon me that the Boston Tea Party was now viewed, in historic retrospect, as a glorified violation of the law of unlawful assembly, that that staunch patriot, Samuel Adams, and others declared that they would take no action against the tea shipment 'until the last legal means of relief had been tried and found wanting.' The historian Fiske comments that 'they had reached a point where the written law had failed them and in their effort to defend the eternal principles of natural justice they were now most reluctantly compelled to fall back upon the paramount law of self-preservation.'"

Brodsky's opinion included a lengthy discussion of the history and practice of unlawful-assembly jurisprudence, which featured quotations from case law and eminent legal commentators. He conducted a civics lesson on the free assembly rights "vouchsafed . . . by the Magna Carta, the Petition of Rights, and the Bill of Rights, the foundation stones of the British constitution and the bases of both our Federal and State constitutions." He combed through every syllable of the relevant statute, Section 2092 of the Penal Law of the State of New York, explaining that "the prohibited intent must be to assemble not only for an unlawful purpose" but "to commit such unlawful act by force." If "either of these two elements are missing, the acts complained of are not within the purpose of the statute.

"The evidence discloses that some of the defendants were under surveillance on the afternoon of July 26, 1935, and that eventually they were trailed to the S.S. *Bremen*," Brodsky said. "At least, one of the defendants was observed talking to some woman. In the evening they were seen in and about the S.S. *Bremen* and just at about the time of sailing of the vessel, which was set for midnight, there was a commotion. Officer Solomon was seen standing with his gun in his right hand, while some person did actually assault him and another sought to take the gun from him. Just about this time he was struck by a person wearing metal knuckles, causing serious injury and immediately thereafter the defendant Drolette was leaving the scene of the commotion, while Officer Moore came toward him, gun in hand, which was discharged causing serious injury to the defendant Drolette.

"There was no evidence of any meeting for the purpose of assembling on the S.S. *Bremen*, nor of any conversations between any of the defendants which took place before they came to the *Bremen*, or after they reached it," Brodsky continued. "Strangely enough, there was no evidence in this case by any of the parties that the ship's emblem had been taken down from its staff. . . . For all that appears from the record (and this is merely guess work) persons may have lawfully asked that the obnoxious emblem be hauled down. Such request may have been met, not only by a refusal on the part of the seamen on the *Bremen*, commissioned to protect what the Master conceived to be their right to fly the flag, but by a show of resistance and possibly by force of arms. Such resistance may have been met by resistance and precipitated what has been called here 'a free-for-all.' I repeat I can only conjecture what happened; there is no proof.

"I am dealing with a criminal offense where nothing must be left to guess or conjecture, but where all the elements constituting the crime must be proven by satisfactory evidence," he said, winding toward his conclusion. "I again repeat that neither the preconceived or common design to commit or the purpose of committing what is claimed here constituted the unlawful assembly was presented for my consideration by the People."

After further quotation of case law, he came to the point:

"I, accordingly, hold that the charge of unlawful assembly has not been prima facie sustained by the evidence presented, and I, accordingly, dismiss the complaint and discharge the defendants."

The outrage against the swastika would not be punished by an American court of law.

"We had a feeling this was going to happen," remembered Bailey.

Brodsky then offered a mixed decision on the secondary incident, the attack on Detective Solomon.

He did not conduct a detailed examination into the veracity of the testimony offered by Detectives Solomon and Moore. Since both Solomon and Moore testified that Drolette had thrown a metal-assisted punch, corroborating each other, Brodsky concluded that "prima facie proof of the commission of the offense has been proved, and I, accordingly, hold the defendant Drolette for assault and possession of the metal knuckles in violation of Section 1897 of the Penal Law."

Brodsky would let a jury make a judgment on the dubious testimony offered by Detectives Solomon and Moore.

A trial in the Court of Special Sessions loomed for Edward Drolette.

Brodsky was less ambivalent on the matter of the other five defendants, who were accused of joining the attack on the Jewish detective. The evidence against Vincent "Low Life" McCormack "did not rise to the point of the dignity of the charge of felonious assault." The evidence against Bailey, Blair, Howe, and Blackwell was nonexistent. "There is not one word of evidence in the entire record connecting them in any way with any crime committed either on the *Bremen* or elsewhere."

The felonious assault charges against the five were thrown out.

Brodsky made no comment on whether Detective Moore's gunshot into Edward Drolette was a justified retaliation against a cop-thrashing predator or a depraved attempt on the life of an unsuspecting protester.

He spent a few paragraphs dismissing or reducing charges against protesters who had been arrested in front of the police precinct on the night of July 26.

Then, he turned back to the Bremen Six.

"As far as Drolette is concerned, I will hold him for the Grand Jury and I will continue the bail in which he is presently held," said Brodsky. "All the defendants are discharged."

"They were let off," remembered Maggie Weaver, who was now living with Arthur Blair, the only noncitizen among the Bremen

Six. "And he left his hat. Blair always wore a hat. And he had been leaving about every ten minutes because he smoked an awful lot. He left the hat in the chair, so the Immigration [officers] that he had seen in the back waiting for him would think that we were coming back. So he was able to leave and go home. I say home now. Blair just stayed in the apartment with me."

———

"Brodsky Frees 5 in Bremen Riot As Incited by 'Pirate' Swastika," blared the front page of the *New York Herald Tribune*, in a typical page-one pronouncement. "Court Sympathetic With Uprising Against Nazis, Notes Bill of Rights Defends Public Assembly and Privilege to Protest Injustice."

The judgment was delivered ten years before the liberation of the death camps. Six years before the Final Solution began in the execution pits of the occupied Soviet Union. Five years before Winston Churchill became Great Britain's wartime prime minister. Four years before the Nazi invasion of Poland launched World War II. Three years before the capitulation at Munich was followed by the pogrom of Kristallnacht.

As described by the *New York Times* in its front-page article, "The action of the magistrate brought a storm of protest."

The Nazi press acted swiftly, publishing attacks in the next morning's newspapers. "The verdict and its motivation," declared Berlin's *Boersen Zeitung*, "represents a far greater insult to Germany than the incident in New York Harbor." The *Lokalanzeiger* asked, "What would the American people and their government say if a German judge were to speak of a 'gangster flag' which must be denied protection?" Joseph Goebbels's *Der Angriff* called Brodsky "an Eastern Jew" who furthered "Jewish-Communistic agitation" with his ruling. "A land in which a judge dares designate the German flag as a pirate flag must realize that this makes all international relations problematical and that there is also something wrong in its own domestic situation," *Allgemeine Zeitung* opined. "It is now up to Washington."

At shortly before noon in Washington on that Saturday, September 7, the short, rotund Nazi ambassador to the United States,

Hans Luther, arrived at the State Department under orders from Berlin. After waiting for several minutes in the ornate diplomatic reception room, Luther was ushered into the office of Secretary of State Cordell Hull.

Both men were just back from their summer vacations.

"The German ambassador came in and said that it was his duty to make earnest complaint about the violent and offensive utterances of a New York City judge relative to the German flag, and to request this government in suitable language to deal with that situation in accordance with the comity existing between nations," wrote Secretary Hull in an internal memo on the meeting.

Luther demanded that the US government show "more concern and more feelings in the nature of regret than it had shown" following the original event on the ship.

Hull said he told Luther that the United States includes "many violent and ultra-radical persons, entertaining every shade of social, political, religious, and other views," individuals who thrive "on controversy and in great headlines in the press growing out of such controversy." Hull didn't see how the US government could "deal with these large numbers of violent, extreme, controversial persons, thus seeking publicity and strife, without increasing such utterances and actions rather than quieting and decreasing them."

Hull blamed the trouble on "awful news reports" coming out of Nazi Germany "about racial and other conditions and controversies." He suggested that if the Nazi regime ceased "the chronic state of incidents" then the "violent utterances" by persons who "relish bitter exchanges of epithets and denunciations" would cease.

"The Ambassador parried this statement and view by making some reference to the interference by one country with the internal affairs of another," wrote Hull.

Hull told Luther that the US government would make no statement about the Brodsky decision until "the full and accurate facts of the reported occurrence" could be reviewed.

"The Ambassador urged me to say something rather definite now," Hull went on.

Hull refused to do so.

Luther "then inquired what he should say to the press, seeking still further to draw from me some expression of regret right now," wrote Hull. "I gave him no satisfaction and he then said he would say nothing to the press."

To the reporters waiting outside, Luther would only say, "I had a very interesting conversation."

After the Nazi ambassador left the office, Secretary Hull dispatched a letter to the governor of New York, Herbert Lehman, informing him of Luther's objection to "Judge Brodsky's reported derogatory expressions with regard to the German flag." Hull asked for "the official facts" to be "assembled and forwarded at your early convenience."

Once he received the communication from Hull, Governor Lehman requested a full report from New York City's chief magistrate, Jacob Gould Schurman.

———

Every mainstream newspaper in America seemed to pen an editorial lamenting that Brodsky had transgressed judicial norms. The *Washington Post* published a ferocious attack on "this New York magistrate" who "seems to have completely lost his judicial bearings" and "had no right to set himself up even incidentally as the judge of a foreign government." The *New York Times* was appalled at Brodsky's "offensive characterization of the *Bremen*" and advised the mayor of New York "to issue a severe rebuke." When sought for comment, Mayor LaGuardia said he would take no action. "I have enough troubles of my own," he said warily. Many editorialists found a nice way of suggesting that Brodsky was a loudmouthed Jew. "But legally—and the magistrate's is a court of law—personal opinions and, above all, emotions, have nothing to do with this case," stated the *New York World-Telegram*. The *Economist* in London felt no need for euphemism. "The fact that the magistrate happens to be a Jew accounts for, without excusing, his behavior."

Brodsky was hailed as a conquering hero by the Yiddish papers while the English-language Jewish press was more cautious in its commentary. "Conservative Jewish leaders here feel that Judge

Brodsky would have done Jewry a better service by not rapping that gravel of his so determinedly," wrote one journalist. He "put the United States government in an uncomfortable spot—and at the same time gave the Nazis something to capitalize on." Supreme Court justice Benjamin Cardozo, the second Jewish member to serve on the nation's highest court, was appalled, writing in a letter to a relative that Brodsky's "shameful utterance" was an "unforgivable" breach of the "standards of judicial propriety." The left-wing press exulted in the exoneration of the five defendants but was loath to celebrate the achievements of a Tammany Hall magistrate. The favorable verdict was instead attributed to "mass pressure and the brilliant legal defense conducted by Congressman Vito Marcantonio," claimed the *Daily Worker*. The International Labor Defense produced a pamphlet called *The Black Flag of Piracy*, which credited "anti-Nazi sentiment throughout the country, and especially New York," with forcing a reluctant Brodsky to issue a decision that made "the brown hordes howl."

Detective Solomon, who was vacationing upstate, was given permission by the New York Police Department (NYPD) to accept a $150 reward from the German shipping line "for his courage in defending the swastika flag," the papers reported.

"By accepting the gift, Solomon muffed a grand opportunity," wrote a columnist for the *Jewish Advocate*. "He could've spurned it and explained that while he defended the flag as he was duty bound to do as an officer of the law, he despised what the flag stood for."

———

Brodsky made his controversial pronouncement at a resonant time on the Nazi calendar. He spoke just days before the opening of the annual party meeting at Nuremberg, the multiday convocation that represented the height of Nazi self-celebration. More than half a million devotees were traveling to the medieval city in northern Bavaria for the festival of mass hypnosis captured so vividly in Leni Riefenstahl's just-released box office hit, *Triumph des Willens* (Triumph of the Will). The Hitler government was celebrating a string of foreign policy successes over the previous year—annexation of the Saar Protectorate on the French border; announcement of military rearmament in repudiation of the Versailles Treaty; signing of the Anglo-German Naval Agreement; and widespread acclamation of Hitler's "peace speech" of May 21, which declared the government's support for a policy that "rejects the prerequisites of war." On the domestic front, the last remaining internal enemies were all but silenced—far-right reactionaries, Catholic priests and nuns, nightclub comedians—while an unprecedented onslaught targeted the Nazi Party's most hated foe, the Jews.

In the weeks leading up to the rally, the Nazi leadership concluded that grassroots actions against Jews had successfully paved the way for top-down legislation. The "acts of terror," according to the Security Service of the SS, could now make way for "effective laws to show the people that the Jewish question is being resolved from above." The word had gone out that Hitler had ordered "individual operations" against Jews to end.

The Nazi state was eager to maintain the stable conditions necessary for a vigorous strategy for economic and military revival. The next major violent attack against the Jewish population would not occur until Kristallnacht (the Night of Broken Glass) in November 1938.

On September 9, the eve of the rally, Joseph Goebbels picked up his pen and updated his diary on the status of the *Bremen* affair. "Judge Brondski [*sic*] in New York insulted the German national flag," he wrote. "I set the press on it. It foams with rage. Our answer: in Nuremberg meets the Reichstag and declares the swastika flag as the sole national flag."

Hitler was summoning the national legislature from Berlin to proclaim that the Nazi Party had completed the task of conquering the German nation-state.

Goebbels' diary entry concluded with giddy admiration for the inspirational leader who would preside over the climactic moment of the Reichsparteitag der Freiheit (Rally of Freedom) in Nuremberg: "Führer is in full flow."

In the afternoon of the following day, September 10, Hitler made his godlike entrance into the Franconian capital, descending from the clouds in his Junkers Ju 52 transport plane. While a band played the Badenweiler March, Hitler stepped from the plane with his chief adjutant, Wilhelm Brueckner, and his chief propagandist, Joseph Goebbels. A huge crowd cheered. After a welcoming ceremony at the airport, he motorcaded to the rustic heart of old Nuremberg in an open-roofed Mercedes-Benz, standing upright in the car with his right arm outstretched in stiff salute to the tens of thousands of cheering faithful lining the streets. Church bells tolled. Following a (second) welcoming ceremony at Nuremberg Town Hall, where Hitler was presented with a ceremonial sword of gold, the evening concluded at the Opera House. Wilhelm Furtwängler, a towering figure in twentieth-century classical music, conducted a gala performance of Hitler's favorite opera, Wagner's *Die Meistersinger*. Swastikas were everywhere.

Over the coming days, uniformed "Aryans" participated in torchlight processions, solemn rituals, political meetings, military displays, and huge assemblies on the famous parade grounds at the Zeppelinfeld, a show of synchronized militancy and devotional commitment that awed foreign visitors and correspondents.

On Thursday, September 12, Secretary of State Hull asked James Clement Dunn, the director of the Division of Western European Affairs, to telephone Governor Lehman of New York and inform him that the State Department was impatient to receive an official copy of Magistrate Brodsky's decision. At ten a.m., Dunn reached one of the governor's senior staffers, who promised to call back. "Not having heard from Mr. Brown, I telephoned him at 2:57 p.m. on the afternoon of the same day to find out what progress was being made," Dunn detailed in a memo. "He informed me that Chief Magistrate Schurman of the City of New York, who had been asked by the Governor for the report, had informed them that the report would not be ready until the middle of the following week." After speaking with Secretary Hull, Dunn placed another call to the governor's office, emphasizing to a second staffer, James J. Mahoney, that a full report wasn't necessary. All that was needed was a certified copy of Brodsky's decision. Mahoney promised to look into the matter and "would let me know with regard to it the following day," Dunn wrote.

By Friday morning, September 13, rumors were spreading about Hitler's plan to convoke a session of the Reichstag. It was said that the entire cabinet, undersecretaries, and heads of key ministries would be present to witness a significant declaration by the government. Western newspapers were full of speculation about the meaning of the "spectacular summons." Informed opinion thought Hitler might announce his intentions regarding Memel, the German-majority city in Lithuania that the Nazis were determined to reincorporate into German territory.

The State Department heard rumors that Hitler was planning a fiery speech that would attack the United States over the *Bremen* incident.

On Friday afternoon, Washington time, James Clement Dunn placed another call to Governor Lehman's office. He again spoke to James Mahoney, who told him the governor was "somewhere in the Adirondacks" and couldn't be reached. The governor's legal counsel, according to Mahoney, "had stated that there was nothing for the Secretary of State to do but wait until we received the report of the Governor which would be transmitted upon its receipt from Chief Magistrate Jacob Gould Schurman." Dunn reiterated that the State Department sought nothing more than a certified copy of Brodsky's decision, noting that "the Secretary was very anxious to make a reply to the German Government within a reasonable time, particularly in view of certain circumstances which had come to our attention and which I was unable to inform him of over the telephone." Dunn wrote, "I further stated that our failure to make reply to the German Government would be construed by them as discourteous and negligent."

On that Friday evening in Nuremberg, after a busy day of fascist pageantry that included an interminable tirade against "the satanic forces of world destruction" delivered by Goebbels, the Führer came to a decision that is still studied by historians. The Reichstag session, which was slated for Sunday night, would not be solely devoted to the elevation of the swastika. Hitler had decided to advance the anti-Semitic ideals that were embodied in the flag. Two Jewish affairs officials in the Interior Ministry were telephoned and instructed to be on the first flight to Nuremberg in the morning.

Early on Saturday, September 14, Bernhard Lösener and Franz Medicus were asked to formulate a "Jewish law" that would forbid sexual relations between Jews and non-Jews and outlaw the employment of "Aryan" servant girls in Jewish households. At intervals throughout the day, Lösener fought his way through the thronged streets to deliver the latest version to the interior minister, Wilhelm Frick, who passed the text on to Hitler. At some point in the afternoon, the two bureaucrats were ordered to come up with another law, one that would remove Jews from the protection of German citizenship, which had been a dream of the Nazi Party since its earliest days. In his postwar account, Lösener was still angry at "Hitler's new mood," which forced the two hacks to keep working even though they were "physically and mentally at the end of their strength."

On that Saturday morning in Washington, James Clement Dunn again placed a call to Governor Lehman's office. He reached James Mahoney, who told Dunn "it was impossible to communicate with the governor" and "impossible to take up any matters with New York City in anticipation of receiving Chief Magistrate Schurman's report." Dunn said he "again pleaded the special circumstances of the case and went over the whole ground again as I had done each time when telephoning to the Governor's office by explaining the fact that it was not necessary to extend the case beyond the actual language used by Magistrate Brodsky in rendering his decision." He "stressed the special circumstances of which we were informed which required that the reply to the German Government be not delayed."

Informed of the intransigence of Governor Lehman's office, Secretary Hull decided he couldn't wait any longer for a Lehman-approved copy of Brodsky's decision.

"The Secretary thereupon asked to have the German Ambassador informed that he would receive him that morning," Dunn wrote.

A call was placed to the German embassy but Hans Luther wasn't available. Rudolf Leitner, the chargé d'affaires who had received the previous (and second) apology a month and a half earlier, was dispatched to the State Department on Pennsylvania Avenue.

After Dr. Leitner arrived and settled into his seat, Hull picked up a piece of paper and read from a five-paragraph statement, speaking with a pronounced lisp and a middle Tennessee accent.

The statement declared that the State Department would take no position on Brodsky's dismissal of the unlawful assembly charges against the Bremen Six, "the correctness of which the department cannot undertake to pass." It would instead address "the statements made by the magistrate in rendering his decision which that government interprets as an unwarranted reflection on it.

"The department is constrained to feel that the magistrate, in restating contentions of the defendants in the case and in commenting on the incident, unfortunately so worded his opinion as to give the reasonable and definite impression that he was going out of his way adversely to criticize the [Nazi] government, which criticism was not a relevant or legitimate part of his judicial decision," Hull said.

After noting "state and municipal officials are not instrumentalities of the federal government," Hull said that the FDR administration "regretted that an official having no responsibility for maintaining relations between the United States and other countries should, regardless of what he may personally think of the laws and policies of other governments, thus indulge in expressions offensive to another government with which we have official relations."

The US government had now issued its third apology since Bill Bailey had flung the swastika into the Hudson.

The evening newspapers in Berlin hailed the US administration's docility, which "inspires hope that friendly relations between the two nations should not be troubled by the hysteria of individuals."

On the following evening, September 15, several hundred Nazi Party grandees packed into the auditorium of the Nuremberg Cultural Association. Motion picture cameras were whirring. A nationwide radio hookup carried the proceedings live. At just after nine p.m., Hermann Goering rose from the presidential chair and gaveled the Reichstag to order. The first item on the agenda called for the effective abolition of the body. Six hundred deputies waived all rules of procedure and voted to put themselves under the "leadership principle." Any pretense of democracy in Germany was formally abandoned.

A grim-faced Adolf Hitler then stepped up to the microphone. He was exhausted after a busy week of rallies, functions, and speeches. In a weakened voice, he delivered a speech that was unlike his usual rants. In a menacing tone that never reached the level of shout, he spoke for just twelve minutes.

He extolled the unity and discipline of the German *Volk*. He characterized the new Wehrmacht as an instrument of peace. He denied any plans to invade neighboring countries, naming Austria, France, and Russia. And he expressed his outrage at the plight of ethnic Germans who were "abused and tortured" in Memel, Lithuania.

Then, he turned to the Jews, who he blamed for all the instability in the world.

"We are further compelled to note that here, as everywhere, it is almost exclusively Jewish elements which are at work as instigators of this campaign to spread animosity and confusion among the peoples," he said. "The insult to the German flag—which was settled most loyally by a statement of the American government—is both an illustration of the attitude of Jewry, even in civil service status, toward Germany and an effective confirmation of the rightness of our National Socialist legislation, the aim of which is to prevent similar incidents in our administration and jurisprudence."

The international agitation has led the Jews of Germany to act in "clear opposition to the German national interests in the Reich" and to commit a wave of "provocative actions" that included the booing of a "basically harmless" anti-Semitic film at a movie theater on the Kurfürstendamm, which was the ostensible reason why Nazi thugs launched the Berlin Riots on July 15.

To prevent Jews from committing further provocative acts that would lead to "quite determined defensive action on the part of the outraged population, the extent of which cannot be foreseen," the Nazi government was adopting "a legislative solution to the problem," Hitler said. The new legislation was "guided by the hope of possibly being able to bring about, by means of a single secular measure, a framework within which the German *Volk* would be in a position to establish tolerable relations with the Jewish people." But "should this hope prove false and intra-German and international Jewish agitation proceed on its course, a new evaluation of the situation would have to take place."

Hitler asked the quiescent Reichstag to adopt the three laws that have come to be known as the Nuremberg Laws.

"The first and second repay a debt of gratitude to the movement, under whose symbol Germany regained its freedom, in that they fulfill a significant item on the program of the National Socialist Party," he said. "The third is an attempt at a legislative solution to a problem which, should it yet again prove insoluble, would have to be assigned to the National Socialist Party for a final solution by law."

Goering then stepped forward to introduce the laws.

"Our newly won freedom requires a new symbol," Goering said. "It is fitting that the new symbol should be the one under which we won our new freedom. The old black, white, and red flag belongs to a glorious period but a period of the past. . . . A soldier from the front lines, Adolf Hitler, pulled us out of the dirt and brought us back to honor. At the same time, we can have no compromise now. The swastika has become for us a holy symbol. It is the anti-Jewish symbol for the world."

The Reichstag deputies cheered so loudly that Goering could barely be heard as he read the law that declared the swastika the national flag of Germany.

The second Nuremberg Law defined a "Reich citizen" as "exclusively a national of German blood, or racially related blood, who demonstrates through his conduct that he is willing and suited to faithfully serve the German *Volk* and Reich." The third— "Law on the Protection of German Blood and German Honor"— outlawed marital and extramarital sexual intercourse between "Jews and nationals of German blood or racially related blood." The deputies laughed uproariously when Goering came to the section that forbade Jews from employing "female nationals of German blood or racially related blood under the age of 45 years in their household."

The laws, which would be subject to a series of supplemental regulations, were adopted without a hint of dissent.

The government of a major European nation had pledged itself to the active purification of its bloodlines.

"For some it appears symbolic that after a beautiful day a steady downpour of rain started just as the Reichstag was let out, and it was also a fitting touch that as Hitler returned to his hotel with a drawn and unsmiling face, in spite of cheering crowds, he was greeted at the entrance by Julius Streicher, anti-Semitic leader, who on his countenance registered his victory," wrote Otto D. Tolischus of the *New York Times*.

Just a few hours later in New York, on the morning of September 16, the *Bremen* docked at Pier 86. "Germany is marvelous," Captain Adolf Ahrens, the regime-approved replacement for Commodore Ziegenbein, gushed to reporters. "And what you call business, well, we brought 2,078 passengers in this ship this trip."

On the next morning, nearly a thousand crew members were mustered on the afterdeck for a formal ceremony. The newspapers said "extra police" were stationed on the pier to provide protection. "Whoever among us sailors is not pledged to this flag is not worthy to sail under it," said Captain Ahrens, reading words that had been dictated over the wireless by Goebbels's propaganda

The triumphal ascent of the swastika on the stern staff of the *Bremen*. The New Jersey side of the Hudson can be seen in the distance. (Jimmy Condon/NY Daily News Archive via Getty Images)

ministry. "Forget all the little hates and clasp your hands in a unity of effort to gain the respect of those who deny respect to our flag today." At the conclusion of the speech, Ahrens led the crew in three "*heil*'s for "the loved Führer, the rehabilitator of German honor, unity, and freedom." A brass band kicked off "Deutschland über Alles" followed by the "Horst Wessel Lied." In his memoirs, Captain Ahrens described how his first officer, Eric Warning, was so overwhelmed with patriotic emotion that he had tears streaming down his cheeks.

The new national emblem was then hoisted for the first time to the position of honor on the stern staff. Press photographers snapped away while the *Bremen*'s band played the Prussian Presentation March. The triumphal ascent of the swastika was sealed with the unquestioning obedience of upraised arms.

Commuters from New Jersey watched from the deck of a passing ferryboat. About a hundred longshoremen glanced over disinterestedly from the wharves. A nearby oil tanker sounded its jeering horn.

CHAPTER FIFTEEN

―――――――

One reason the Western world failed to rouse itself more promptly to the Nazi menace was surely this tendency to dismiss as impossible fantasy the many warnings the Nazis themselves gave us.

—VARIAN FRY, DECEMBER 21, 1942

I N THE WAKE of the "black flag of piracy" verdict, the Bremen Six hit the left-wing speaking circuit, raising consciousness about Edward Drolette's upcoming trial and urging greater engagement with the Nazi threat. "From then on, you were constantly on a soapbox," Bailey said. "No matter where an anti-Nazi rally was being held, somehow, one of the guys was there. You know, rallying the people, telling them, 'Don't stop now! We got the bastards on the run!'" Bailey, still just twenty years old, remained the spokesman for the group. He was quoted in a Communist pamphlet describing how the "rag under which thousands of workers are being beaten and murdered, that filthy swastika which represents the ruling class of Germany, was ripped from the flag staff, torn in half and thrown overboard into the Hudson River sewage where it belongs." Bailey and his largely Celtic coconspirators had performed a quintessentially Irish act of rebellion, which called for an advance guard of "bold Fenian men" to commit an insurrectionary spectacle to inspire the people to join the noble cause.

Reporters stalked Magistrate Louis B. Brodsky to his chambers and his weekend home in Connecticut. "In the United States, a judge is not a Jewish judge, a Catholic judge or a Protestant judge, but an American judge dealing out justice to the human beings before him," he told a man from the *World-Telegram*, declining to make a specific comment on his judgment. "I have tried to live up to that ideal." While dining at a Broadway restaurant, he became so enraged by dinnerware marked "Made in Germany 1935"—a violation of the boycott—that he called the owner over, gave him a stern rebuke, and handed over a copy of the court decision, which he apparently kept at the ready. Brodsky received thousands of letters from all over the world, "congratulating him for his statesmanlike courage, his long range view of history, and his technical acumen in meeting the immediate situation with a legally unchallengeable opinion," wrote a journalist. A gossip columnist for the Jewish press was offered a glance at the trove of correspondence. "Amazing as it sounds he is submerged with mail from Germany commending (yes commending) him for his courageous remarks in his celebrated verdict anent the swastika," wrote Phineas J. Biron in his syndicated "Strictly Confidential" column. "We were shown open postcards postmarked Berlin hailing in German Brodsky's words and declaring that they reflected the sentiment of every German."

Emil Ludwig, an eminent German author whose books had been burned by the Nazi regime, offered high praise for Brodsky during a wide-ranging session with reporters in his suite at the St. Moritz Hotel on Central Park.

"You have no idea what repercussions it has had in Europe," Ludwig said of the verdict. "It is on everyone's lips. Everyone talks of Brodsky. Where is Brodsky? I should very much like to see him. I want to congratulate him."

One of the reporters said he would be back in fifteen or twenty minutes. Brodsky lived a dozen blocks away in a West Seventy-Second Street apartment just off the park.

Ludwig was answering a question about Jewish emigration to Palestine when Judge Brodsky was brought into the suite and introduced by the reporter who retrieved him.

"No other picture than that of a child being told that Santa Claus has just arrived could convey the reaction of Herr Ludwig to this announcement," wrote journalist Meyer F. Steinglass. "Breaking through our circle he rushed to greet the man whose words concerning the swastika have made the whole world resound with his name."

"Judge Brodsky, how are you, judge?" Ludwig said. "You don't know how happy I am to meet you. When I left my home in Switzerland, I told my wife that I was going to America to congratulate you and embrace you."

Ludwig rose from his chair and "proceeded to carry out his promise."

"The judge was visibly very much touched by the compliments which the internationally famed biographer showered on him," wrote Steinglass.

"You have no conception, judge, of what a tremendous effect your courageous words had upon the world," Ludwig said.

"Thank you, Herr Ludwig," responded Brodsky.

The judge described the many letters of support he had received from citizens of Nazi Germany.

"Doesn't that appear to you to be a definite sign of internal weakness that may bring about a revolution?" Brodsky asked.

"I am afraid I can't agree with you on that, judge," Ludwig responded. "You see, the German temperament does not support this view. It is almost safe to say that the German people value discipline and regimentation or what you would call the 'goose step' more highly than certainly their religion and, one might even say, their bread. No, I don't think there will be a revolution in Germany."

After numerous adjournments and delays, Edward Drolette went to trial in the Court of General Sessions before Judge Morris Koenig and a jury of twelve men.

Detectives Solomon and Moore took the stand and repeated the New York City Police Department (NYPD) version of the night of July 26, 1935.

Drolette testified in his own defense, denying that he delivered the metal-knuckle punch to the right eye of Detective Solomon.

Edward Drolette
speaking at a
victory party for
the Bremen Six.
(Tamiment Library,
New York University)

He described how he tried to save the Jewish detective from "members of the *Bremen*'s crew." George Blackwell, an admitted member of the Bremen Six, told the jury that Drolette had been frantically concerned for Solomon's fate. "They are killing that man!" Drolette shouted, according to Blackwell. The star witness for the defense was Alice Hughes, a society columnist for the conservative *New York American*, who was one of the guests of the sailing party. It was *Bremen* crew members, she affirmed, who attacked the plainclothesman and attempted to throw him overboard.

The jury needed just an hour to acquit Drolette.

The Bremen Six had been exonerated of all wrongdoing.

"The tearing down of the swastika on July 26, 1935, has caused the unmasking of the Hitler regime for, lo and behold, we read in the press of the nation that the German flag has been decreed to be no longer her national emblem and that in her place and stead, there has been substituted the swastika," wrote Congressman Vito

Marcantonio in an article for a labor publication. "The Nazis can no longer hide behind the German flag. They now have been forced to raise aloft as a challenge to civilization the swastika, symbol of cowardice and ignorance. The *Bremen* incident has caused this unmasking. I am proud to have played my little part in this far-reaching event."

Such lofty sentiments offered little solace to Bill Bailey in the autumn of 1935. He hadn't received any letters from his bride-to-be, Pele, who had been attending a Communist youth conference in Moscow. In desperation, he went to see Jacob "Pop" Mindel, the secretary of the national committee of the Young Communist League. "You don't know?" Mindel said. "Why, she left here an hour ago to catch the Limited back to Chicago." Bailey rushed to Grand Central Station. But the train was gone.

Bailey dashed off a letter by special delivery to Chicago, nervously hoping Pele would provide an innocent explanation for why she'd been avoiding him. He received a Dear John letter in return. She said she'd met a young German antifascist in Moscow. He had been arrested and tortured by the Nazis but had managed to escape Germany. The two had fallen for each other.

"She was in love with this comrade and that was that," Bailey wrote. "There was nothing she could do about it, but our romance was over. While it may have been easy for her to call the romance ended, it was not so easy for me. For many years thereafter, I would be haunted by this aborted affair."

Bailey was promptly kicked out of the East Coast branch of the International Seamen's Union (ISU), which condemned him as a "paid Moscow agent, trained and financed by Moscow gold." He arranged a workaround by gaining admittance into the less doctrinaire West Coast branch of the ISU. After a brief stint as an oiler on the *Alaskan*, which traveled between New York and San Francisco, Bailey returned to the New York waterfront. He helped put out a rank-and-file newspaper with a group of fellow radicals that included his old mentor from his first days in activism, John Quigley

"Robbie" Robinson, and his pal from the raid on the *Bremen*, Arthur "Mac" Blair. The paper's editorial strategy was to attack the "gangster officials of the ISU," which responded by dispatching goons to rough up anyone seen reading its mimeographed pages. In the spring of 1936, Bailey was assigned to Baltimore, where he urged crews to stage walkouts in protest of unfair hiring practices, lack of overtime pay, and miserable working conditions. He was assaulted one evening by a Baltimore cop, who struck him three times with a nightstick, breaking his nose and jaw. "How come you're not talking like you were last week on that soapbox?" the officer taunted. "How come?" Bailey was thrashed so severely that even the cops at the station house were shocked and concerned.

He went back to New York, where he declined the soul-deadening opportunity to be a desk bureaucrat and shipped out for the West Coast on the *President Garfield*. Near the end of the trip, which included stops in Havana and Panama, Bailey and two other crew members presented the captain with a list of demands for basic improvements in the living and eating quarters, which were grudgingly made once the ship arrived in San Francisco. Bailey decided to stay in port to participate in a planned strike of the maritime workforce, becoming editor of a newspaper for engine-room seamen (the *Black Gang News*) and winning election as a delegate to two separate strike committees. The waterfront "hit the bricks" on October 29, 1936. "Everybody went out together—walked off ships, walked off piers, shut it down!" Bailey told an interviewer. The strike ended ninety-eight days later, after the workers won concessions on such issues as hiring protocols, overtime pay, and job security.

In Germany, Lawrence Simpson was freed. He had languished for eighteen months in Nazi jails and concentration camps, twelve of which were spent in solitary confinement, for the crime of attempting to smuggle antiregime propaganda into Germany. "I was never beaten and they treated me fairly enough but were trying to force me to answer questions," said Simpson when he reached New York. "What they did was keep me in constant fear of death by indirect threats." He published a pamphlet called *The Blessings of Fascism* and traveled the country, delivering speeches about his experience. "As a class-conscious worker and as an American believing in democracy," he wrote in the pamphlet, "I thought it my duty to aid my fellow workers abroad in their efforts to throw off the fascist yoke and to establish democratic government."

Following the success of the 1936–1937 strike, Bailey was asked by Party leadership to spread the Communist gospel in the Hawaiian Islands. Landing in Honolulu, he found lodging in a brothel, where he met clandestinely with a small collection of would-be revolutionaries, some of whom would go on to become important figures of organized labor in Hawaii. Bailey took the interisland steamer to Maui, where he delivered speeches outside of sugarcane plantations and urged the Filipino laborers to organize for equitable treatment. At a plantation near Wailuku, he was heckled by an abusive group of *lunas* (plantation foremen), which led him to deliver an intemperate riff that local authorities interpreted as a violation of the Criminal Syndicalism Law of 1919. "Perhaps one day these hills I'm now facing will run with the blood of those who today snicker and sneer and oppress the workers of Maui!" Back in Honolulu, a waterfront cop took him aside and advised him to be on the next boat to the mainland. After receiving the blessing from his circle of comrades, Bailey hired onto the *Lurline* for San Francisco.

"I want to go to Spain in the worst way," he told his group in Honolulu. "I feel I gotta be there."

Bill Bailey was headed to the Spanish Civil War.

He joined the roughly 2,800 Americans who defied US law— the Neutrality Act had been amended to ban arms sales to both sides of the Spanish conflict and the State Department barred American citizens from traveling to Spain—to come to the aid of the democratically elected Popular Front government, a coalition of liberals, Socialists, and Communists. The Spanish Republic was fighting to retain power in the face of the fascist insurgency led by Generalissimo Francisco Franco, who kept a photograph of Adolf Hitler on his desk. The US volunteers, part of an International Brigade of thirty-five thousand men and women from all over the world, served in a number of battalions and units but were collectively known as the Abraham Lincoln Brigade. While the Soviet Union sold arms and lent assistance to the Republican (or Loyalist) forces in Spain, Great Britain and even France, which was led by a Popular Front government, adopted a policy of nonintervention. The proto-Axis alliance had no such qualms. General Franco received matériel and troops from Mussolini's Italy (the victor in the Italo-Ethiopian War) and Hitler's Germany, which was eager to provide Hermann Goering's new air force, the Luftwaffe, with a chance to practice aerial bombardment on undefended cities, such as Guernica in the Basque country.

"As a Communist, I was convinced beyond a doubt that what was happening in Spain would have a profound impact upon the struggle against fascism," Bailey wrote in an article for the *Harvard Educational Review* in 1985. "I felt that the defeat of fascists in Spain would be the best inducement for the Italian people to dispose of their country's fascists. Would the German people, seeing the defeat of fascism in Spain, fail to dispose of their Nazi leaders? These were questions that the struggle in Spain could answer."

The forces of European fascism, it was becoming clear, could not be deterred by anything other than force of arms.

The boycott campaign led by Samuel Untermyer, the oft-quoted founder of the Non-Sectarian Anti-Nazi League, hadn't dissuaded the world from convening in Berlin for the Olympic Games in 1936. The boycotters failed to prevent the heavyweight title bouts between Joe Louis and Max Schmeling, the fistic legend of Nazi Germany who will "take American money to Germany and to that extent destroy the efficacy of the boycott," said Untermyer. While the *Bremen* was losing business to the new European superliners, the *Normandie* and the *Queen Mary*, the German liner's passenger lists remained filled with prominent and notable names. Two of the biggest stars in Hollywood, Clark Gable and Henry Fonda, had no problem sailing under the swastika. By 1937, Nazi Germany was in the midst of a robust and enduring recovery. The unemployed had been put to work in war plants and public works projects, causing the jobless rate to plummet. A program of economic self-sufficiency allowed for a decrease in imported goods, a devastating blow for an international boycott. "Let everyone do his share, and we shall win out in the end," wrote Untermyer in a letter to a supporter who feared the boycott was doomed. "I believe in the justice of our cause, and that as time passes it appeals more and more to the people. Just wait until I have restored my health, and we shall soon make things buzz."

At the passport office in San Francisco, Bailey wrote on the application form that he was a "studen" heading to the Paris Exposition. The clerk glanced up at him, added a *t* to "studen," and said, "Don't forget to keep your head down." With the assistance of the Communist Party, he took a Greyhound bus to New York, boarded an English liner with twenty-five other volunteers (who he was told to avoid), arrived at Le Havre on the French coast, and rode a passenger train to Paris. On the following afternoon, an American coordinator informed the men that tight security at the border meant they'd have to "hoof it across the Pyrenees." From Paris, the group traveled south, escorted by party contacts waiting at prearranged locations along the way, eventually reaching Perpignan, where an old bus took them to within a half mile of the border. A sixty-year-old mountain guide carrying a cane led the way up into the hills. For hours, the volunteers trudged across the rough terrain separating the two countries—snow-capped peaks, swift-running streams—until reaching a long valley with a house in the distance.

"The guide stopped and pointed toward the farmhouse," Bailey wrote. "'Casa,' he said. He motioned for us to go on, then clenched his right fist, and raised it a few inches above his head."

Bailey spent eighteen months in Spain, using his birth name of Mike as a nom de guerre and serving in the Lincoln-Washington Battalion with a machine-gun company of fellow seamen. "I felt right back in the old fo'c'sle again, with a good crew," he said. "You felt that nothing could happen to you as long as you were with that group." He was awed by foreign volunteers eager to fight the good fight against tyranny, touched by the warmth and generosity of the Spanish people, and impressed by the Soviet Union's

willingness to lend support for the Republican cause. Bailey twice
ran into Ernest Hemingway, who was reporting on the war for the
North American Newspaper Alliance. On the second meeting,
Bailey asked Hemingway whether he had a cigarette. "Out came a
pack of American cigarettes," Bailey said. "I remember taking one
out, handing it back. He said, 'Go ahead, keep the whole pack.'
To us it was like keeping a million dollars." Even as the war turned
steadily against the Spanish Republic, Bailey maintained his opti-
mism. He wrote to a friend that it was "written in the books that
victory shall be ours regardless of what extremes the enemy might
go to."

"Mike is a real rough but gentle guy," one of his fellow soldiers,
Harry Hakam, wrote in a letter home in 1938. "To hear him talk
it's Popeye the Sailor come to life. . . . He was the guy who tore
the flag off the *Bremen* and tossed it into the harbor. This should
give you an idea of what a tough man he is." Perley Payne, another
Lincoln volunteer, was immediately drawn to the tallest soldier in
the battalion. "As a small town boy who never had much adven-
ture, here was a guy who had done so many things and I won't say
awe but I really liked him," Payne said in a postwar interview. "He
had been in a lot of battles and stuff like this deal on the *Bremen*. I
adopted Bill because he was big and I could see him. When he'd
fall down, I'd fall down, when they were bombing or something."

Bailey experienced the worst of a brutal war. He and his comrades struggled with lackluster weaponry, barely sufficient training, tattered uniforms, lice infestation, extreme weather, rotten
food, and the constant specter of death. In the late summer and
autumn of 1937, he participated in the battles of the Zaragoza
offensive, witnessing gruesome scenes that would remain with him
for the rest of his life. He learned "what it meant to see a man with
the whole side of his head blown off and the brain still pouring
out, you know," Bailey said. "And he was turning to ash and he
was still pulsating, you know. And he was one of your guys." Bailey
fought house-to-house in the famous battle of Belchite and felt a
sense of accomplishment at liberating the town. But victory came

at a steep cost. "Our dead were everyplace," he said. "Every street had men lying dead in it."

After the retreats of the first months of 1938, Bailey joined the last major Republican offensive of the war, the Battle of the Ebro, a nearly four-month clash that ended with a decisive victory for the fascists. One of the thousands who perished was Bailey's close friend Joe Bianca, a mustachioed braveheart who was regarded as the best soldier in the battalion. The two had made plans to travel after the war to Mexico, where they would load up a few mules with supplies, head into the mountains, and pan for gold and silver. But Bianca was struck and killed by enemy fire on Hill 666 in the Serra de Pàndols. "Many men died in Spain, and no one had time for tears," Bailey wrote. "Tears were something personal. We accepted death as part of the struggle against those who gloried in it, those who were always shouting '*Viva Muerte*'—the fascists. But when Joe Bianca died none of us tried to hold back the tears."

Bailey would later describe his frustration over the unwillingness of left-wing factions to set aside internecine differences in service to the greater cause. He would forever be disgusted by the injustice that was visited upon an American volunteer named Paul White, who, after returning to the battalion following a brief attempt to go AWOL, was executed by a firing squad for desertion. Bailey even felt remorse for once refusing to provide a fascist prisoner of war with a cigarette, a simple failure of compassion that gnawed at him for years. Yet he never regretted going to Spain, which, as he told a newspaper reporter in 1981, was "really a necessary thing."

"It's just that Spain, as the old matadors say, was the moment of truth."

Bailey was one of three members of the Bremen Six who fought in Spain. The others were Vincent "Low Life" McCormack and William Howe, whose real name was William Jamieson. Mac Blair, who suffered from TB during the *Bremen* episode, volunteered to join the fight but was turned down because of his poor lungs. He and his new wife, the former Margaret "Maggie" Weaver, moved to

San Pedro, California, where they agitated among maritime workers in the port of Los Angeles. Robbie Robinson recruited seamen for the war before going himself, eventually serving as a political commissar. On the other side of the ledger, Ernst Hanfstaengl, the Nazi propagandist and Harvard graduate who appears several times in our story, *almost* went to Spain. After falling out of favor with senior Nazi leadership, "Putzi" was ordered by Hitler to travel to Franco's territory to assist German correspondents reporting on the war. While the plane was in midflight, however, the pilot revealed that the plan was to drop him behind Republican lines. During a brief stopover in Leipzig, Hanfstaengl fled in terror. He never believed the story that the whole thing was an elaborate practical joke hatched by Hitler and Goebbels to punish him for unkind remarks he'd made about German troops in Spain. After stops in Switzerland, Great Britain, and Canada, Hanfstaengl reached the United States, where he spent World War II providing the US government with intelligence on Nazi leaders.

William Howe/Jamieson—who was part of the starboard-side team that diverted *Bremen* sailors while the port-side team rushed for the swastika—grew so disillusioned in Spain that he deserted and, upon his return to New York, sat down with a State Department official to expose the Communist Party's attempts to subvert neutrality and passport laws. "After you get to Spain, things start to change," he said, "you find out the score. You don't go there to be dictated to as a volunteer, believing you are going to fight for Democracy. That's what I went there for—not to fight for Stalin but for principles, but it turned out different." He offered a paranoid account of the party's efforts to use subterfuge to transport recruits across the ocean, through France, and into Spain. He named Robbie Robinson as one of those involved in the nefarious scheme. But "the brains of the whole thing," he rambled, were "the Russian Jews." In the course of the interrogation, Howe/Jamieson told the story of the *Bremen*, noting that he was close to Eddie Drolette when Detective Moore fired his famous bullet. "At that time I was wrestling with a Heinie, who was twice as big as myself," he said. "I haven't quite gotten over the effects of the beating I got on that ship." He then provided the State Department with a Hitlerian interpretation of the *Bremen* incident. The party leadership in the United States, he said, "got a number of us fellows—Irish and Christians—to start trouble, concealing the fact that the Jews were behind it."

"Howie," as Bailey called him, had undergone a bizarre and troubling transformation. He disappeared from the movement.

———

After the Spanish government announced that the International Brigades would leave the country—in the (blinkered) hope that global opinion would pressure Franco to ask the Germans and Italians to return home, too—Bailey marched in the emotional farewell parade through the flower-strewn streets of Barcelona on October 29, 1938, passing in review before the republic's president, premier, cabinet ministers, and army chiefs. "It was very sad to leave something that you've already lost," he said. "And I think one of the saddest moments of my life was when they put on a big parade for us in Barcelona. It was a parade you could never forget. Every person in Barcelona and the adjoining area turned out for that parade. You couldn't help but say, 'These are the people I'm leaving—what's going to happen to them?' Because you know sooner or later, Franco was gonna move in." Now twenty-three years old, Bailey made the long journey back to San Francisco, where he paid his back dues to the Marine Firemen's Union and resumed his life in the engine rooms of oceangoing vessels. He was sailing in the Mediterranean on the *President Monroe* when he learned that Franco's forces had conquered Madrid on March 28, 1939. The war was officially over three days later.

Bailey was at sea when the *New Yorker* magazine published a short story by Irwin Shaw called "Sailor off the Bremen," which included a fictionalized account of the swastika incident. In the chaos after the flag was cut down, a character named Ernest—a devoted Communist described as a "Red Saint with the long view"—was beaten so severely by a *Bremen* steward that he lost an eye. "They organized like lightning," another character said of the crew members' response to the disturbance. "Method. How to treat a riot on a ship. Every steward, every oiler, every sailor, was there in a minute and a half. Two men would hold a comrade, the other would beat him. Nothing left to accident." The story described how Ernest made a vain attempt to convince his friends to abort a plan to exact revenge on the steward who administered his beating. "'It's not a personal thing,' Ernest said in a tired voice. 'It is the movement of Fascism. You don't stop Fascism with a personal crusade against one German. If I thought it would do some good, I'd say, sure go ahead. . . . '"

In New York, Louis B. Brodsky was no longer at the center of the world's great controversies. He made the papers when a once-infamous but now passé burlesque dancer named Faith Bacon was charged with disorderly conduct for wearing "wisps of chiffon" while walking a fawn on a leash on Park Avenue. Ms. Bacon claimed she didn't mean for her publicity stunt to disrupt traffic. Brodsky dismissed the charge. The judge was less lenient toward a handicapped panhandler who, it turned out, maintained residences in Queens and Manhattan and enjoyed the services of a valet. He sentenced the man to two years' probation and instructed him to stay out of all the boroughs of New York except Queens. On July 1, 1939, Brodsky retired from the Magistrates' Courts, ending fifteen years of idiosyncratic opinions, an improvisational humanitarian destined to be replaced by bureaucratic drones. "I came to look upon each case not only as a case but as a social problem, and I tried to dispose of the cases in this court in a manner befitting a poor man's court," he said in his farewell statement on July 1. "I hope this court will always be regarded as a poor man's court." Brodsky would spend the remainder of his career in private practice.

On August 23, 1939, the shocking news was broadcast that Nazi Germany and the Soviet Union had reached a nonaggression pact, which gave Hitler the freedom he needed to begin World War II with the invasion of Poland. Bailey was "absolutely appalled" that the leader of world Communism had joined hands with the *Führer* of the fascist cause. "I thought that Stalin should be leading the fight, plunging right into this rotten bastard," he said. "I looked for an explanation and the explanation given to me from the Party was that the Soviet Union was biding for time. They needed this extra time so Stalin could prepare the Red Army to eventually meet the onslaught of fascism. Well, maybe it made a little sense if you rationalize it, like you can almost rationalize anything." Bailey didn't leave the party as many did after the Hitler-Stalin Pact. He maintained his radical activism among his fellow seamen and, with no hope of sharing his life with the beloved Pele, entered into a hasty marriage with a woman whose boyfriend had been killed in Spain.

On September 1, while the German armed forces launched the blitzkrieg against Poland, the *Bremen* was speeding across the Atlantic Ocean in a desperate attempt to reach safe harbor before Great Britain declared war on Nazi Germany and sought to sink the jewel of Hitler's commercial fleet. The ship had left New York for the last time two days earlier, sailing with a full crew but no passengers under the command of now commodore Adolf Ahrens. On September 3, when the British and French issued war declarations, the *Bremen* was headed toward the Denmark Strait between Iceland and Greenland. Commodore Ahrens had issued a "darken ship" order. All topside and navigational lights were extinguished. Wolfram Büttner, a dishwasher, was punished for smoking a cigarette on deck. Plans were laid to scuttle the ship if an enemy warship was spotted. A few thousand mattresses were hauled to the promenade deck, where they could be doused with petrol and set on fire when the signal was given. The crew hung from the lifeboats and slathered gray paint over the black hull to match the overcast conditions. The name of the ship was blotted out. The *Bremen* was a fugitive vessel of an outlaw regime. A pirate ship, you might call it.

The ship's location was a matter of widespread speculation in the world's media. Rumors spread about a dash for the Mexican port of Veracruz. The Admiralty denied a story that the Royal Navy captured the liner in the North Atlantic. The Associated Press reported that it was sunk off the coast of Brazil. In fact, the *Bremen* slipped past the notice of two British cruisers, the HMS *Berwick* and HMS *York*, and sailed to the Barents Sea port of Murmansk, safely within the territory of Germany's new ally, the Soviet Union. "The German liner *Bremen* is believed to be in a northern Russian port," announced Winston Churchill, then holding the position of first lord of the admiralty. Two months later, the ship made a second covert trip, arriving back in its homeport of Bremerhaven on December 13. Work began to transform the luxury liner into a troop transport for the planned (but never attempted) invasion of Great Britain. Large loading doors were cut into the hull to accommodate military cargo. The deck was outfitted with 88 mm antiaircraft guns. The name *Bremen* was retired in favor of ship number 802.

Samuel Untermyer died on March 16, 1940, at the age of eighty-two. He did not live to see the Nazi state attempt to carry out his prediction of a "cold-bloodedly planned and already partially executed campaign for the extermination of a proud, gentle, loyal, law-abiding people," which he made over the public airwaves in 1933.

"He organized and headed the first widescale boycott of German goods in the United States, and at one time he called Secretary of State Cordell Hull 'spineless' in the government's attitude toward Germany," the Associated Press wrote in its obituary. "He had not been as active in recent years as formerly, although periodically he came out with a denunciation of German treatment of Jews."

After Hitler invaded France in June 1940, Varian Fry, the young American journalist who had provided the world with such a powerful firsthand account of the Berlin Riots of July 1935, traveled to Marseilles on behalf of the Emergency Rescue Committee, a private relief organization that he helped found. Fry and a network of accomplices used mostly illegal means to spirit some two thousand anti-Nazi political and intellectual refugees, Jews and non-Jews alike, out of Vichy France. Such luminaries of world culture as Hannah Arendt, Pablo Casals, Max Ernst, and Marc Chagall were prevented from falling into Nazi hands. German and French officials lodged complaints with Secretary of State Cordell Hull, who asked the US ambassador in Paris to prevent Fry from "evading the laws of countries with which the United States maintains friendly relations." After thirteen months of rescue work, Fry was expelled from the country by the French government.

Edward Drolette remained an outspoken and eloquent advocate for the rights of seamen, serving in leadership roles in the marine engineers' union and even testifying before a US Senate subcommittee about conditions in the "sweatshops at sea." On July 25, 1940, he jousted with senators over arcane points of maritime law, displaying a depth of knowledge unusual for someone who never made it past eighth grade.

"If you read through the rules and regulations of the Steamboat Inspection Service, somewhere—I had to read all of their supplements and everything else—I read somewhere that whatever the American Bureau of Shipping may specify, those standards shall be accepted as law by that body," Drolette said. "That is hidden away somewhere in a big long paragraph."

"I know there are a good many hundreds of pages, although I have never read them," said Senator Wallace White, a Republican from Maine.

"I have read every bit of them," Drolette responded.

On March 16, 1941, a fire broke out on the troopship formerly known as the *Bremen*, which remained berthed in Bremerhaven. The inferno raged for hours until the ship listed to starboard, collapsing into the pier. Initial reports indicated that a single RAF warplane had scored a direct hit. "While the main Royal Air Force attack that night was on Hamburg, one of the bombers apparently missed its way and attacked the docks at Bremerhaven, which had been assigned as an alternative target," according to a newspaper report. But the Nazi authorities denied that the great ship had been felled by enemy attack. Hitler and Goering demanded an investigation. "I need a perpetrator," said Heinrich Himmler, the leader of the SS. Suspicion soon fell on a young sailor, a member of the *Bremen* crew, who was identified as a saboteur. The story was that the fire was an inside job. Gustav Schmidt was tried and summarily executed.

The wreck was towed up the Weser River, where the engines, boilers, generators, and turbines were removed. The superstructure was salvaged for scrap metal.

The ship's remains today rest in the Weser Estuary at a place called Blexen Reede. All that survives is the rusting lower deck skeleton, which can still be seen at low tide, peeking out of the shallows.

Bailey spent early 1941 working as a maintenance man in the engine room of the *President Johnson*, which made a four-month journey to Southeast Asia that included stops in Rangoon and Manila. He arrived back in San Francisco a few weeks before World War II took another startling turn. On June 22, 1941, Nazi Germany repudiated the Hitler-Stalin Pact and commenced the massive invasion of the Soviet Union, marking the beginning of the genocide of European Jewry. A million Jews would be killed in the "Holocaust by Bullets" in the swath of territory between the Baltic and Black Seas, which occurred outside the range of such extermination camps as Auschwitz and Treblinka.

With the woman he had impulsively married after returning from Spain, Bailey returned to New York, where he won election to a leadership position in the Marine Firemen's Union, which was officially known as the Marine Firemen, Oilers, Watertenders, and Wipers Association. He was now port agent, responsible for "protecting our engine room members against the money-grubbing, union-hating ship owners." But the marriage was unraveling. She was a copious drinker with a fondness for nightclubs. He was an abstemious subversive who had to get up early each morning for the waterfront.

On December 7, 1941, Bailey was in a movie theater when the lights came on and the announcement was made that the forces of imperial Japan had bombed Pearl Harbor. On the following day, the United States declared war on Japan. On December 11, Nazi Germany and Fascist Italy declared war on the United States.

"There were no more pretenses about war, nor about our responsibilities," Bailey wrote. "We were up to our ears in it on all fronts."

With the US entry into World War II, Bailey was given new responsibilities in his role as port agent. His task was to take young
civilians who had been rushed through a two-week training course
and assign them to the engine rooms of hastily constructed Liberty and Victory ships delivering food, weapons, and ammunition
to US allies Great Britain and the Soviet Union. Few wartime duties were more perilous than working three stories below the deck
of a cargo vessel while wolf packs of German U-boats menaced
the shipping lanes of the North Atlantic. Bailey described how
the young men who came through his office were "bursting with
enthusiasm" to contribute to the war effort. But as the months
passed, he grew increasingly uncomfortable letting others bear
the brunt of the struggle. "I decided I couldn't take it any longer,
you know, watching these kids coming in," he told an interviewer.
"I said to myself, 'How the fuck can I go through this war—when
people ask me 'What did you do during the war?'—all I'll be able
to say will be 'I helped win by pushing kids out, by manning ships.'"

Bailey resigned from his position as port agent in New York,
separated from his wife, and traveled to the West Coast. He studied for his engineer's license, which would enable him to sail as an
officer in the US merchant marine.

After he passed the exam and received his certificate—he
wished Miss O'Rafferty from back in Hoboken could've seen the
greatest academic triumph of his life—Bailey shipped out, serving
on a series of vessels traversing huge expanses of the Pacific. On
the *John Paul Jones*, he made a storm-tossed journey of nearly a
month from New Guinea to Tocopilla, Chile, where the ship was
loaded with nitrate supplies necessary for munitions production.
He next labored on the *Cape Grieg*, which voyaged from Jacksonville, Florida, to the Allied installations in the Mariana Islands and
the New Hebrides, delivering a shipment that included significant quantities of beer, wine, and whiskey. The liquor, a military
officer said, served "medicinal purposes." For nearly four months,
the *Samuel Gompers* ferried materials to American troops fighting
to end the Japanese occupation of the Aleutian Islands, which
was achieved in the summer of 1943. Bailey worried about the

possibility of a torpedo strike in the frigid waters off of Alaska. "But we came through okay." In early 1945, on the *George Powell*, he and his shipmates supported the Allied campaign to retake the Philippines, landing near Manila to deliver supplies in the midst of the fighting. The smell of decaying corpses reminded him of Spain.

On the Western Front, Patrick Gavin was participating in the final Allied onslaught against Hitler.

Gavin, the County Mayo native who had boarded the *Bremen* with Bailey and deployed his Irish accent to avoid arrest by the NYPD, had been serving with the US Army since 1941. He had risen to the rank of technician fourth grade, which meant that he would've been addressed as sergeant. "He was always a good man to have at your side in the event of trouble," Bailey said of him. Gavin appears to have fought in the Battle of the Bulge, the German military's last major counteroffensive from mid-December 1944 to late January 1945. When Paddy Gavin died in the fighting on March 19, the war against Hitler was all but won.

The Allied Expeditionary Force in southern Germany had already issued a set of regulations abrogating Nazi laws in the occupied zones.

The first regulation repealed the Nazi policy protecting the dignity and honor of the swastika.

On August 6, 1945, Bailey was en route to Okinawa on a Victory ship known as the *Laredo Victory*. "Our radio operator picked up some garbled message," he wrote. "He couldn't restrain himself. He came rushing down to us with the news that a guy named Adam had invented some bomb which was just dropped on Hiroshima." Three days later, a second atomic bomb was dropped on Japan, this time striking Nagasaki. "The cry for surrender came loud and clear." After the *Laredo Victory* reached the Okinawan port of Naha, Bailey was unsettled by an encounter with a naval officer, who let loose a string of racial epithets against the Germans, Italians, and Japanese. "So let's finish the job and go after those Russian bastards!" he barked. "Then we can all sit back and enjoy our victory. Right, sailor?"

On the return trip to San Francisco, the *Laredo Victory* sailed with open portholes and lights aglow.

"We were alive with discussions about what the new world would be like now that fascism had been destroyed," Bailey wrote. "As we talked about the future, I could not dismiss from my mind that gold-braid bastard I met who wanted to take on the Russians."

CHAPTER SIXTEEN

Revolution only needs good dreamers who remember their dreams.

—TENNESSEE WILLIAMS

I N A PROPER world, the name Bill Bailey would call to mind an indelible figure in the confrontation against international fascism rather than a moldy vaudeville number that pleads, "Won't you come home, Bill Bailey/Won't you come home?" He was a slum kid from a destitute Irish family, a reformed juvenile delinquent with a Hell's Kitchen twang, who developed a political conscience by working in the decrepit freighters of the Depression-era seafaring trade. At a time when the young men who would storm the beaches of Nazi-occupied Normandy were still in the fourth grade, he was one of the vanishing few to ascend the public stage and exhort the unheeding masses to confront a criminal regime of world-historical scope. While he longed for a world where "guns and weapons of destruction would be a thing of the past," he believed a fight with Hitler and his ilk could not be avoided. He was lucky to survive a year and a half in Spain, where he lived through the savage rigors of a dirty war. In the struggle to end the Japanese variant of fascism in the Pacific, he went below decks in munitions- and supply-laden ships, exposed to an enemy attack that would've come without warning and with little chance for escape.

But he was returning to an America that was entering the Cold War. The Soviet Union was no longer our ally in the common fight against the Axis powers. Stalin's dictatorship had emerged from World War II as the world's only other superpower, an expansionist regime with newly acquired satellite states in Eastern and Central Europe. The tiny community of American Communists, which numbered some fifty-five thousand men and women at the end of the war, would come to be seen as a fifth column preparing the ground for a Soviet takeover of the United States. "The Reds, phonies, and 'parlor pinks' seem to be banded together and are becoming a national danger," President Harry S. Truman wrote in his diary on September 20, 1946. "I am afraid they are a sabotage front for Uncle Joe Stalin." Bill Bailey would not be celebrated as a patriot. He was an enemy of the state.

In the months after he returned from the war, Bailey entered into a second marriage, wedding a fellow believer in the cause, Ruth (Kujawsky) Kaye, the American-born daughter of Polish Jews who was eight or nine years old when she joined the Young Pioneers, the Communist Party's youth group. The marriage wouldn't last. He blamed the long absences that were an occupational hazard of the seaman's life with preventing "any type of a decent social relationship with your family, your wife." Bailey would regret his failure to accept his wife as an equal whose political work was as important as his, instead expecting her to handle the domestic duties that represented "stultifying and crushing drudgery," in Lenin's phrase. The couple had a son, Michael, who meant more to Bailey than anything. "If I had to sit down and think of the happiest moments of my life, I would have to say when he put his arms around you and hugged you," he said. "There was just something special about it that never happens again and so, like I tell all people who have little kids, cherish it." Mike would follow his father's example and make his career as a merchant seaman.

Bailey and the handful of Reds in his branch of the Marine Firemen's Union put on "an act of bravado" when the anti-

Communist panic descended upon the United States. President Truman signed an executive order creating a comprehensive program to root out any "disloyal or subversive person" employed by the federal bureaucracy. J. Edgar Hoover's FBI began infiltrating and disrupting Communist and Communist-affiliated organizations. Federal prosecutors brought charges against Communist leaders for violating the Smith Act (1940), which made it a crime to be a member of any group or society that advocated the violent overthrow of the government. The House Un-American Activities Committee (HUAC), which had been originally constituted to expose Nazi sympathizers in the United States, commenced the most infamous phase of its history. The movie business in Hollywood and other private industries drew up blacklists to prevent suspected Communists from gainful employment. In Wheeling, West Virginia, the junior senator from Wisconsin delivered the speech that made him a national star. "I have here in my hand a list of 205, a list of names," said Senator Joseph McCarthy, "that were made known to the Secretary of State as being members of the Communist Party and who nevertheless are still working and shaping policy in the State Department." Or was it fifty-seven names? Senator McCarthy could never keep his story straight.

Arthur "Mac" Blair, who never became an American citizen, was hounded by the authorities until he fled with his wife, Maggie, into Mexico, where he lived out the rest of his life.

The real trouble started for Bailey when the Communist regime in North Korea invaded South Korea on June 25, 1950. Two days later, President Truman announced that he was dispatching US troops to the Korean peninsula, where the fighting lasted for three cruel years until an armistice established Korea as a divided nation. Only one member of the House of Representatives voiced opposition to Truman's failure to seek congressional approval for the Korean War. "The power to declare and make war is vested in the people through the Congress of the United States," said Representative Vito Marcantonio, who was four years away from dying of a heart attack on a sidewalk in lower Manhattan at the age of fifty-one. "That power has been usurped. . . . We here in

Congress have finally accepted this usurpation of our rights as representatives of the American people. We abdicated. I have heard no protest. Not a single word." The wave of anti-Communist actions that followed the commencement of hostilities included the Magnuson Act, which was signed into law by Truman on August 9, 1950. The law required the Coast Guard to deny security validation—and thus employment—to marine workers "whose character and habits of life were such as to authorize the belief that his presence on vessels and waterfront facilities would be inimical to the security of the United States."

The right-wing leadership of the Marine Firemen's Union was only too eager to hand over the names of its Communists to the Coast Guard. Bailey was officially declared a national security threat. He was screened off the waterfront, which prevented him from obtaining work on or near merchant vessels. The livelihood he had known since he was fourteen years old had been taken from him.

"It is not a pleasant feeling to wake up one morning and discover you have been cut off from all your shipmates, or your shipmates have been cut off from you," he wrote. "The union hall had been declared off limits for all the 'screened out' characters. The union newspaper would not print my letters of protest, and the membership would be putting their livelihoods in jeopardy just by being seen with me."

Bailey and his fellow outcasts fought back by restarting the *Black Gang News*, which offered a left-wing perspective on union affairs for rank-and-file marine firemen. He picketed and leafleted and petitioned to end the war in Korea. In defiance of the blacklist, he sought work in the maritime industry. He was hired as a machinist repairing ships on the San Francisco waterfront, but was let go after his black mark was discovered. "No clearance, no work," he was told. He arranged another machinist job, this time working across the bay in an Oakland shipyard. After a week, he was asked not to return. He was lucky to find a position at Pacific Gas and Electric, a public utility, which often hired engine-room

Bailey and his attorney, Doris Brin Walker,
before HUAC on December 5, 1953. (Michael Bailey)

seamen who were between ships. He lasted three or four months
before he ran into an old colleague, who passed word of Bailey's
presence to the Marine Firemen's Union and thence to J. Edgar
Hoover's men. He was summoned to a supervisor's office. "Well,
I'm glad the FBI told us that we have a number-one Communist
here and we found out in time before you blew up the plant," he
was told. A security guard escorted Bailey to his locker, where he
retrieved a few items, and then ejected him from the building. "I
left the plant just humiliated."

In time, he received "the subpoena."

The House Un-American Activities Committee, then chaired
by Congressman Harold Velde of Illinois, brought its noxious
road show to San Francisco for a week of hearings in late 1953.
Bailey, now thirty-eight, was the first witness to appear in the afternoon session on December 5. He was accompanied by his party-
assigned attorney, Doris Brin Walker, who he described as "able

and dedicated." Bailey took his chair in the oak-paneled Board of Supervisors hearing room in San Francisco City Hall, clutching his carefully composed statement denouncing the committee's work as a hysterical and defamatory attack on progressive unionism. His testimony was broadcast live over the radio airwaves.

"What is your name, please, sir?" asked Frank Tavenner, the committee's counsel.

"William J. Bailey," he said. He gave his birthdate as "January 23, 1910," failing to note that he was born Michael Bailey on June 13, 1915. Bailey briefly outlined his limited experience with formal education.

"What is your present occupation?" Tavenner asked.

"I don't think that concerns this committee," Bailey responded.

Tavenner asked Chairman Velde to direct the witness to answer.

"Yes, it does concern the committee as I have explained previously, Mr. Witness, and you are directed to answer the question," said Velde.

"I am willing to answer the question, Mr. Velde, if you would tell me how it would pertain to the committee," said Bailey.

Velde described how the committee was "authorized and directed by a resolution of the House of Representatives to investigative subversive activities and propaganda and to recommend remedial legislation which would capably handle the problem of subversion." He said the committee was interested in "how far Communists and other subversive activities have penetrated into all types of employment." The issue of "your employment" is thus "a very pertinent matter to this committee."

"Now," Velde continued, "will you answer the question, under direction, where are you presented employed?"

"I am unemployed," Bailey said.

"After all the hemming and hawing on the subject, springing this answer left the audience laughing and the committee stunned," Bailey later recalled.

"How were you employed in 1946?" Tavenner shot back.

After a brief conference with his lawyer, Bailey declined to answer, invoking his Fifth Amendment right against self-incrimination.

In the uproar that followed, Bailey said he could "save the committee a lot of time" if he would be allowed to read his prepared statement.

"Does this statement show where you were employed in 1946, Mr. Witness?" Velde said.

"I don't know if it does or not," Bailey said. "If you allow me to read it."

"Did you write it or did somebody else write it for you?" said Congressman Gordon Scherer of Ohio.

At this point, Bailey raised his voice, which took on a distinctively New York/New Jersey timbre.

"I am quite capable of writing my own statements, Mr. Congressman," he snapped. "Why do you make that type of an inference? Do I look like an idiot or a dummy here that I have to have ghostwriters make statements for me?"

Chairman Velde asked to see the statement, which he read. "There is nothing in here relative to your employment in 1946," he said.

Tavenner then came to the point.

"Were you at any time in 1946 acting as the West Coast coordinator of the seamen's branches or waterfront branches of the Communist Party?" he asked.

"Where would you get that information?" asked Bailey.

"Is it wrong?" said Tavenner.

"Well, where would you get that information?"

"Is it wrong?"

"Well, Mr. Chairman," said Bailey.

"Will you answer the question?" said Tavenner.

"I decline to answer that question or any other questions dealing with organizations, names, or anything else," said Bailey.

Velde said Bailey was "purely in contempt of this committee" and demanded that he answer the question.

Bailey refused.

"Are you a member of the Communist Party?" Velde asked suddenly.

Bailey declined to answer, noting that the Fifth Amendment was still the law of the land.

"Are you a member of the Communist Party?" Velde asked again.

"Well, frankly, Mr. Chairman, I don't think that is any of your business," said Bailey.

"Well, regardless of whether it is our business or not," said Velde.

"I would give you the same answer I have given the FBI, riot squads, police department, and everybody else, that it is *just none of your business!*"

Velde paused.

"Let the record show," he said slowly, "that the witness has raised his voice in contempt of the committee of Congress."

The *San Francisco Chronicle* characterized Bailey's "none-of-your-business" line as a "shout."

The committee gave up on Bailey. He was dismissed from the stand.

The next witness, James Kendall, was the proverbial "stool pigeon," the committee informant, who gleefully named names. He testified about attending a meeting in 1946 during which "it was announced that Bill Bailey was the West Coast coordinator or that he had been given the job of the West Coast coordinator for the waterfront sections of the Communist Party." Kendall emphasized that he was referring "to the witness that was here a few minutes ago when he had a lapse of memory about 1946."

========

Bailey's circumstances were such that he felt he had to flee San Francisco. He ran into an old friend who held a senior position with the International Longshore and Warehouse Union (ILWU), which, under the leadership of the dauntless Harry Bridges, had been steadfast in its defiance of McCarthyism. The friend suggested that Bailey travel up to the sleepy lumber port of Eureka, where he might find work loading and unloading ships with the

ILWU Local 14. Armed with an introduction letter, Bailey slipped out of the Bay area, dropping a few hints to friends that he was thinking of traveling to New York to visit a sick relative. During his exile in northern California, Bailey found a new life as a long-shoreman. He eventually assumed a leadership role in the local and spearheaded a campaign to institute needed reforms. He urged the adoption of a nondiscrimination policy that led to the local's first African American member. Such was the nature of the radicalism of this enemy of the American republic.

After years of frustrations with half-witted directives, inexplicable policy shifts, and arbitrary internal punishments, Bailey finally quit the Communist Party. "I would not fold while the Party was under attack," he wrote. But by 1956, with the Red Scare subsiding, he felt he wouldn't be lending aid and comfort to the witch-hunters. He was appalled by the Soviet Union's violent suppression of the Hungarian Uprising, seeing himself not in the armored units of the superpower but in the students marching in the streets. He understood now that Joseph Stalin was a murderous thug who had killed millions of his own people. "He was nothing but a paranoid, sick SOB in many cases," Bailey said. "And these people who were purged came from the background of fighting for the great ideals of socialism. They went through all the aches and pains and the terror to create this society only to be taken out later as dogs and shot?" A few days after he informed the party leadership of his decision, he heard a knock at the door. His girlfriend answered to find two special agents of the FBI, who had come to offer congratulations and propose a meeting. Bailey slammed the door in their faces.

Bailey returned to San Francisco, where he settled into life as a longshoreman with Local 10 of the ILWU. After a laborious day of handling dusty and hazardous cargo on the waterfront, he would ascend to the picturesque heights of Telegraph Hill, where he rented a quaint one-room cottage that was likely once a garage for a Model T. "As an ex-seamen used to living in cramped quarters aboard ship, this small amount of space did not change my life-style much," he said. He would spend his free time pounding away on his typewriter, writing both short and long fiction. A novel he composed about a ship's crew delivering munitions to the Russian Civil War (1917–1922) was published in the Soviet Union. By the end of the 1960s, his work on behalf of San Francisco's dockworkers led to his election as vice president of Local 10.

"Guys loved to work with him," said Brian McWilliams, a colleague of Bailey's who would go on to become international president of the ILWU. "He was full of stories and wisdom and experience."

In retirement, Bailey remained committed to the causes that animated his life. He described himself as a believer in the principles of socialism who never lost his love for street agitation. "I feel envious when I see people out there on the picket lines fighting and demonstrating," he said. "My God, I wish I'd get the hell out there and join up with them." In 1978, he and a few of his old lefty friends began a Thursday-morning ritual of walking along San Francisco Bay to Fort Point at the base of the southern anchorage of the Golden Gate Bridge, where they touched the chain-link fence bordering the park, a gesture of hope that they would return one more time. The tradition lives on today, decades later, among the descendants, friends, and admirers of the original "Fort Point Gang." Back in the early days, the walk would conclude at Eppler's Bakery on Chestnut Street. Nowadays, the group convenes for coffee at the Seal Rock Inn on Point Lobos Avenue. The presiding matriarch is Corine Thornton, who, now in her midnineties, remembers reading about the *Bremen* incident in the *Kansas City Star* when she was a young teenager.

In the early 1980s, Bailey began thinking about the importance of preserving the memory of his life and times. With a group of creaky seagoing rebels, he founded the Marine Workers Historical Association, which was established to record the history of the unions "for the young people coming into the industry who don't know from nothing, so they don't get the idea that all that stuff was handed to them on a silver platter or that it came from heaven," he said. The back issues of the association's newsletter, the *Hawsepipe*, contain Bailey's writings on everything from hopping freight trains during the Depression to the "creeping Reagan

Bailey in 1988. "I'm fighting for the conditions of the youngsters that are yet to come into this country." (*San Francisco Examiner*)

Bailey with his Spanish Civil War rifle.

attitude affecting many young people today, 'I'm okay, Jack, the hell with you, what's in it for me?'" Bailey started putting together his autobiography with the assistance of Lynn Damme, a young theater student who had arrived in town from Minneapolis. Damme served as Bailey's editor, visiting him as often as three or four times a week to pick up the latest typewritten installment. She recalled how he was "desperate" to complete the work. "He felt it was the best thing he could leave behind," Damme said. "He believed in the power of history."

Bailey became something of a celebrity after he began appearing as a talking head in historical documentaries—including *Seeing Red* (1983) about the Communist Party in the United States; *The Spanish Civil War* (1983), a multipart series for British television; and *The Good Fight: The Abraham Lincoln Brigade in the Spanish Civil War* (1984). Journalists, authors, scholars, photographers, and filmmakers made the trek up to his Telegraph Hill sanctuary, which was now filled with memorabilia from a lifetime of activism and presided over by his beloved Siamese cats,

Mr. and Mrs. Fagin. "Craggy-faced, bespectacled, six feet three, he's right out of a Rockwell Kent woodcut, crossed with American gothic," wrote Studs Terkel. He is "a big man with reddish hair, a rumpled, well-lived-in face and a colorful manner of speaking," according to Blake Green in the *Chronicle*. "Bill Bailey is without question one of the great men of San Francisco and one of the grander men of our time," wrote legendary gonzo journalist Warren Hinckle. He gave radical walking tours of the San Francisco waterfront and traveled the country delivering talks, spreading his message that "to witness an injustice and do nothing—that is the biggest crime."

"You have that good feeling inside of you that, dammit, no matter how old you are, you can do something, you can change a government, you can change a system," he said of his activism. "When I fight for conditions today, I say I am fighting not just for myself but I'm fighting for the conditions of the youngsters that are yet to come into this country or into this world, so they can sit back and say some poor son of a bitch got his head batted in 30, 40, 50 years ago so that I can have these halfway decent conditions today. And that tradition goes on and on because that is our heritage. Without heritage, without some traits, we ain't nothing. We're just a mass of little wiggly worms."

Bailey's telegenic documentary appearances brought interest from Hollywood. He starred opposite Bruce Dern in Rob Nilsson's *On the Edge* (1986), playing a grouchy revolutionist who lived in a junkyard and tried to teach his parrot to say "Workers of the World Unite!" Bailey was a "natural actor" whose performance was "an unexpected treat," wrote the *New York Times*. "Bill was always humble, completely co-operative, and great because he didn't act," said Nilsson. "He couldn't avoid being himself, which fulfills Thelonious Monk's idea: 'A genius is one most like himself.'" He appeared in a walk-on part as an MGM security guard in Irwin Winkler's drama about the Hollywood blacklist, *Guilty by Suspicion* (1991). "They took me into this office and there's De Niro laying out on a couch," Bailey told the *Oakland Tribune* of the experience of advising the film's star about McCarthyism. "Irwin Winkler is there and some other people. They introduce me and De Niro comes over and wants to talk. 'Look, did you feel wiped out?' he asked me. He wanted to know about all the stuff that happened to us."

But Bailey regarded the movie business as a "corrupted sort of existence," a superficial world where everyone was nice to you whether you deserved it or not. He spoke much more fondly about the recognition bestowed on him by members of the Marine Firemen's Union, who voted to end the ban on Communists and reinstate Bailey's membership with honor. Our protagonist had been accepted by society at last. His trials and disappointments were over. He had lived long enough, as he said in the waterfront vernacular, to piss on his enemies' graves.

In 1993, he published his autobiography, *The Kid from Hoboken*, with printing costs covered by donations from a few hundred friends and supporters, including Representative Nancy Pelosi ($250), the Irish Republican Army gunrunner George Harrison ($125), and the California Wholesale Meat Company ($250). Bailey dedicated the book to his beloved son, Michael. "You are the best thing in my life," he wrote. "I tried to leave you a better world." By now, Bailey was ill, suffering from what he described as "a long complication of lung problems." Lynn Damme recalls how he would complain about phone calls from Robert De Niro, who wanted him to come to New York to talk about a film idea. "I'm too sick," Bailey would say. "I can't make the trip." He died on February 27, 1995. Three weeks later, Congresswoman Pelosi rose in the House of Representatives and read a statement into the record, praising Bailey's "lifelong commitment to social and economic justice, continuing his activities until his dying day." It had been forty-one years since the same House of Representatives had smeared him as "un-American."

"I was reading the paper and . . . turned for some reason to the obituaries and there was William Bailey," wrote Don Bajema, an actor who met Bailey on the set of Rob Nilsson's film *Heat and Sunlight*. "A long piece revealing the modesty of the man. It was there in three long columns. He had done more, said more, seen more, and put more at stake than those of us who met him later in life could have dreamed."

Bill Bailey was unusually gifted in the arts of oral storytelling, an ability he'd honed in mess rooms and hiring halls over the course of decades. He could set a scene, establish a plot line, create vivid characters, build to a climax, and offer a moral lesson. He wasn't a blarney-spouting fabulist. The historical record confirms that he spoke with startling consistency and accuracy. He had an exceptional memory. Bailey told tales that revealed his view of life—his anger over the struggles of his put-upon mother, his wonder at the world beyond his poor upbringing, his delight in joining arms with likeminded compatriots to fight for a better world, and his rage at the ignorant and foolish who defended the systems of injustice. He had a favorite story that he told many times over the years. It was a parable about the ragged effort in the early days of the Nazi regime to convince the world that Adolf Hitler had to be confronted.

Maria Brooks, a filmmaker who became close to Bailey at the end of his life, recalls traveling with him to a nursing home populated with aging left-wingers in the Bay area.

"He was tired and frail by this time," she recalled. "The old-timers knew him. They were excited to see him. Bill asked what story they'd like to hear. Hands were raised. It was the *Bremen*. They wanted to hear that story again."

ACKNOWLEDGMENTS

Michael Bailey, Bill Bailey's son, was a patient guide to his father's life. I will always be grateful for his generosity and openheartedness. Thanks also to Corine Thornton; Lynn Damme; Maria Brooks; Brian McWilliams; Harvey Schwartz; Robin Walker of the International Longshore and Warehouse Union; John Rocco of SUNY Maritime College; Daniel Czitrom; Jeff Cuyubamba; Rob Nilsson; Don Bajema; Janon Fisher; Nina Sheldon; Hannah Palin of the University of Washington Libraries; New Jersey State Archives; National Archives and Records Administration of College Park, Maryland; Columbia University Archives; the Library of Congress; Bancroft Library of the University of California, Berkeley; New York Public Library; and Tamiment Library and Robert F. Wagner Labor Archives at New York University. My agent, Mary Evans, was, as always, a forceful and determined advocate. Ben Adams, my editor at PublicAffairs, was a believer in Bill Bailey's story from the beginning. Iris Bass and Sandra Beris at PublicAffairs are consummate pros. The book would've been scarcely worth the effort without the love and support of Laura and El.

NOTES

Prologue

1   *"And then," as Virgil:* Robert Fitzgerald, "Passages from Virgil's First Georgic," in *Spring Shade: Poems 1931–1970* (New York: New Directions, 1971), 170.

1   *A Riverside Drive:* "Sleepless Doctor Leaps to Death," *New York Herald Tribune,* July 13, 1935.

2   *"we're down here eating* boint liva*":* Bill Bailey interview, *Seeing Red: Stories of American Communists,* dir. Julia Reichert and James Klein, Heartland Productions, 1983.

3   *boasting the highest percentage:* "1934 Traffic Mark Set by Bremen and Europa," *New York Times,* February 3, 1935.

3   *"vast seagoing cathedral":* John Malcolm Brinnen and Kenneth Gaulin, *Grand Luxe: The Transatlantic Style* (New York: Henry Holt and Co., 1988), 140.

3   *"The Great Pyramid of":* "Steam Song," *New Yorker,* July 19, 1930.

3   *a cherished tradition:* "Night Sailings Are New Events," *New York Times,* April 1, 1928.

4   *It would later be estimated:* "Text of Police Department's Report on the Bremen Riot," *New York Times,* August 2, 1935; "Police Reports in Connection with the Bremen Incident," *Public Papers of Governor Herbert H. Lehman* (Albany: J. B. Lyon Co., 1935), 708–715.

5   *"It looked like it was"*: Bill Bailey interview, "The Day We Tore the Nazi Flag off the Bremen," Bancroft Library, call no. 85/171, University of California, Berkeley.

6   *"never-ending uphill battle"*: Bill Bailey, *The Kid from Hoboken: An Autobiography* (San Francisco: Circus Lithographic Prepress, 1993), 423.

7   *"inspired servant of the"*: Jacques Maritain, *Man and the State* (Chicago: University of Chicago Press, 1966), 141.

7   *"I asked Bill once"*: Author interview with Maria Brooks.

Chapter One

9   *The first thing to know:* Michael Bailey, Bill Bailey's son, confirmed that his father's birth name was Michael and celebrated his birthday in June. According to the birth certificate on file with the State of New Jersey, a male child was born to William Bailey and Elizabeth Nolan on June 13, 1915.

9   *In his autobiography:* Bill Bailey, *The Kid from Hoboken: An Autobiography* (San Francisco: Circus Lithographic Prepress, 1993), 20.

10   *"I only remember one"*: Bill Bailey interview transcript for *The Good Fight* documentary, 1981, box 1, folders 39 and 40, Abraham Lincoln Brigade Archives (ALBA), Tamiment Library, New York University.

12   *"She told me that as far"*: Bill Bailey interview with John Gerassi, August 8, 1980, John Gerassi Oral History Collection, ALBA Audio 18, Tamiment Library, New York University.

13   *"It was my mother's way"*: Bailey, *Kid from Hoboken*, 37.

13   *And if, when all a vigil:* Thomas Osborne Davis, *The Poems of Thomas Davis* (Dublin: James Duffy, 1857), 10.

14   *"Who the bloody hell"*: Bailey, *Kid from Hoboken*, 30.

15   *"The Lord ran around"*: Bailey interview, *Good Fight*.

18   *"Ships had always wormed"*: Bailey, *Kid from Hoboken*, 71.

19   *"So I just happened to go aboard"*: Bill Bailey interview with Howard Kimeldorf, September 15, 1981, container 8/55, John Ahlquist and Margaret Levi research materials, Special Collections University of Washington Libraries.

Chapter Two

21   *The ships built in that:* Michael Anton, "The Age of Ships," *City Journal*, Autumn 2001.

21 *Kaiser Wilhelm II's naval fleet:* Milan Vego, *Operational Warfare at Sea: Theory and Practice* (Abingdon, Oxfordshire, UK: Routledge, 2009), 6.

22 *the German Navy was permitted:* Bruce Watson, *Atlantic Convoys and Nazi Raiders: The Deadly Voyage of HMS Jervis Bay* (Westport, CT: Praeger, 2006), 20.

22 *The two venerable German:* Otto J. Seiler, *Bridge Across the Atlantic: The Story of Hapag-Lloyd's North American Liner Services* (Herford, Germany: Verlag Mittler, 1991), 36–55.

23 *"Resuming service, their small":* John Malcolm Brinnin, *The Sway of the Grand Saloon* (New York: Delacorte, 1971), 451.

23 *"They claim that in addition":* "Ship Men Doubt Wisdom of Fast German Liners," *New York Herald Tribune,* December 27, 1926.

23 *In recognition of its position:* "The Liner Bremen Is Christened by Hindenburg," *New York Herald Tribune,* August 17, 1928; "Bremen Is Launched While 50,000 Sing," *New York Times,* August 17, 1928.

24 *"Like a thunderclap":* Eduard Zimmerman, *Flag-Ship Bremen: The Story of a Ship's Dynasty* (Bremen, Germany: Norddeutscher Lloyd, 1959), 44.

24 *"bacillus and fermenting":* Richard Evans, *Lying About Hitler* (New York: Basic Books, 2001), 78.

25 *"to secure for the German people":* Lucy Dawidowicz, *The War Against the Jews: 1933–1945* (New York: Bantam, 1975), 91.

25 *"almost mathematical":* Volker Ullrich, *Hitler: Ascent 1889–1939,* trans. Jefferson Chase (New York: Knopf, 2016), 216.

26 *"Every day 7,500 men":* "Bremen Will Bid for Atlantic's 'Blue Ribbon,'" *New York Herald Tribune,* May 12, 1929.

26 *"It was breathtaking":* Frank O. Braynard, *The Bremen and the Europa* (New York, Fort Schuyler Press, 2005), 15.

27 *The ship weighed:* "The Bremen: Main Particulars of the S.S. Bremen," *Marine Engineering and Shipping Age,* July 1, 1930; "German Super Liner Enters Service," *Marine Engineering and Shipping Age,* August 1, 1929.

27 *Its most prominent exterior:* "New German Liners Resemble Cruisers," *New York Times,* March 11, 1929.

27 *"cut and audacity of a destroyer":* Brinnin, *Sway of the Grand Saloon,* 452.

27 *The interior was lauded:* John Malcolm Brinnin, *Sway of the Grand Saloon,* 454.

27 *The ship featured:* "Bremen Will Bid for Atlantic's 'Blue Ribbon," *New York Herald Tribune,* May 12, 1929; "Bremen Sails on Her First Trip Tuesday," *New York Herald Tribune,* July 14, 1929. The details on the

interior features of the ship are included in the many articles that were published at the time of the ship's launch.

27   *A forbidding oil painting:* "Der Champion," *New Yorker*, September 14, 1929.

28   *A crew of 950 kept:* "New Queen of Sea Breaks All Records," *American Monthly*, August 1, 1929.

29   *A message to the* Evening Post*":* "Bremen Plane in Port, Liner Few Hours Off," *New York Evening Post,* July 22, 1929.

30   *At 1:05 p.m., 20 miles:* "Bremen in, Cuts 9 Hours off Atlantic Speed Mark; Harbor Roars Welcome," *New York Herald Tribune,* July 23, 1929. See several other stories in the same edition of the paper.

30   *"The reception given to the* Bremen*":* "Bremen in, Smashes Record for Atlantic by 9 Hours," *New York Times,* July 23, 1929. See several other stories in the same edition of the paper.

32   *The* Post*'s man on the:* "Bremen Speeds in Quest of New Record Eastward," *New York Evening Post,* July 27, 1929.

33   *"carried with it the":* E. B. White, *Here Is New York* (New York: Little Bookroom, 2011), 23.

Chapter Three

35   *"a slow ship, a real":* Bill Bailey, *The Kid from Hoboken: An Autobiography* (San Francisco: Circus Lithographic Prepress, 1993), 74.

35   *"How can the ship sail":* Bill Bailey interview, with Howard Kimeldorf, September 15, 1981, container 8/55, John Ahlquist and Margaret Levi research materials, Special Collections University of Washington Libraries.

37   *"Going to sea in those days":* Bailey interview, Kimeldorf.

37   *"thieves, smugglers and users of":* Bruce Nelson, *Workers on the Waterfront: Seamen, Longshoremen, and Unionism in the 1930s* (Urbana: University of Illinois Press, 1988), 20.

37   *Showboat Quinn, Boxcar Flaherty:* Gloria Emerson, "Haskell Wexler Zooms in on Nicaragua," *Mother Jones,* August–September 1985. *They were the gypsies":* Helen Lawrenson, *Stranger at the Party: A Memoir* (New York: Random House, 1975), 212.

41   *Steamship firemen were:* "Firemen on Steamships," *Scientific American,* October 30, 1852.

41   *"working like a dog, eating":* Bailey interview, Kimeldorf.

41   *"Put one of 'em down here":* Eugene O'Neill, *Early Plays* (New York: Penguin, 2001), 362.

41 *"You'd get off a ship"*: "Activist Bailey Takes on New Challenge as Actor in Films," *Oakland Tribune*, May 6, 1984.

42 *"already running all over"*: Bill Bailey interview transcript for *The Good Fight* documentary, 1981, box 1, folders 39 and 40, Abraham Lincoln Brigade Archives (ALBA), Tamiment Library, New York University.

42 *"I was beginning to see"*: Howard Kimeldorf, *Reds or Rackets?: The Making of Radical and Conservative Unions on the Waterfront* (Berkeley: University of California Press, 1988), 21.

Chapter Four

43 *Our flag is fluttering*: Hilmar Hoffmann, *The Triumph of Propaganda: Film and National Socialism, 1933–1945*, trans. John A. Broadwin and V. R. Berghahn (Oxford: Berghahn, 1996), 49.

44 *On a not-atypical journey*: "Bremen Carries Notables," *Brooklyn Daily Eagle*, May 13, 1931.

44 *By the summer of 1932*: "Liner Bremen, Record Holder, Starts 4th Year," *New York Herald Tribune*, July 20, 1932.

44 *In late 1932, when a*: "Marilyn Miller Marooned on Ship Without Luggage," *Washington Post*, December 2, 1932.

45 *"like a dream, a fairy-tale"*: Thomas Childers, *The Third Reich: A History of Nazi Germany* (New York: Simon and Schuster, 2017), 225.

46 *Passenger liners were a priority*: Ernest Hamburger, "A Peculiar Pattern of the Fifth Column: The Organization of the German Seamen," *Social Research* 9 (1942), 495–509. The details on the political organization of the *Bremen*'s crew that appear throughout this chapter are gleaned from this source.

47 *For at least a portion*: Peter A. Huchthausen, *Shadow Voyage: The Extraordinary Wartime Escape of the Legendary S.S. Bremen* (New York: John Wiley and Sons, 2005), 17.

47 *The motif of four interlocking*: Steven Heller, *The Swastika: Symbol Beyond Redemption?* (New York: Allworth Press, 2000), 17–39.

48 *"The swastika here in"*: Timothy W. Ryback, *Hitler's Private Library: The Books That Shaped His Life* (London: Bodley Head, 2009), 130.

48 *cranks like Lanz von Liebenfels*: Brigitte Hamann, *Hitler's Vienna: A Dictator's Apprenticeship*, trans. Thomas Thornton (New York: Oxford University Press, 1999), 209.

48 *ideas of Guido von List*: Hamann, *Hitler's Vienna*, 206–207.

49 *"All those who busy themselves"*: Adolf Hitler, *Mein Kampf* (Stockholm: White Wolf Publishing, 2014), 210–212.

51   *The average Nazi Party:* Hoffmann, *Triumph of Propaganda,* 19.

52   *Hitler often boasted:* "Hitler Plans to Replace Flag of Reich with 'Nazi' Banner," *New York Times,* December 7, 1931.

52   *At two p.m. on March 12:* "Hindenburg Drops Flag of Republic," *New York Times,* March 13, 1933; "Hindenburg Dips Republic Flag, Unfurls Nazi and Empire Colors," *New York Herald Tribune,* March 13, 1933.

52   *On the* Bremen: "3 German Liners Here to Change Flags Today," *New York Times,* September 17, 1935.

Chapter Five

53   *To trade with Germany:* "Nazism Must Lead to War," *Economic Bulletin,* published monthly by the Non-Sectarian Anti-Nazi League to Champion Human Right, April 1935.

53   *In the propaganda-fueled:* Peter Longerich, *Holocaust: The Nazi Persecution and Murder of the Jews* (Oxford: Oxford University Press, 2010), 33–41.

53   *"Since Monday I have been":* "Refuses to Act on Boycott of Jewish Shops," *Baltimore Sun,* March 11, 1933.

54   *Jewish judges and lawyers:* Saul Friedländer, *Nazi Germany and the Jews,* vol. 1, *The Years of Persecution, 1933–1939* (New York: HarperCollins, 1997), 29.

54   *Although editorial pages:* Deborah E. Lipstadt, *Beyond Belief: The American Press and the Coming of the Holocaust, 1933–1945* (New York: Free Press, 1986), 13–18.

54   *"the chancellor authorized me":* Lipstadt, *Beyond Belief,* 18.

55   *By the third week of March:* Moshe Gottlieb, *American Anti-Nazi Resistance: An Historical Analysis, 1933–1941* (New York: Ktav, 1982), 45–47, 49–51.

55   *On March 23, seven hundred:* "10,000 Veterans in Protest Parade Against Nazi Terror," *Daily Worker,* March 24, 1933; "O'Brien Reviews 4,000 Hitler Foes," *New York Times,* March 24, 1933.

55   *The contingent of seamen:* "Seamen Picket German Consul as Crowds Cheer," *Daily Worker,* March 24, 1933.

56   *On March 25, Hermann Goering:* "Jewry Is Safe in Germany, Goering Says," *New York Herald Tribune,* March 26, 1933.

57   *"We unequivocally demand":* Gulie Ne'eman Arad, *America, Its Jews, and the Rise of Nazism* (Bloomington: Indiana University Press, 2000), 145–146.

57 *under Secretary of State Cordell Hull's:* "German Violence Against Jews Ends," *New York Herald Tribune,* March 27, 1933.

57 *On March 27, the American Jewish:* "Hitlerism Protest Meeting Draws 60,000 to Garden," *New York Daily News,* March 28, 1933.

58 *the Nazi government announced:* "Hitlerites Order Boycott Against Jews in Business, Professions and Schools," *New York Times,* March 29, 1933. The story appeared in the top right of page 1 with a three-line headline across two columns.

59 *A week later, the first:* Friedländer, *Nazi Germany and the Jews,* 26–36; Peter Longerich, *Holocaust,* 38–42.

60 *His most dedicated:* "Nazi Ambassador Arrives in N.Y. on Bremen This Morning; United Front Committee Calls Protest," *Daily Worker,* April 14, 1933.

61 *Consul General Kiep reached:* "Luther Arrives; Consul Bars Talk," *New York Evening Post,* April 14, 1933; "Bremen Gags Luther, Here as New Envoy," *New York Daily News,* April 15, 1933.

62 *Civic leader of fabulous wealth:* Untermyer resided with his champion collies on a 170-acre estate overlooking the Hudson River north of New York City, a baronial manor with castlelike main residence of gray granite, sixty greenhouses tended by a team of horticultural specialists, and a system of terraced gardens with faux-Grecian fountains, pools, statues, a temple, and a colonnaded amphitheater.

62 *During a speech at Symphony:* "Untermyer Urges German Boycott," *New York Times,* May 8, 1933.

62 *Untermyer was invited:* Gottlieb, *American Anti-Nazi Resistance,* 47–49, 119–121.

62 *Although many Jewish leaders:* The American Jewish Committee and the B'nai B'rith both regarded closed-door diplomatic appeal as the *only* proper way to respond to the Nazi crisis. Neither organization would join the boycott. The American Jewish Congress came around to support the boycott idea but refused to combine forces with Untermyer's effort. It instead allied with the Jewish Labor Committee to form the Joint Boycott Council. The Jewish Agency of Palestine defied the boycott by reaching the Transfer Agreement (*Ha'avara*) with the Nazi government, which allowed some German Jews to immigrate to Palestine as long as they took their assets in the form of German exports, thereby *expanding* German business interests in the Middle East. The Board of Deputies of British Jews in England and the Alliance Israélite Universelle in France both opposed the boycott.

62 *At around dawn on May:* "Protest Arrival of Nazi Agent," *Daily Worker,* May 24, 1933.

63 *At Quarantine, Weidemann:* "Demonstration at Pier Distrubs Goebbels' Aide, Arriving as Nazi Envoy to Chicago Fair," Jewish Telegraphic Agency, May 26, 1933.

64 *The NYPD then ordered:* "Anti-Nazi Protest Meets Weidemann Arrival in U.S.," *Daily Worker*, May 26, 1933; "Nazi Art Envoy Escapes Reds' Brooklyn Riot," *New York Herald Tribune*, May 26, 1933.

64 *They had been hearing:* "Antwerp Longshoremen Make Nazi Captains 64 Flag," *Daily Worker*, May 29, 1933.

65 *When the master of:* "Force Ships to Strike Nazi Flag," *Marine Workers Voice,* June 1933.

65 *In Seville, the captain:* "Swastika Irks Spaniards, So Nazis Fly Alfonso Flag," *New York Herald Tribune*, May 27, 1933.

65 *Careful note has been:* "From the State Department," *Jewish Examiner*, August 9, 1935.

66 *On August 7, after returning:* "Text of Untermyer's Address," *New York Times*, August 8, 1933.

66 *During an August 27 address:* "Address of Samuel Untermyer at the Annual Reunion of the Tri-State Lodges, Order of B'nai B'rith, at Youngstown, Ohio," August 27, 1933, box 142, Papers of the Non-Sectarian Anti-Nazi League (NSANL), Rare Book and Manuscript Library, Butler Library, Columbia University.

Chapter Six

67 *"A friendly guy":* Bill Bailey interview, with Howard Kimeldorf, September 15, 1981, container 8/55, John Ahlquist and Margaret Levi research materials, Special Collections University of Washington Libraries.

68 *"Everybody became so demoralized":* Bill Bailey interview, Janet Clinger, *Our Elders: Six Bay Area Life Stories* (Bloomington, IN: Xlibris, 2003), 121.

69 *"His profanity was rich and metaphorical":* Cecil D. Eby, *Comrades and Commissars: The Lincoln Battalion in the Spanish Civil War* (University Park: Pennsylvania State University Press, 2007), 207.

69 *published Bailey's first act:* "Stowaway Suicides," *Marine Workers Voice*, February 1934.

70 *He volunteered:* Bill Bailey, *The Kid from Hoboken: An Autobiography* (San Francisco: Circus Lithographic Prepress, 1993), 203–207.

71 *"And you get up there":* Bill Bailey interview, *Seeing Red: Stories of American Communists*, dir. Julia Reichert and James Klein, Heartland Productions, 1983.

72   *"When I got into the Communist":* Bill Bailey interview with Maria Brooks,
      LifeStory: Bill Bailey, a film by Maria Brooks, Al Allen collection on the
      International Longshore and Warehouse Union, 1939–2016, Uni-
      versity of Washington Libraries/Special Collections.

73   *In his autobiography, he writes about:* Bailey, *Kid from Hoboken,* 238–241.
      The identity of "Pele" remains elusive. Was she Pele de Lappe, a
      gifted artist who was active in Communist causes in the 1930s and
      became an acquaintance of Bailey's later in life? (Pele de Lappe's
      first name was pronounced "Pee-Lee.") The details of de Lappe's
      life differ from those of the "Pele" described in Bailey's autobiog-
      raphy. De Lappe was not from Chicago, was not an organizer in
      the stockyards, doesn't seem to have attended a Communist train-
      ing school, didn't travel to a Moscow youth conference in 1935,
      and didn't marry a German antifascist. Lynn Damme, who edited
      Bailey's autobiography, said that Bailey didn't share details about
      "Pele" with her during the editing process. When Damme asked
      Bailey whether he was sure he wanted to use the name "Pele" in
      the book—Damme was mindful that Pele de Lappe was a known
      figure in radical circles in San Francisco—Bailey "insisted" that
      the name "Pele" be published. During an interview with the au-
      thor, de Lappe's daughter, Nina Sheldon, said she was unaware of
      any romance between Bailey and her mother in the mid-1930s. To
      heighten the mystery, Pele de Lappe drew the cover art for Bailey's
      autobiography.

Chapter Seven

75   *We wish only to be:* "Interview with Hitler: German People Wish to Be
      Peaceful and Happy," *South China Morning Post,* March 19, 1935.

75   *Beginning in early 1934:* "North German Lloyd Uses Buses to Aid Pas-
      sengers: Act to Avert Confusion in Shift to New Terminal," *New York
      Herald Tribune,* January 21, 1934.

76   *achieving some successes:* Richard A. Hawkins, "Hitler's Bitterest Foe:
      Samuel Untermyer and the Boycott of Nazi Germany, 1933–1938,"
      American Jewish History 93 (March 2007): 11.

76   *The research department of:* "Letter to Hugo Strauss of Macy's," box 380,
      August 28, 1935, NSANL Papers, Columbia University.

76   *Among those singled:* "Jewish Banker Sails on Europa," Jewish
      Telegraphic Agency, April 28, 1935; "Arliss Sends Apology for Sail-
      ing to Europe on Nazi Liner Bremen," Jewish Telegraphic Agency,
      June 8, 1934; "'Andy' Goes Abroad on 'Verboten' Nazi Liner," Jewish
      Telegraphic Agency, July 19, 1934.

76 *boasted of an* increase: "Bremen Starts Its Sixth Year," *New York Herald Tribune*, July 19, 1934.

76 *Cole Porter felt no:* "Cole Porter's Gloomiest Minute Is When the Curtain Goes Up," Lucius Beebe, *New York Herald Tribune*, November 18, 1934.

77 *"But beyond these relatively":* "Alarmists Fail to Stir U.S. on Foreign Threat," *Christian Science Monitor*, May 19, 1934.

78 *"The Jews who already":* Richard Menkis and Harold Troper, *More Than Just Games: Canada and the 1936 Olympics* (Toronto: University of Toronto Press, 2015), 14.

78 *At Quarantine, forty reporters:* "Jeering Faced by Hanfstaengl, Arriving Today," *New York Herald Tribune*, June 16, 1934; "5,000 Anti-Nazis Protest on Hanfy," *New York Post*, June 16, 1934; "Hanfstaengl Here, Avoids Foes at Pier," *New York Times*, June 17, 1934; "Hanfstaengl Arrives and Flees Jeerers," *New York Herald Tribune*, June 17, 1934; "Pier Mob Jeers 'Double' As Hanfstaengl Is Taken off Liner Europa by Tug," *New York World-Telegram*, June 16, 1938; "2,000 Greet Hanfstaengl with 'Boos,'" *Daily Worker*, June 17, 1934.

79 *In his memoirs, Hanfstaengl:* Ernst Hanfstaengl, *Hitler: The Missing Years* (New York: Arcade, 1994), 243–244.

79 *"About those little things":* "Dr. Hanfstaengl Mixes Rhetoric and Ball Game," *New York Herald Tribune*, June 18, 1934.

80 *"To object to the presence":* Andrew Nagorski, *Hitlerland: American Eyewitnesses to the Nazi Rise to Power* (New York: Simon and Schuster, 2012), 210.

80 *The only trouble came:* "Girls in Anti-Nazi Move at Harvard," *Daily Boston Globe*, June 22, 1934.

80 *"I was sitting in the Astor":* Hanfstaengl, *Hitler: The Missing Years*, 245.

80 *he was back at Pier 86:* "Hanfstaengl off, Cheered by Crowd," *New York Times*, July 8, 1934.

81 *After learning of Hindenburg's:* "Roosevelt's Regret to Hitler," *Daily Boston Globe*, August 3, 1934.

81 *interview with (yes) Putzi:* "Hearst Is Quoted as Hailing Nazi Vote," *New York Times*, August 23, 1934.

82 *"a very large and influential":* David Nasaw, *The Chief: The Life of William Randolph Hearst* (Boston: Houghton Mifflin, 2000), 497.

82 *Mindful of the bad publicity:* Ben Procter, *William Randolph Hearst: The Later Years, 1911–1951* (New York: Oxford University Press, 2007), 187.

82 *"He was aboard the Nazi":* "Hearst, Grown Fond of Nazis, Is Silent on Jewish Question," *Jewish Telegraph Agency*, September 28, 1934.

82 *"Everything was much more":* "Hearst Returns, Distrustful of Ship Reporters," *New York Herald Tribune,* September 28, 1934.

84 *US government was silent:* "Conferees Meet at White House on Reich Arms," *New York Herald Tribune,* March 17, 1935.

84 *"a believer in democracy":* Robert Dallek, *Franklin D. Roosevelt and American Foreign Policy, 1932–1945* (New York: Oxford University Press, 1979), 95. Dallek included the quotes from both senators.

Chapter Eight

85 *"Nobody wanted to holler":* Bill Bailey interview, with Howard Kimeldorf, September 15, 1981, container 8/55, John Ahlquist and Margaret Levi research materials, Special Collections University of Washington Libraries.

85 *"I could feel important things":* Bill Bailey, *The Kid from Hoboken: An Autobiography* (San Francisco: Circus Lithographic Prepress, 1993), 254.

86 *"From the time I awoke":* Bailey, *Kid from Hoboken,* 242.

87 *"When the hell are you coming":* Bailey, *Kid from Hoboken,* 257.

87 *Nazi storm troopers in the German provinces:* Peter Longerich, *Holocaust: The Nazi Persecution and Murder of the Jews* (Oxford: Oxford University Press, 2010), 54–57.

88 *"the cleansing of our foul":* Randall L. Bytwerk, *Julius Streicher: Nazi Editor of the Notorious Anti-Semitic Newspaper Der Stürmer* (New York: Cooper Square Press, 2001), 35.

88 *"single cohabitation of a Jew":* Richard Lawrence Miller, *Nazi Justiz: Law of the Holocaust* (Westport, CT.: Praeger, 1995), 27.

88 *"racial disgrace of a character":* William Dodd to Cordell Hull, July 17, 1935, US Department of State, *Foreign Relations of the United States,* vol. 2, 1935, 401.

89 *During the spring and summer:* "Nazis Open New Catholic War," *New York World-Telegram,* July 18, 1935; "New Law Forbids Publication of Religious Organs," *New York Post,* April 25, 1935; "Nazis Arrest Many in Catholic Orders," *New York Times,* April 28, 1935; "New Nazi Drive Hits Catholics," *New York Post,* May 8, 1935; "Vatican Protests Nazi 'Brutality,'" *New York Post,* May 23, 1935.

89 *"Many of the nuns arrested":* "Nazis Arrest Many in Catholic Orders," *New York Times,* April 28, 1935.

89 *Sister Neophytia, the mother superior:* "Nazis Sentence Two More Nuns for Smuggling," *New York Herald Tribune,* May 23, 1935.

89 *another trial, Sister Wernera:* "Nazis Sent Nun to Prison," *Chicago Tribune,* May 18, 1935.

89   *While the regime was:* Lawrence Simpson, *The Blessings of Fascism: My 18 Months in Nazi Hells* (New York: National Lawrence Simpson Tour Arrangements Committee, 1937), 1–31.

91   *"As for Coney Island on":* Arthur Miller, "Before Air Conditioning," *New Yorker,* June 22, 1998.

91   *On Thursday, July 11:* "Mercury at 90; 5 Die in Hottest Day of Summer," *New York Herald Tribune,* July 12, 1935; "City Is Cooled by Rain After 14 Die in 91.4 Record Heat," *New York Herald Tribune,* July 13, 1935; "2,000,000 Flee City for Beaches as Mercury Again Soars to 89," *New York Times,* July 15, 1935.

92   *He would later be described:* Reginald Gibbons and Terrence Des Pres, eds., *Thomas McGrath: Life and the Poem* (Urbana and Chicago: University of Illinois Press 1992), 181.

92   *"I felt terrible":* Bailey, *Kid from Hoboken,* 258.

92   *Margaret Weaver took pity:* Margaret Blair, Audio Interview with Vera Hickman, May 7, 1984, Scholarship @ the Beach, the California State University Long Beach Digital Depository. All subsequent Margaret "Maggie" Weaver quotations come from this interview.

93   *On July 15, 1935:* Moshe Gottlieb, "The Berlin Riots and Their Repercussions in America," *American Historical Jewish Quarterly* 59 (March 1970), 302–328.

93   *"All along the Kurfürstendamm":* "Editor Describes Rioting in Berlin: Varian Fry of the Living Age Tells of Seeing Women and Men Beaten and Kicked," *New York Times,* July 17, 1935.

93   *The police prevented:* "Reaction to Riots Alarms Germans; Baiting Continues," *New York Times,* July 17, 1935; "Berlin Jews Hide From Terror," *New York Post,* July 16, 1935; "New Terrorism Feared by Jews After Nazi Riot," *New York World-Telegram,* July 16, 1935.

94   *A Polish Jew named:* "Beaten Berlin Jew Dies," *New York Times,* August 2, 1935.

94   *"inspiration of these disgraceful":* "An 'Aryan' Diversion," *New York Herald Tribune,* July 17, 1935.

95   *"It is primarily necessary":* Miller, *Nazi Justiz,* 41.

95   *On July 15, the first day:* "Pope's Note to Nazis Flays Pact Violation," *New York Daily News,* July 17, 1935.

95   *Hermann Goering was so incensed:* "Reich Strikes at Catholics; Rules Attacks on Priests Are Assault on Nazi State," *New York Times,* July 19, 1935.

96   *"clearly within their rights":* "US Aids Sailor Jailed by Nazis: But State Department Avoids Row over Seizure of Citizen from S.S. Manhattan," *New York Post,* July 20, 1935.

96 *"There was nothing in my soul":* Bill Bailey interview, *Seeing Red: Stories of American Communists,* dir. Julia Reichert and James Klein, Heartland Productions, 1983.

96 *"Hitler was telling the Catholics":* Bill Bailey interview transcript for *The Good Fight* documentary, 1981, box 1, folders 39 and 40, Abraham Lincoln Brigade Archives (ALBA), Tamiment Library, New York University.

96 *"an affront and an insult":* Bill Bailey interview, "The Day We Tore the Nazi Flag off the Bremen," Bancroft Library, call no. 85/171, University of California, Berkeley.

96 *"We decided between all":* Bailey interview, Kimeldorf.

96 *"So we passed the word":* Bill Bailey interview with John Gerassi, August 8, 1980, John Gerassi Oral History Collection, ALBA Audio 18, Tamiment Library, New York University.

Chapter Nine

97 *Intensification of campaign:* William Dodd to Cordell Hull, July 17, 1935, RG 59, box 6787, National Archives and Records Administration (NARA), College Park, Maryland.

97 *The hammer fell on:* "Nazi Intensify Drive on Jews and Catholics: War Veterans Also Harassed Anew in Push for Absolute Power," *Brooklyn Daily Eagle,* July 20, 1935. The story also describes actions taken against "cabaret, vaudeville and circus" artists.

98 *In Magdeburg, a man:* "Prosecutors Advised on Catholic Action," *New York World-Telegram,* July 20, 1935.

98 *On Sunday, July 21, after:* "Priests Who Assail Nazi 'Purge' Today Will Be Arrested," *New York Times,* July 21, 1935.

98 *On the same morning:* "Catholics of New York!" flier, July 21, 1935, RG 59, box 6787, NARA.

99 *"Every ship sailing is":* "Answer the Nazi Provocations at Pier 86 in New York Friday," *Daily Worker,* July 24, 1935.

100 *"And it came down":* Bill Bailey interview transcript for *The Good Fight* documentary, 1981, box 1, folders 39 and 40, Abraham Lincoln Brigade Archives (ALBA), Tamiment Library, New York University.

100 *"What was the crew supposed":* Bill Bailey interview, Janet Clinger, *Our Elders: Six Bay Area Life Stories* (Bloomington, IN: Xlibris, 2003), 133.

100 *"Sometimes, I don't know":* Bill Bailey interview with John Gerassi, August 8, 1980, John Gerassi Oral History Collection, ALBA Audio 18, Tamiment Library, New York University.

100   *"Today's Nazi press"*: "Catholic Priests Silent on Nazi-Church Dispute, Except in South Germany," *New York Times*, July 22, 1935.

101   *Mayor Fiorello LaGuardia released*: "Mayor Puts Curb on Germans Here," *New York Times*, July 24, 1935.

102   *the blunt-speaking Samuel Untermyer*: "Hitler Doomed, Says Untermyer," *New York Post*, July 23, 1935.

102   *The State Department was receiving*: Numerous enclosures, RG 59, box 6787, NARA.

103   *On July 24, Senator*: "Senator King to Ask Nazi Probe," *New York World-Telegram*, July 24, 1935.

103   *According to a memo*: William Philips memo, August 3, 1935, RG 59, box 6787, NARA.

103   *On the morning of the twenty-fifth*: "Dickstein Calls Hitler Madman," *New York World-Telegram*, July 25 1935; "Dickstein in Clash in House on Reich," *New York Times*, July 26, 1935.

104   *The* Bremen *"came in"*: "Ship News on the Gangplank," *New York American*, July 26, 1935.

105   *For the two gentlemen from*: "Reich Divided on Way to Treat Jews," *New York Herald Tribune*, July 26, 1935; "Editor Holds Riots Inspired by Nazis," *New York Times*, July 26, 1935.

105   *"I only half believed"*: Varian Fry, "The Massacre of the Jews," *New Republic*, December 21, 1942.

105   *During these hours*: Margaret Blair interview, the California State University Long Beach Digital Depository.

106   *"If we get arrested"*: Bailey interview, Gerassi.

106   *In the early afternoon*: "Mercury Drop Points to End of Heat Wave," *New York Post*, July 25, 1935.

Chapter Ten

107   *Hear it, boys, hear it*: Clifford Odets, *Waiting for Lefty and Other Plays* (New York: Grove Press, 1994), 31.

107   *During the overnight*: "Humidity Goes into a Tailspin," *New York Post*, July 26, 1935; "Rain Ends Grip of 21-Day Heat Wave Here," *New York Times*, July 26, 1935; "Rain Ushers in Cool Spell," *Brooklyn Daily Eagle*, July 26, 1935.

108   *Reached for comment*: "Nazi Denies Fry Report," *New York Times*, July 28, 1935.

108   *The fact that no Jews*: Jeremy Schaap, *Triumph: The Untold Story of Jesse Owen and Hitler's Olympics* (Boston and New York: Houghton Mifflin,

2007), 72. Nazi authorities eventually yielded to international pressure, permitting a half-Jewish fencer named Helene Mayer to compete for the German Olympic team.

108   *In Washington, DC, on the same:* "Jewish Groups Protest to U.S. Against Nazis," *New York Herald Tribune,* July 27, 1935.

109   *"I have been to sea":* Edward Drolette testimony, July 25, 1940, Hearings before a Subcommittee of the Committee on Commerce on H.R. 6881 An Act to Implement the Provisions of the Shipowners' Liability (Sick and Injured Seamen) Convention of 1936, United States Senate, 261–270. See also Edward Drolette, "An Open Letter is Issued to Ship Officers," *Daily Worker,* October 11, 1934.

110   *By 3:30 p.m. on the appointed day:* The actions of NYPD on July 26 are gleaned from Trial Transcript and Accompanying Materials, RG 59, box 6763, National Archives and Records Administration (NARA), College Park, Maryland; "Text of Police Department's Report on the Bremen Riot," *New York Times,* August 2, 1935; and "Police Reports in Connection with the Bremen Incident," *Public Papers of Governor Herbert H. Lehman* (Albany: J. B. Lyon Co., 1935), 708–715.

110   *Harold F. Moore was:* "'Fats' M'Carthy, Gangster, Slain in Albany Raid: Long-Sought Coll Follower Trapped by Police; Wife, Pal, Detective Wounded, 2nd Companion Seized, Ex-Clerk in Wall St. Lead to Captors to Hide-Out," *New York Herald Tribune,* July 12, 1932; "Detective Coming Home: Moore, Wounded Slayer of McCarthy, to be Brought from Albany," *New York Times;* August 23, 1932; "H.F. Moore is Dead; Detective Hero, 50: Ex-Lieutenant Here Won Top Honor for Slaying Gangster in 1932—Cited 10 Times," *New York Times,* June 12, 1951.

110   *Matthew Solomon was:* "Shot, Unarmed Policeman Nabs Broadway Thief," *New York Herald Tribune,* March 1, 1926; "Police Hero to Retire: Patrolman Matthew Solomon was Hurt in Bremen Riot," *New York Times,* September 12, 1941.

110   *At four p.m. in Washington:* "Press Conference, Executive Offices of the White House, July 26, 1935, 4 p.m.," *Franklin D. Roosevelt and Foreign Affairs,* ed. Edgar B. Nixon, vol. 2, March 1934–August 1935 (Cambridge, MA: Belknap Press of Harvard University Press, 1969), 582–583.

112   *"We dressed in our best":* Bill Bailey, *The Kid from Hoboken: An Autobiography* (San Francisco: Circus Lithographic Prepress, 1993), 259.

112   *"We never touched":* Bill Bailey interview with John Gerassi, August 8, 1980, John Gerassi Oral History Collection, ALBA Audio 18, Tamiment Library, New York University.

113   *"Had we known that":* Bailey interview, Gerassi.

114　*"Reich Jews 'Eliminated'":* "Reich Jews 'Eliminated' from Olympics," *New York Post,* July 26, 1935.

114　*"We went down to see":* Lucius Beebe, "This New York," *New York Herald Tribune,* July 28, 1935.

116　*"The* Bremen *stood motionless":* Bailey, *Kid from Hoboken,* 260.

117　*Onward marched an assortment:* See the following daily newspaper coverage of the event: "Red Riot on Bremen Here; 1 Shot, 16 Hurt," *New York Daily News,* July 27, 1935; "Reds Rip Flag off Bremen, Throw It into Hudson; 2,000 Battle the Police," *New York Times,* July 27, 1935; "Rioters Here Rip Nazi Flag off Bremen, *New York Herald Tribune,* July 27, 1935; "4 Held as Bremen Riot Leaders," *New York World-Telegram,* July 27, 1935; "Reds Rip Flag from Bremen," Associated Press, July 27, 1935; "Nazis Demand Bremen Apology," *New York Post,* July 27, 1935; "Court Under Guard as 15 of Red Rioters Draw Sympathizers," *Brooklyn Daily Eagle,* July 27, 1935; "Bremen Fight Spurs Drive on Terror," *Daily Worker,* July 29, 1935.

118　*would boast to his brother-in-law:* Steven T. Usdin, *Engineering Communism: How Two Americans Spied for Stalin and Founded the Soviet Silicon Valley* (New Haven, CT: Yale University Press, 2005), 288.

118　*"It was eleven at night":* "Bremen Demonstration is Turned into Riot by Police Tactics," *Catholic Worker,* September 1935.

119　*"Many have made the ocean":* "Bremen Sailings Inspire Writer," *Brooklyn Daily Eagle,* August 18, 1933.

120　*"We got our own":* Bailey interview, Gerassi.

122　*"Watch that flag!":* Janet Ginn, "The Shot That Rang Around the World," *Labor Defender,* September 1935.

122　*"So I turned around":* Bill Bailey interview transcript for *The Good Fight* documentary, 1981, box 1, folders 39 and 40, Abraham Lincoln Brigade Archives (ALBA), Tamiment Library, New York University.

123　*Adrian Duffy, short and wiry:* Duffy went on to become a leading figure in the National Maritime Union (NMU), which was founded in 1937. In 1948, "he was elected Vice President in the 'clean sweep' election that ousted Communist Party functionaries from union office," according to his obituary in the NMU's newspaper, *The Pilot.* He served for ten years as vice president in charge of organizing for the NMU until he returned to sea. "I didn't get around to asking him how come he wasn't still in NMU 'politics,'" wrote a fellow seaman who met Duffy on the deck of a ship in 1963. "I had the impression—maybe it's the one I wanted to have—that he felt that the air was cleaner where he was then than where he had been formerly." Gilbert Mers, *Working the Waterfront: The Ups and Downs of a Rebel Longshoreman* (Austin: University of Texas Press, 1988), 167. Duffy died in 1973.

Chapter Eleven

125 *The shot that wounded:* Janet Ginn, "The Shot That Rang Around the World," *Labor Defender*, September 1935.

125 *"No matter where you look":* Bill Bailey interview transcript for *The Good Fight* documentary, 1981, box 1, folders 39 and 40, Abraham Lincoln Brigade Archives (ALBA), Tamiment Library, New York University.

125 *"figuring this bastard's":* Bill Bailey interview, "The Day We Tore the Nazi Flag off the Bremen," Bancroft Library, call no. 85/171, University of California, Berkeley.

125 *"I could swear to this day":* Bill Bailey interview, Janet Clinger, *Our Elders: Six Bay Area Life Stories* (Bloomington, IN: Xlibris, 2003).

127 *Drolette had a different version:* "It Was Worth It, Says Heroic Seaman Shot in Bremen Affray," *Daily Worker*, August 24, 1935.

128 *"The crowds stood motionless":* "But the Swastika Fell," *New Masses*, August 6, 1935.

129 *"I hate to say this":* Bill Bailey interview with John Gerassi, August 8, 1980, John Gerassi Oral History Collection, ALBA Audio 18, Tamiment Library, New York University.

130 *"next thing was takin' names":* Bailey interview, Gerassi.

131 *Although it is hard:* Peter A. Huchthausen, *Shadow Voyage: The Extraordinary Wartime Escape of the Legendary S.S.* Bremen (New York: John Wiley and Sons, 2005), 75.

131 *"It was a big relief":* Bailey interview, Gerassi.

132 *"Thus prompted those thugs:* "Bremen Demonstration Is Turned into Riot by Police Tactics," *Catholic Worker*, September 1935.

134 *"There isn't the slightest reason":* Trial Transcript and Accompanying Materials, RG 59, box 6763, National Archives and Records Administration (NARA), College Park, Maryland.

Chapter Twelve

137 *As an American citizen I demand:* Adam Bernard to Secretary of State Hull, August 5, 1935, RG 59, box 6763, National Archives and Records Administration (NARA), College Park, Maryland.

139 *On Sunday, July 28:* "Germans Hail Bremen Crew," *Sunday Mirror*, July 28, 1935.

139 *Upon arrival in Bremerhaven:* "L. Ziegenbein Dies; Bremen's Captain," *New York Times*, June 23, 1950. According to the story, the two *Bremen* officers were imprisoned because they failed to make any "attempt to

prevent anti-Nazi demonstrators here from tearing down her swastika flag."

139 *Goebbels wrote in his diary:* Joseph Goebbels, diary entry dated July 29, 1935, in Elke Fröhlich, ed., *Die Tagebücher von Joseph Goebbels,* vol. 3/1, April 1934–February 1936 (Munich: De Gruyter Saur, 2005), 268.

140 *Howe/Jamieson later told:* William E. Chapman, American consul, Gibraltar, "American deserters from armed forces in Spain," May 10, 1938, RG 59, file 852.2226/18, NARA.

140 *"I had one beer aboard":* "Alien in Lineup After Recovering from Cop Beating," *New York Post,* August 3, 1935.

140 *requested an adjournment:* Trial Transcript and Accompanying Documents, NARA.

141 *"Solomon was forced to choose":* "Riot in New York at German Ship *Bremen;* Swastika Torn Down and Thrown into Hudson River," *Forverts,* July 28, 1935.

141 *"Late in the evening of July 26":* Copy of Leitner protest letter with English translation, July 29, 1935, RG 59, box 6763, NARA.

142 *"American people are always":* William Phillips to William Dodd, July 31, 1935, US Department of State, *Foreign Relations of the United States,* vol. 2, 1935, 404.

142 *"Everything possible has been":* "Berlin Protests Flag Riot, U.S. Ask Lehman Report; Nazi Resume Violence," *New York Herald Tribune,* July 31, 1935.

143 *Phillips urged New York governor:* Phillips to Lehman, July 30, 1935, RG 59, box 6763, NARA.

143 *When Mayor LaGuardia learned:* LaGuardia to Hull, July 30, 1935, RG 59, box 6763, NARA.

143 *On that night in the:* "Mayor Denounced by 6,000 Germans," *New York Times,* July 31, 1935.

144 *On the following morning, August 1:* Phillips to President Roosevelt, August 1, 1935, RG 59, Box 6763, NARA.

144 *Within hours, the US government:* "U.S. Defends City in Bremen Rioting: Phillips in Reply to German Protest Praises Police—Stress Prompt Arrests. Regrets Insult to Flag. Note Says Line Officials Were Lax in Precautions. Case Is Considered Closed," *New York Times,* August 2, 1935.

145 *on August 4, Joseph Goebbels:* "Dr. Goebbels Speech in Essen of August 4," State Department memo, August 5, 1935, RG 59, box 6787, NARA.

146 *A "Provisional Committee":* "Conference on Thursday to Aid Flag Case Heroes," *Daily Worker,* August 7, 1935.

147   *The shouts and jeers from:* "1 Bremen Rioter Is Convicted; 6 Cases Continued," *New York Post*, August 7, 1935; "Court Scene Storm at Bremen Case Trial; US Backs Nazi Arrest," *Daily Worker*, August 8, 1935; "Court in Uproar at Ship Riot Trial," *New York Times*, August 8, 1935.

148   *On the following evening, August 8:* "Nazi Foes Urge That U.S. Shun Olympic Games," *New York Herald Tribune*, August 9, 1935; "Bremen Rioters Cheered by 20,000," *New York Post*, August 9, 1935; "Bremen Rioters Cheered by 20,000," *New York Times*, August 9, 1935; "20,000 Hail Anti-Nazi Fight," *Daily Worker*, August 10, 1935.

Chapter Thirteen

151   *The spirit of the Boston:* "But Germany Is Not Taking Us for Tea," *New York Post*, August 5, 1935.

151   *"We were the 'wheat Brodskys'":* "No Apology or Explanation Needed, Brodsky Declares," *New York World-Telegram*, August 10, 1935.

152   *To a newsboy who:* "Apologies for City to Newsboy in Court," *New York Times*, October 11, 1925.

152   *He lauded an elderly:* "Woman Feeding Birds Is Arrested in Park," *New York Times*, April 10, 1934.

153   *When a young Salvador Dalí:* "Art Changed, Dali Goes on Rampage in Store, Crashes Through Window into Arms of the Law," *New York Times*, March 17, 1939.

153   *rights of striking fur workers:* "Fur Strike Pickets Upheld by Court," *New York Times*, May 25, 1926.

153   *burlesque dancers:* "Court Upholds Nudity," *New York Times*, April 7, 1935.

153   *and litterateurs:* "Brodsky Rules Against Sumner as Book Censor," *New York Herald Tribune*, November 11, 1931.

153   *He was proud of the:* Edna Brand Mann, "Judge Brodsky and the Bremen Case," *American Spectator*, November 1935.

153   *"He wears a pince-nez":* Mann, "Judge Brodsky and the Bremen Case."

154   *"Keep an honest judge":* "Broun Contributes Slogan to Democratic Opponent," *New York Herald Tribune*, September 21, 1930.

154   *He was known around town:* Herbert Mitgang, *The Man Who Rode the Tiger: The Life and Times of Judge Samuel Seabury* (New York: Fordham University Press, 1996), 190.

154   *According to a document in the:* Abraham Gravitsky to Judge Brodsky, September 5, 1933, box 142, NSANL papers, Columbia University.

154   *The title was the:* "Boycott Best Weapon Against Hitler, Says Brodsky in Broadcast," Jewish Telegraphic Agency, August 19, 1934.

155   *"long, high-ceilinged, utterly":* "Endless Drama of Magistrate's Court: At the Bar the Common People Present Their Common Woes in an Atmosphere That Is Sometimes Tense," *New York Times,* February 2, 1930.

155   *"It was worth getting shot":* "It Was Worth It, Says Heroic Seaman Shot in Bremen Affray," *Daily Worker,* August 24, 1935.

156   *"The district attorney may say":* The court testimony in this chapter comes from Trial Transcript and Accompanying Materials, RG 59, box 6763, National Archives and Records Administration (NARA), College Park, Maryland.

160   *His exalted reputation didn't":* "Shot in Gun Battle at Apartment House," *New York Times,* August 17, 1927.

160   *His constituents paid little heed:* Gerald Meyer, *Vito Marcantonio: Radical Politician, 1902–1954* (Albany: SUNY Press, 1989), 121.

161   *"in the reasonably clear and precise":* Richard H. Rovere, "Vito Marcantonio: Machine Politician, New Style," *Harper's Magazine,* April, 1944.

162   *"In one of our court appearances":* Bill Bailey, *The Kid from Hoboken: An Autobiography* (San Francisco: Circus Lithographic Prepress, 1993), 267.

162   *"The courtroom was crowded":* "Riot Hearing Put Off," *New York Times,* August 29, 1935.

165   *A veteran of World War I who:* "Head of Bomb Squad Will Serve the Navy," *New York Times,* December 16, 1943.

165   *The Italian government honored:* "Lieut. Pyke to Be Decorated," *New York Times,* November 25, 1934.

Chapter Fourteen

169   *These walls breathe out:* Dudley Fitts, ed., *Four Greek Plays,* trans., Fitts and Robert Fitzgerald (New York: Harcourt, Brace and Co., 1960), 50.

169   *"We drove to the pier":* Bill Bailey, *The Kid from Hoboken: An Autobiography* (San Francisco: Circus Lithographic Prepress, 1993), 268.

170   *As on other occasions":* "Calls Bremen 'Pirate Ship' and Frees 8," *New York World-Telegram,* September 6, 1935.

176   *"The German ambassador came in":* "Memorandum of Conversation between Secretary Hull and the German Ambassador, Herr Hans Luther," Papers of Cordell Hull, box 58, Library of Congress.

177 *"After the Nazi ambassador left:* Hull to Lehman, September 7, 1935, RG 59, box 6763, National Archives and Records Administration (NARA), College Park, Maryland.

177 *The* Washington Post *published:* "Highly Injudicious," *Washington Post,* September 8, 1935.

177 *The* New York Times *was appalled:* "An Unfortunate Decision," *New York Times,* September 9, 1935.

177 *"But legally—and the magistrate's":* "A Dangerous Precedent," *New York World-Telegram,* September 9, 1935.

177 *"The fact that the":* "British Score Brodsky Ruling," *New York Times,* September 14, 1935.

177 *"Conservative Jewish leaders":* H.W., "Our New York Letter," *Jewish Advocate,* September 24, 1935.

178 *Supreme Court justice Benjamin:* Richard Polenberg, *The World of Benjamin Cardozo: Personal Values and the Judicial Process* (Cambridge, MA: Harvard University Press, 1997), 184–185.

178 *The International Labor Defense produced:* Mike Walsh, *The Black Flag of Piracy* (New York: International Labor Defense, 1935), 9.

178 *Detective Solomon, who was:* "Detective Gets Reward," *New York Times,* September 7, 1935.

179 *"The acts of terror":* Volker Ullrich, *Hitler: Ascent 1889–1939,* trans. Jefferson Chase (New York: Knopf, 2016), 552.

179 *On September 9, the eve:* Goebbels, diary entry dated September 11, 1935, in Elke Fröhlich, ed., *Die Tagebücher von Joseph Goebbels,* vol. 3/1, April 1934–February 1936 (Munich: De Gruyter Saur, 2005), 290–291.

180 *In the afternoon of the following:* Hamilton T. Burden, *The Nuremberg Party Rallies* (New York: Praeger, 1967), 100–112.

180 *On Thursday, September 12, Secretary of:* "Memorandum," James Clement Dunn, RG 59, box 6763, NARA. Mr. Dunn's seven-page memo provides a comprehensive narrative of the behind-the-scenes diplomatic maneuvering that preceded the US government's September 14 apology.

182 *Early on Saturday, September 14:* Ullrich, *Hitler: Ascent 1889–1939,* 554–559.

183 *The statement declared that:* "Hull Apologizes for Brodsky Talk Against Nazi Rule," *New York Times,* September 15, 1935.

186 *"For some it appears symbolic":* "Reich Adopts Swastika as Nation's Official Flag; Hitler's Reply to Insult," *New York Times,* September 16, 1935.

186   *Just a few hours later:* "Swastika Raised on Bremen and Hailed as Battle Flag," *New York World-Telegram,* September 17, 1935; "Swastika Raised on Bremen Here," *New York Post,* September 17, 1935; "Bremen Hoists Swastika Here at 8 a.m. Today," *New York Herald Tribune,* September 17, 1935; "Bremen Raises Swastika," *New York Journal,* September 17, 1935; "Bremen Raises Swastika Flag at Hudson Pier," *New York Herald Tribune,* September 18, 1935; "Swastika Raised over 3 German Liners in N.Y.," *Chicago Tribune,* September 18, 1935; "Nazi Swastika Raised on 3 Liners Here; Bremen Captain Leads Ceremony on Deck," *New York Times,* September 18, 1935.

Chapter Fifteen

189   *One reason the Western world:* Varian Fry, "The Massacre of the Jews," *New Republic,* December 21, 1942.

189   *He was quoted in:* Mike Walsh, *The Black Flag of Piracy* (New York: International Labor Defense, 1935), 6.

190   *"In the United States, a judge is":* "No Apology or Explanation Needed, Brodsky Declares," *New York World-Telegram,* August 10, 1935.

190   *"Amazing as it sounds":* Phineas Biron, "Strictly Confidential," *American Israelite,* October 10, 1935.

190   *"You have no idea":* "Emil Ludwig Before the Judge," *Jewish Criterion,* October 23, 1935.

191   *Drolette testified in his:* "Seaman Is Acquitted in Bremen Assault," *New York Times,* March 25, 1937; "Sailor in Bremen Riot Freed of Assault Charge," *New York Herald Tribune,* March 25, 1937.

192   *"The tearing down of the":* Vito Marcantonio, "A Modern Boston Tea-Party," *Labor Defender,* October 1935.

193   *"She was in love":* Bill Bailey, *The Kid from Hoboken: An Autobiography* (San Francisco: Circus Lithographic Prepress, 1993), 269.

194   *"I was never beaten":* "Ex-Nazi Prisoner Is Hailed at Dock," *Baltimore Sun,* January 4, 1937.

195   *"I want to go to Spain":* Bill Bailey interview with Howard Kimeldorf, September 15, 1981, container 8/55, John Ahlquist and Margaret Levi research materials, Special Collections University of Washington Libraries.

196   *"As a Communist, I was convinced":* Bill Bailey, "One Man's Education: A Testimony to Internationalism," *Harvard Educational Review* 55, no. 1 (February 1985).

197   *"Let everyone do his share":* Untermyer to J. George Fredman, January 23, 1936, box 77, NSANL Papers, Columbia University.

197 *"The guide stopped":* Bailey, *Kid from Hoboken,* 328.

197 *"I felt right back":* Bill Bailey interview transcript for *The Good Fight* documentary, 1981, box 1, folders 39 and 40, Abraham Lincoln Brigade Archives (ALBA), Tamiment Library, New York University.

198 *"Out came a pack":* Bill Bailey interview, Janet Clinger, *Our Elders: Six Bay Area Life Stories* (Bloomington, IN: Xlibris, 2003).

198 *"written in the books":* Bill Bailey to Marjorie Polon, September 29, 1938, Marjorie Polon Papers, ALBA no. 159, Tamiment Library, New York University.

198 *"Mike is a real rough":* Harry Hakam to Marjorie Polon, June 19, 1938, Marjorie Polon Papers, ALBA no. 159, Tamiment Library, New York University.

198 *"As a small town boy":* Bill Bailey interview with Maria Brooks, *LifeStory: Bill Bailey,* a film by Maria Brooks, Al Allen collection on the International Longshore and Warehouse Union, 1939–2016, University of Washington Libraries/Special Collections.

198 *"what it meant to see a man":* Bailey interview, *Good Fight.*

199 *"Many men died in Spain":* Bill Bailey, "Memories of Joe Bianca and Spain," Hawsepipe: Newsletter of the Marine Workers Historical Association (Summer 1988): 18–19.

199 *He would forever be disgusted:* Bill Bailey interview, Manny Harriman Oral History Project, box 1, V 48-010, Abraham Lincoln Brigade Archives (ALBA), Tamiment Library, New York University.

199 *Bailey even felt remorse:* Bailey interview, Clinger.

199 *"really a necessary thing":* "Spain Was a Moment of Truth," *San Francisco Chronicle,* February 7, 1981.

200 *On the other side of:* Andrew Nagorski, *Hitlerland: American Eyewitnesses to the Nazi Rise to Power* (New York: Simon and Schuster, 2012), 213–215.

200 *sat down with a State Department official:* "Memorandum," June 15, 1938, RG 59, file 852.2221/1133, National Archives and Records Administration (NARA), College Park, Maryland.

201 *"It was very sad to leave":* Bailey interview, Brooks.

201 *the New Yorker magazine published:* Irwin Shaw, *Sailor off the Bremen and Other Stories* (New York: Random House, 1939).

202 *"wisps of chiffon":* "Faun a Rarity, Dancer Freed," *New York Herald Tribune,* April 25, 1939.

202 *The judge was less lenient:* "Beggar with 'Valet' Is Warned by Court," *New York Times,* April 27, 1939.

202 *On July 1, 1939, Brodsky:* "Brodsky Quits Bench: Magistrate Hails Gains in Court as He Retires," *New York Times,* July 1, 1939. Brodsky

died on April 29, 1970, at the age eighty-six. The story of his *Bremen* verdict took up two paragraphs in his six-paragraph obituary in the *New York Times*.

202 *"I thought that Stalin":* Bailey interview, Brooks.

203 *the* Bremen *was speeding:* Peter Huchthausen's *Shadow Voyage* tells full story of the *Bremen's* flight.

204 *Samuel Untermyer died:* "Untermyer Dies; Noted for Fight on Anti-Semitism," *Chicago Tribune*, March 17, 1940.

204 *Fry and a network of accomplices:* See Sheila Isenberg, *A Hero of Our Own: The Story of Varian Fry* (New York: Random House, 2001) and Andy Marino, *A Quiet American: The Secret War of Varian Fry* (New York: St. Martin's Press, 1999).

205 *Edward Drolette remained:* Drolette, who was married from 1937 to 1941 to a Polish-born woman named Sylvia Kraft, died on February 5, 1950. He is buried in the Long Island National Cemetery in East Farmingdale, New York. Drolette was eligible for interment in a US military cemetery because of his service in World War I.

205 *"If you read through":* Edward Drolette testimony, July 25, 1940, Hearings before a Subcommittee of the Committee on Commerce on H.R. 6881, 261–270.

205 *"While the main Royal Air Force":* "British Say Lone Raider Set Fire to the Bremen," *New York Herald Tribune*, March 22, 1941.

205 *"I need a perpetrator":* Frank O. Braynard, *The Bremen and the Europa* (New York, Fort Schuyler Press, 2005), 191–195.

206 *"There were no more":* Bailey, *Kid from Hoboken*, 341.

207 *"I decided I couldn't":* Bill Bailey interview, Michael Gillen, *Merchant Marine Survivors of World War II: Oral Histories of Cargo Carrying Under Fire* (Jefferson, NC: McFarland, 2015), 7–11.

208 *The first regulation repealed:* Malcolm Quinn, *The Swastika: Constructing the Symbol* (London and New York: Routledge, 1994), 3.

209 *"We were alive with":* Bailey, *Kid from Hoboken*, 386.

Chapter Sixteen

211 *Revolution only needs good:* Tennessee Williams, *The Theatre of Tennessee Williams*, vol. 2 (New York: New Directions, 1971), 450.

212 *"Reds, phonies, and 'parlor pinks'":* Ted Morgan, *Reds: McCarthyism in America* (New York: Random House, 2004), 307.

212 *"any type of a decent":* Bill Bailey interview with Maria Brooks, *LifeStory: Bill Bailey*, a film by Maria Brooks, Al Allen collection on the

International Longshore and Warehouse Union, 1939–2016, University of Washington Libraries/Special Collections.

212   *Bailey would regret:* Constance Coiner, *Better Red: The Writing and Resistance of Tillie Olsen and Meridel LeSueur* (London: Oxford University Press, 1995), 53.

213   *Arthur "Mac" Blair, who never:* The Blairs lived in a number of locations in Mexico before settling in Guadalajara. Mac died in 1979. After her husband's death, Margaret Blair returned to California, where she was active in peace and justice causes. She eventually became the chairwoman of the Long Beach branch of the Gray Panthers, the militant senior citizens' group that confronted ageism in the United States. In 1985, she wrote a letter to the editor of the *Los Angeles Times,* objecting to a comment made by the mayor of Long Beach, who felt the city should do its patriotic duty and allow the US Navy to bring nuclear weapons into Long Beach waters. "According to my understanding of American democracy, it is not only the right but the duty of citizens to express their opinions on what they consider vital public issues," she wrote. "They should not be told to 'shut up.'" Margaret Blair died on June 10, 2002.

213   *The real trouble started:* Bill Bailey interview, Griffin Fariello, *Red Scare: Memories of an American Inquisition, An Oral History* (New York: W. W. Norton, 1995).

213   *"The power to declare":* "Truman Based Korea Order on UN Resolution," *New York Herald Tribune,* June 28, 1950.

214   *"It is not a pleasant feeling":* Bill Bailey, *The Kid from Hoboken: An Autobiography* (San Francisco: Circus Lithographic Prepress, 1993), 397.

219   *"I would not fold":* Bailey, *Kid from Hoboken,* 419.

219   *"He was nothing but":* The Spanish Civil War, Granada TV (United Kingdom), 1983.

219   *"As an ex-seamen used":* Richard Sexton, *The Cottage Book* (San Francisco: Chronicle Books, 1998), 62–63.

220   *"Guys loved to work":* Author interview with Brian McWilliams.

220   *"I feel envious when I":* Bill Bailey interview transcript for *The Good Fight* documentary, 1981, box 1, folders 39 and 40, Abraham Lincoln Brigade Archives (ALBA), Tamiment Library, New York University.

220   *"a gesture of hope":* Constance Coiner, *Better Red: The Writing and Resistance of Tillie Olsen and Meridel Le Sueur* (New York: Oxford University Press, 1995), 255–256.

220   *The presiding matriarch:* Author interview with Corine Thornton.

220   *"for the young people coming":* Bill Bailey interview, Janet Clinger, *Our Elders: Six Bay Area Life Stories* (Bloomington, IN: Xlibris, 2003).

221   *She recalled how he:* Author interview with Lynn Damme.

221   *"Craggy-faced, bespectacled":* Studs Terkel, *The Good War: An Oral History of World War II* (New York: New Press, 1984), 98.

222   *"a big man with reddish hair":* Blake Green, "From Radical to Star," *San Francisco Chronicle*, April 3, 1984.

222   *"Bill Bailey is without question":* Warren Hinckle's column on Bailey was reprinted in Bob Callahan, ed., *The Big Book of American Irish Culture* (New York: Penguin Books, 1987), 194.

222   *"You have that good feeling":* Bailey interview, Brooks.

222   *"Bill was always humble":* Author interview with Rob Nilsson.

222   *"They took me into this":* "Activist Bailey Takes on New Challenge as Actor in Films," *Oakland Tribune*, May 6, 1984.

223   *"corrupted sort of existence":* Bailey interview, Clinger.

223   *"I was reading the paper":* Don Bajema, *Winged Shoes and a Shield: Collected Stories* (San Francisco: City Lights Books, 2012), 289.

224   *"He was tired":* Author interview with Maria Brooks.

INDEX

activism, of Bailey, B., 6–7, 222
  Indian stowaway and, 67–69
  ISU and, 74, 85, 193, 194
  Marine Firemen's Union and,
    206, 212–213, 214, 223
  Marine Workers Voice and, 69–70,
    71
  MWIU and, 70–74
  Nazi Germany impacting, 96
  Robinson, J., and, 69
  socialism and, 220
activism (US), against Nazi
    Germany, 54
  action-now, 65
  arrests and, 64
  Bremen Six support and, 131,
    132, 133 (photo)
  Catholic Church and,
    98–99
  Committee for Action Against
    Fascism and, 60
  Croll and, 117–118
  ground protesters at Bremen
    Riot and, 117–119, 128
  Hanfstaengl and, 77–79, 80

Jewish War Veterans march as,
    55–56
  maritime strike committees and,
    194
  NYPD and, 63–64, 78–79
  Pier 86 demonstration as, 78–79,
    99
  Weidemann and, 62–63, 64
  See also Untermyer, Samuel
Adams, Samuel, 172
Ahrens, Adolf, 186–187, 203
Alaskan (ship), 193
American Jewish Committee, 57,
    108
American Jewish Congress,
    108
  national day of prayer, fasting,
    and protest by, 57–58
Anti-Nazi Federation of New York,
    138
  Bremen Six and, 148 (photo),
    149
  rally of, 148–149
Anton, Michael, 21
April Laws, 59, 87–88

Aryans, 24–25
    April Laws and, 59
    mixed couples and, 88, 93, 94,
        145, 182
    swastika and, 48, 50
Aurelio, Thomas A., 147–148

Bacon, Faith, 202
Baer, Hans, 78–79
Bailey, Bill, 19 (photo), 86 (photo),
        148 (photo), 215 (photo),
        221 (photo)
    See also specific topics
Bailey, Elizabeth (mother), 18, 19
        (photo), 41
    immigration of, 9–10
    marital violence and, 10, 16–17
    occupation of, 11, 12, 16
    politics of, 12–13
    religion for, 11–12
    second marriage of, 13, 16–17
    St. Peter school and, 14–15
Bailey, William (father), 10
Bajema, Don, 223–224
Baltimore, Maryland, 74
    MWIU office in, 73
    police brutality against Bailey, B.
        in, 194
Beebe, Lucius, 114
Bell, "Ding Dong," 70–71
Berlin, Irving, 32
Berlin Riots. See Kurfürstendamm
Bianca, Joe, 199
Biddle, Anthony J. Drexel, 115
Biron, Phineas J., 190
Black Gang News, 194
    Cold War and, 214
Blackwell, George, 139, 148
        (photo), 192
Blair, Arthur "Mac," 148 (photo)
    background of, 92

Bremen Riot and, 109, 112–113,
        116–117, 121–122, 129
    in Bremen Six, 140
    injuries of, 129
    in Mexico, 213
    newspaper work of, 193–194
    in Spanish Civil War, 199
    at Trial of Bremen Six, 174–175
    Weaver and, 92, 140, 174, 199,
        213
The Blessings of Fascism (Simpson),
        194–195
Blood Flag (Blutfahne), 51
B'nai B'rith, 57, 66
Bone, Homer T., 84
Boston Tea Party, 168, 172
boycott of German goods, 55, 76,
        118
    Brodsky and, 154, 190
    Untermyer and, 65–66, 102, 196,
        204
Bremen, SS (ship), 25 (photo), 105
        (photo)
    Ahrens as captain of, 186–187,
        203
    alcohol on, 31–32
    architects designing, 27
    cell leaders on, 46–47
    crew, 28
    "darken ship" order for, 203
    famous passengers on, 44,
        76–77, 82, 114–115, 196
    features of, 27–28
    first return trip of, 31
    Great Depression and, 43
    Hindenburg and, 23–24, 27–28
    hype for, 26
    inaugural journey of, 29–31
    Luther on, 60–61
    midnight sailing tradition on,
        32–33

NDL building, 23–24

Pier 86 demonstration and, 78–79, 99

propaganda on, 47–49, 186–187

reception for, 30–31

sabotage of, 205–206

Schulwitz as ideological director of, 47

in Soviet Union territory, 203–204

Studnitz on, 28, 30

swastika flag on, 186–187, 187 (photo), 192–193

tests for, 25–26

Untermyer and, 62

Walker, J., on, 31

war and, 203–204, 205–206

Ziegenbein as captain of, 28, 30, 31, 104

Bremen Riot, 3, 126 (photo), 224

Bailey, B., and, 5, 99–100, 106, 112, 116–117, 121–123, 125–126, 131

Blair and, 109, 112–113, 116–117, 121–122, 129

Catholics and, 106, 112–113, 130

crowd aboard, 4, 119–120, 128

Day and, 118, 122, 132

Drolette and, 109–116, 120, 127–129

Duffy and, 122–123, 130

evacuation and, 119, 120–121

famous passengers aboard during, 114–115

Friends of the New Germany and, 119

Gavin and, 109, 112–113, 116, 121

ground protestors at, 117–119, 128

Hapag-Lloyd and, 111

McCormack and, 121, 129, 133

Murphy and, 128

NYPD and, 4, 5, 109–110, 119, 128–129, 131

planning, 96, 99–100, 106, 112–113, 120

Red Squad at, 115–116, 120, 127–128

Robinson and, 99

Rosenberg, J., and, 118

in "Sailor off the Bremen," 201–202

significance of assault on, 5–6

Solomon during, 126–127

swastika flag and, 4–5, 52, 99–100, 116, 122–123, 128–129, 170, 171, 175

violence during, 121–122, 125–130

Weaver and, 105–106, 109, 121, 123, 132, 133, 155

Ziegenbein and, 119–120, 131, 139

Bremen Riot aftermath

Anti-Nazi Federation of New York and, 138

Carr and, 135, 138

German Americans and, 143

Goebbels and, 139, 145–146

Hapag-Lloyd and, 142–143

Hitler on, 184

LaGuardia on, 142

Nazi Germany and, 137–138, 139, 141–142

newspapers on, 137–138

NYPD report in, 144–145, 165

Roosevelt administration and, 135, 142, 144

Solomon and, 141, 178

swastika flag and, 192–193

Bremen Six, 6
  activists supporting, 131, 132,
    133 (photo)
  at Anti-Nazi Federation rally, 148
    (photo), 149
  Aurelio and, 147–148
  bail for, 135, 141, 143–144
  Bailey, B., of, 139, 149
  Blackwell of, 139, 148 (photo),
    192
  Blair of, 140
  Brody and, 140, 146
  charges against, 134, 146–147
  Drolette of, 140
  fake backgrounds of, 134
  felonious assault booking of, 134
  Ford as magistrate for, 134–135
  ILD and, 146, 147
  interrogation of, 133
  Jamieson of, 139–140
  McCormack of, 139, 148 (photo)
  in Spanish Civil War, 199
  speaking circuit of, 189
  Tauber and, 147
  Unger representing, 131,
    134–135, 141, 143
  See also Trial of Bremen Six
Bridges, Harry, 218
Brodsky, Louis B., 152 (photo)
  Bacon verdict by, 202
  boycott of German goods and,
    154, 190
  congratulatory letters for, 190
  Dalí and, 153
  early life of, 151–152
  Jewish roots of, 154
  Ludwig and, 190–191
  politics and, 153
  retirement of, 202
  on swastika flag, 170, 171, 175,
    177

  Trial of Bremen Six and, 156,
    164, 165, 166–167, 168,
    170–174, 177, 180–183, 189
  unorthodox verdicts of, 152–153
  US media on decision of, 175,
    177–178
  wealth of, 154
Brody, Morris, 140, 146
Brooks, Maria, 7, 224
Brundage, Avery, 108

Cannon, Hughie, 10, 211
Cardozo, Benjamin, 178
Carr, Wilbur J., 135, 138
Catholic Church, in Nazi Germany,
    2–3, 44, 56, 88, 100, 145
  byzantine currency laws and, 89
  Goering attacking, 95
  laws against, 101
  US activism against Nazi
    Germany and, 98–99
Catholic Church, US
  Bremen Riot and, 106, 112–113,
    130
  in early life of Bailey, B., 14–15,
    96
cell leaders (Zellenleiter), 46–47
Churchill, Winston, 175, 204
Cohan, George M., 40
Cold War
  Bailey, B., impacted by, 6–7, 212,
    213–215
  Black Gang News and, 214
  Korean War and, 213–214
  Magnuson Act in, 214
  Smith Act and, 213
Committee for Action Against
    Fascism, 60
Communist Party, Germany
  Nazi Party and, 42
  Thälmann and, 45, 117

Communist Party, US, 36, 42
  Bailey, B., and, 2, 7, 72–73, 86,
    195, 197, 203, 214, 218, 219
  on Hawaiian Islands, 195
  Hitler-Stalin Pact impacting, 203
  Marine Firemen's Union and
    names of, 214
  MWIU and, 71
  Pele and, 73–74, 87, 169–170,
    193, 203
  Smith Act and, 213
  Spanish Civil War and, 197, 200
  training course for, 73–74
  Truman and, 212–213
  Weaver and, 92
  See also Bremen Riot
Conant, James B., 80
Correll, Charles, 76
Croll, June, 117–118
Crouse, Russel, 29

Dalí, Salvador, 153
Damme, Lynn, 221, 223
DAP. See German Workers' Party
Davis, Thomas, 13
Day, Dorothy, 118, 122, 132
De Niro, Robert, 222–223
Der Stürmer (cartoon publication),
    88, 94
Dickstein, Samuel, 103–104
  House Un-American Activities
    Committee and, 77
Dillinger, John, 77
Dodd, William, 97
Dodge, Geraldine Rockefeller, 115
Dorsey, Tommy, 32
Drechsel, William, 77
Drolette, Edward, 192 (photo)
  brass knuckles on, 129
  Bremen Riot and, 109–116, 120,
    127–129
    in Bremen Six, 140
    Moore shooting, 127–128
    Red Squad and, 110–116, 120
    trial of, 191–192
    Trial of Bremen Six and, 156,
      157, 159, 162–164, 165–166,
      167, 173, 174
    US Senate subcommittee
      testimony of, 205
    in World War I, 109
Duffy, Adrian, 122–123, 130
Dunn, James Clement, 183
  Brodsky decision and, 180–181,
    182

Earle, George H., 115
early life, of Bailey, B., 2
  Catholic school in, 14–15, 96
  delinquency in, 16, 17–18, 140
  at Farm for Wayward Boys, 16
  First Communion in, 15
  Hudson Street building in, 11
  Irish nationalism in, 12–13
  name change in, 9, 20
  newsboy job in, 12, 17
  parents and, 9–11
  public school in, 16
  railroad traveling in, 38–40
  siblings in, 9–10
  storytelling in, 15
  virginity lost in, 36–37
Ehrhardt Brigade, 49
Eliot, T. S., 78
Europa, SS (ship), 43, 75
  construction of, 23, 25
  fire on, 26
  swastika flag on, 80

family, of Bailey, B.
  Bailey, W., as father, 10
  marriage and, 203, 206, 207

family, of Bailey, B. (*continued*)
   siblings as, 9–10, 12, 13–14
   son as, 212, 223
   stepfather as, 13, 16–17
   See also Bailey, Elizabeth
      (mother)
Farm for Wayward Boys, 16
fascism, 63, 64, 87, 98–99, 202,
      203, 209
   The Blessings of Fascism,
      194–195
   Committee for Action Against
      Fascism, 60
   European, 196
   MWIU against, 55–56
   refugee committees and, 78
   in Spain, 196, 199
   Wise on, 148
   See also Italy
Florida, 38
Fonda, Henry, 196
forcible coordination
      (*Gleichschaltung*), 46
Ford, Michael A., 134–135
Forrestal, James, 115
Fort Point Gang, 220
France, 83, 196
   Hitler invading, 204
   in World War I, 109
Franco, Francisco, 195, 196, 200,
      201
Frick, Wilhelm, 182
Friends of the New Germany, 80
   Bremen Riot and, 119
   LaGuardia and, 119
   Schuster and, 102
Fry, Varian, 93, 94, 189
   at Emergency Rescue
      Committee, 204
   Hanfstaengl and, 105, 107,
      108
   on Ku'damm riots, 104–105,
      107–108, 204
   refugees and, 204–205

Gable, Clark, 196
Gavin, Pat
   Bremen Riot and, 109, 112–113,
      116, 121
   in World War II, 208
German merchant fleet
   Hapag, 22–23, 46, 55, 76
   Hapag-Lloyd and, 76, 77, 111,
      142–143
   House Un-American Activities
      Committee and, 77
   Imperator (ship) in, 21–22
   nazification campaign and, 22,
      46
   NDL and, 22–23, 25–26, 43, 46,
      55, 75, 76, 80
   Treaty of Versailles and, 22, 24
   Vaterland (ship) in, 22
   See also specific ships
German Workers' Party (DAP), 49
Germany
   Second Reich in, 49
   See also German merchant
      fleet; Nazi Germany; Weimar
      Germany
Gleichschaltung (forcible
      coordination), 46
Goebbels, Joseph, 25, 45, 181, 200
   Bremen Riot aftermath and, 139,
      145–146
   Der Angriff and, 93, 175
   military draft and, 83
   on Trial of Bremen Six, 175, 179
   Weidemann and, 64, 79
Goering, Hermann, 56–57, 184
   Catholic Church attacked by, 95
   Luftwaffe and, 83, 196

Nuremberg Laws and, 185–186
  as Police Commissioner, 53–54
Goodman, Benjamin, 79
Great Britain, 83, 196, 207
  Churchill, 175, 204
  planned invasion of, 204
  policy of appeasement, 84
  War on Nazi Germany and,
    203–204
Great Depression, 35, 71
  jobs during, 39
  SS *Bremen* (ship) during, 43
  unemployment rate in, 40
Grimminger, Jakob, 51

The Hairy Ape (O'Neill), 41
Hakam, Harry, 198
Hakenkreuz (hooked cross), 47–48
Hamburg-America Line (Hapag),
    22–23, 55
  Hapag-Lloyd merger of, 76
  nazification campaign and, 46
Hanfstaengl, Ernst "Putzi," 54
  demonstrations against, 77–79, 80
  Fry and, 105, 107, 108
  Harvard and, 80
  Hearst and, 82
  Hitler and, 78
Hapag. *See* Hamburg-America Line
Hapag-Lloyd
  Bremen Riot aftermath and,
    142–143
  Bremen Riot and, 111
  Drechsel and, 77
  merger under, 76
Harvard University, 80
Hawaiian Islands, 195
Hawsepipe, 220–221
Hearst, William Randolph, 81
  Hanfstaengl and, 82
  Hitler and, 82–83

heat wave, New York City, 1, 91–92
  end of, 107, 108
  Rockaways and, 103
Hemingway, Ernest, 198
Hess, Rudolf, 46
Hindenburg, Paul von
  conservative nationalists and,
    52
  death of, 81
  Hitler made chancellor by, 45
  Nazi Germany and, 45, 52, 59,
    81
  SS *Bremen* (ship) and, 23–24,
    27–28
historical documentaries, 221, 222
Hitler, Adolf, 2, 6, 75
  on Bremen Riot aftermath, 184
  DAP joined by, 49
  France invaded by, 204
  Hanfstaengl and, 78
  Hearst and, 82–83
  Hindenburg making, chancellor,
    45
  Mein Kampf by, 24–25, 49,
    87–88
  Nazi Party joined by, 49
  Night of the Long Knives and,
    80
  presidential powers of, 81
  Roosevelt and, 81, 84
  Spanish Civil War and, 196
  swastika and, 48–52
Hitler-Stalin Pact (nonaggression
    pact), 202–203, 206
hobbies, Bailey, B.
  Fort Point Gang and, 220
  oral storytelling as, 7, 15, 224
  writing as, 219–221, 223
Hoffmann, Hilmar, 51
hooked cross *(Hakenkreuz)*, 47–48
Hoover, Herbert, 41

House Un-American Activities
     Committee (HUAC), 213
   Bailey, B., at, 6–7, 215–218, 215
     (photo)
   Dickstein convening, 77
   Kendall and, 218
   in San Francisco, 215–216
   Scherer and, 217
   Tavenner and, 216, 217
   Velde chairing, 215, 216,
     217–218
   Walker, D., and, 25 (photo),
     215–216
Howe, William. See Jamieson,
     William
HUAC. See House Un-American
     Activities Committee
Hughes, Alice, 192
Hull, Cordell, 57, 84, 143, 204
   Leitner and, 183
   Luther and, 176–177
Hungarian Uprising, 7, 219

ILD. See International Labor Defense
ILWU. See International Longshore
     and Warehouse Union
Indian stowaway, 67–68
   Marine Workers Voice story on,
     69–70
Industrial Workers of the World
     (IWW), 36
international Jewish leaders, 54–55
International Labor Defense (ILD),
     146
   Kuntz and, 155, 158–159
   Tauber and, 147, 155–156, 158,
     159–160, 165, 166
   Unger and, 131, 134–136, 141,
     143, 155, 156
International Longshore and
     Warehouse Union (ILWU)

Bailey, B., and, 218–219
   Bridges and, 218
International Seamen's Union
     (ISU)
   Bailey, B., at, 74, 85, 193, 194
   newspaper attacking, 194
   police brutality and, 194
International Workers Of The
     World, 35
Irish War of Independence, 12
ISU. See International Seamen's
     Union
Italy, 83, 85, 86 (photo)
   Ethiopia and, 111, 196
   Pyke and, 165
   Rex (ship) in, 43, 75
IWW. See Industrial Workers of the
     World

jail
   delinquency and, 16, 17–18
   Great Depression and, 39
   resalable metal extraction and,
     40
   stowaway and, 38
Jamieson, William, 148 (photo)
   in Bremen Six, 139–140
   in Spanish Civil War, 199–200
   transformation of, 201
Jewish organizations
   American Jewish Committee, 57,
     108
   American Jewish Congress,
     57–58, 108
   B'nai B'rith, 57, 66
   in Germany, 57
   Jewish War Veterans, 55–56
Jewish Telegraphic Agency (JTA),
     145–146
Jewish War Veterans, 55–56
Jim Crow Laws, 36

jobs and volunteer work, of Bailey, B.
  at *Black Gang News*, 194, 214
  cargo loading as, 18
  during Cold War, 214–215
  film acting as, 222–223
  historical documentaries as, 221,
    222
  at ILWU, 218–219
  Marine Workers Historical
    Association and, 220–221
  as newsboy, 12, 17
  newspaper, 193–194
  retirement from, 220
  See also activism, of Bailey, B.;
    merchant seaman jobs, of
    Bailey, B.
JTA. *See* Jewish Telegraphic Agency

Kaye, Ruth (Kujawsky), 212
Kendall, James, 218
The Kid from Hoboken (Bailey), 221
  supporters of, 223
Kiep, Otto, 60–61
Kimball, James H., 103
King, William, 103
Korean War
  Marcantonio and, 213–214
  Truman and, 213
Kristallnacht (Night of Broken
    Glass), 179
Krohn, Friedrich, 49, 50
Ku'damm. *See* Kurfürstendamm
Kuntz, Edward, 155, 158–159
Kurfürstendamm (Ku'damm),
    93–95, 146, 185
  Fry on riots at, 104–105,
    107–108, 204

El Lago (ship), 36, 38
LaGuardia, Fiorello, 138, 161 (photo)
  on Bremen Riot aftermath, 142

discrimination against German
    citizens by, 101–102, 119
  Friends of the New Germany
    and, 119
  Marcantonio and, 160
Lake Gaither (ship)
  merchant seaman job on, 20,
    35–36
  mistakes on, 36
Landi, Elissa, 114
Laredo Victory (ship), 208–209
later years, of Bailey, B.
  film acting in, 222–223
  Hawsepipe in, 220–221
  historical documentaries and,
    221, 222
  hobbies in, 219–221, 224
  ILWU and, 218–219
  leaving Communist Party in, 7, 219
  retirement in, 220
  storytelling in, 224
  writers on Bailey, B., in, 221–222
Lawrenson, Helen, 37–38
Lehman, Herbert, 143
  Brodsky decision and, 177, 180,
    181, 182
Leitner, Rudolf
  Hull and, 183
  Phillips and, 141–142
Liebenfels, Lanz von, 48
List, Guido von, 48
London, Jack, 38
Lösener, Bernhard, 182
Ludwig, Emil, 190–191
Lurline (ship), 195
Luther, Hans, 79
  Hull and, 176–177
  on SS *Bremen* (ship), 60–61
  on Trial of Bremen Six ruling,
    175–176
Luxury Liner Row, 75

Magnuson Act, 214

Manhattan, SS (ship), 90, 92, 96

Marcantonio, Vito, 149, 161
(photo)
death of, 213
Korean War and, 213–214
LaGuardia and, 160
on swastika flag, 192–193
Trial of Bremen Six and, 155,
160–164, 165–168

Marine Firemen, Oilers,
Watertenders, and Wipers
Association (Marine Firemen's
Union), 206, 212–213
Communists identified in, 214
recognition from, 223

Marine Workers Historical
Association, 220–221

Marine Workers Industrial Union
(MWIU)
Bailey, B., at, 70–74
Baltimore office of, 73
Bell at, 70–71
Communism and, 71
fascism and, 55–56
Munson Line freighter and, 73
Port Organizing Committee of,
70
Robinson, J., at, 69, 74

Marine Workers Voice, 69–70, 71

Maritain, Jacques, 7

McCarthy, Joseph, 213

McCormack, Vincent "Low Life"
Bremen Riot and, 121, 129, 133
in Bremen Six, 139, 148 (photo)
Spanish Civil War and, 199
at Trial of Bremen Six, 163

McGrath, Thomas, 92

McLean, Wilhelm, 26

media, US
on Bremen Riot, 137–138

Nazi Germany in, 54, 94
on Trial of Bremen Six, 175,
177–178

Medicus, Franz, 182

Mein Kampf (Hitler), 24–25, 49,
87–88

Merchant Marine, US, 109, 207
Laredo Victory (ship) and,
208–209

merchant seaman jobs, of Bailey, B.,
1, 6–7
on *Alaskan* (ship), 193
desire for, 18–19
in Europe, 67–68, 85
on *Exchange* (ship), 86, 87
first, 19–20
hiring agents for, 38
Indian stowaway and, 67–69
international travels and, 41–42
on *John Jay* (ship), 41
on *El Lago* (ship), 36, 38
on *Lake Gaither* (ship), 20, 35–36
on *Lurline* (ship), 195
on Munson Line freighter, 73
personality types for, 37–38
on *President Johnson* (ship), 206
quarters for, 37
on *Southern Cross* (ship), 41
steamship fireman as, 41
US merchant marines in World
War II and, 207–209

Miller, Arthur, 91

Miller, Marilyn, 44

Mindel, Jacob "Pop," 193

Minor, Robert, 78–79

mixed couples, in Nazi Germany,
88, 93, 94, 145, 182

Moore, Harold F.
Drolette shot by, 127–128
on Red Squad, 110, 112, 114,
116, 127–128

reputation of, 160
Trial of Bremen Six and, 160,
    162–163, 165–166, 174
trial of Drolette and, 191
Morgan, Henry S., 114–115
Morgenthau, Henry, Sr., 62
Murphy (detective)
Bremen Riot and, 128
Trial of Bremen Six and, 163,
    164, 165
Mussolini, Benito, 43
Spanish Civil War and, 196
MWIU. *See* Marine Workers
    Industrial Union

National Socialist German Workers'
    Party. *See* Nazi Party
National Socialist mob, 45
Nazi Germany
    activism of Bailey, B., impacted
        by, 96
    anti-Jewish laws in, 58–60, 87–88,
        89, 101, 182, 185–186
    antiregime and, 2–3
    April Laws in, 59, 87–88
    Bremen Riot aftermath and,
        137–138, 139, 141–142
    Catholic Church in, 2–3, 44, 56,
        88–89, 95, 98–99, 100–101, 145
    economic recovery in, 196–197
    forced sterilization law in, 89
    Great Britain and war on,
        203–204
    Hanfstaengl in, 54
    Hearst and, 81–83
    Hindenburg and, 45, 52, 59, 81
    Hitler-Stalin Pact with Soviet
        Union and, 202–203, 206
    "Holocaust by Bullets" and, 206
    international Jewish leaders and,
        54–55

international media messages of,
    56–57
Jewish stores in, 53–54, 59
Kristallnacht in, 179
Ku'damm violence in, 93–95,
    104–105, 107–108
Luftwaffe in, 83, 196
Luther and, 60–61, 79, 175–177
military draft in, 83
mixed couples in, 88, 93, 94,
    145, 182
Night of the Long Knives and, 80
Nuremberg Laws in, 185–186
Nuremberg Rallies in, 6, 51
Olympics (1936) and, 108
press on Trial of Bremen Six, 175
propaganda in, 47–49, 178,
    186–187
refugees from, 204–205
Reichsparteitag der Freiheit in,
    179–180
Reichstag session in, 181–182,
    184
Roosevelt first statement on, 57
Saar Protectorate in, 83
Simpson in, 89–91, 96, 146,
    194–195
Social Democrats and, 44, 45,
    56
Stahlhelm in, 97–98
storm troopers in, 58, 87, 95
Streicher in, 58, 88, 94
swastika as official flag of,
    192–193
territorial acquisitions of, 83
US media on, 54, 94
See also activism, against Nazi
    Germany, US; Goebbels,
    Joseph; Goering, Hermann;
    Hitler, Adolf; US politicians,
    opposing Nazi Germany

Nazi Party
  Communist Party and, 42
  Enabling Act and, 56
  forcible coordination by, 46
  Hitler joining, 49
  swastika and, 49, 192–193
  Thule Society and, 49
  unemployment discontent and,
    42
  votes in 1928 for, 25
  votes in 1932 for, 44
  votes in 1933 for, 42
  youth marching song for, 43
NDL. *See* North German Lloyd line
Neutrality Act, 155
  Spanish Civil War and, 195
New Deal, 142
New York Police Department
    (NYPD)
  activism against Nazi Germany
    and, 63–64, 78–79
  Bremen Riot and, 4, 5, 109–110,
    119, 128–129, 131
  Bremen Riot report by, 144–145,
    165
  Goodman at, 79
  Murphy in, 128, 163, 164,
    165
  See also Red Squad
Night of Broken Glass
    (Kristallnacht), 179
Night of the Long Knives, 80
Nilsson, Rob, 222
Non-Sectarian Anti-Nazi League
    (NSANL), 53
  Untermyer and, 62, 76, 102,
    154, 196
Normandie (ship), 43, 104, 196
North German Lloyd line (NDL),
    22, 55
  Hapag-Lloyd merger of, 76

  nazification campaign and, 46
  SS *Europa* (ship) and, 23, 25–26,
    43, 75, 80
  See also Bremen, SS (ship)
Nuremberg Laws, 185
  Reich citizen in, 186
Nuremberg Rally
  consecration of flags at, 51
  of 1935, 6
NYPD. *See* New York Police
    Department

Oakland, California, 39
Odets, Clifford, 107
Olympic Games (1936)
  Nazi Germany and, 108
  US boycott of, 148, 196
On the Edge (movie), 222
O'Neill, Eugene, 41
Order of the New Templars (Ordo
    Novi Templi), 48

Payne, Perley, 198
Pearl Harbor bombing, 206
Pele (romantic interest), 73–74,
    87, 203
  in Moscow, 169–170, 193
  wedding plans of, 169
Pelosi, Nancy, 223
personal characteristics, Bailey, B.
  accent as, 2, 7
  appearance as, 1–2, 73
Phillips, William, 108, 144
  Leitner and, 141–142
police brutality, 194
politicians (US), opposing Nazi
    Germany
  Bone as, 84
  Dickstein and, 103–104
  Hull as, 84
  King as, 103

LaGuardia as, 101–102
Marcantonio as, 149
Porter, Cole, 76–77
Pound, Ezra, 115
President Johnson (ship), 206
Prohibition laws, 31
propaganda, German
Riefenstahl and, 47, 178
on SS *Bremen* (ship), 47–49,
186–187
Pyke, James A.
background of, 165
Italy and, 165
Red Squad and, 111, 116
Trial of Bremen Six and,
165–167

Queen Mary (ship), 43, 196

railroad travelers, 38–40
Rally of Freedom (Reichsparteitag
der Freiheit), 179–180
Red Squad, 5, 64, 78, 100
at Bremen Riot, 115–116, 120,
127–128
Drolette and, 110–116, 120
Moore on, 110, 112, 114, 116,
127–128
Pyke and, 111, 116
Solomon on, 110, 112, 114, 116,
126–127
Reichsparteitag der Freiheit (Rally
of Freedom), 179–180
relationships and romance, of
Bailey, B.
first marriage as, 203, 206, 207
losing virginity and, 36–37
Pele and, 73–74, 87, 169–170,
193, 203
second marriage as, 212
Rex (ship), 43, 75

Riefenstahl, Leni, 47, 178
Robinson, John Quigley "Robbie,"
73, 90
Bremen Riot and, 99
MWIU and, 69, 74
newspaper of, 193–194
Roosevelt, Franklin Delano, 40–41
first statement on Nazi Germany
by, 57
Good Neighbor policy of,
110–111
grandson of, 115, 144
Hitler and, 81, 84
inaugural address of, 54
Morgenthau and, 62
Roosevelt administration, on Nazi
Germany
apologies by, 165, 183
Bremen Riot aftermath and, 135,
142, 144
Brodsky decision and, 180–183
first statement on Nazi Germany
by, 57
letters to, 102–103
Phillips and, 108
Simpson and, 96
Rosenberg, Alfred, 82
Rosenberg, Julius, 118

"Sailor off the Bremen" (Shaw),
201–202
San Francisco, California, 197, 206,
209, 214, 218, 222
Bailey, B., as longshoreman in,
7, 219
Fort Point Gang in, 220
HUAC in, 215–216
unemployment in, 39
Schall, Thomas D., 84
Scherer, Gordon, 217
Schmidt, Gustav, 205

Schneider, Gotthold, 63

Schulwitz, Erwin, 47

Schuster, Joseph, 102

Second Reich, 49

Shaw, Irwin, 201–202

Sherman, William O'Neil, 29–30

Simpson, Lawrence, 89, 146
    anti-Nazi propaganda of, 90
    arrest of, 90–91
    The Blessings of Fascism by,
        194–195
    in concentration camp, 91
    freedom of, 194
    Roosevelt administration on, 96

Smith Act, 213

Social Democrats, 44, 45, 56

Solomon, Matthew
    Bremen Riot aftermath and, 141,
        178
    Bremen Riot and, 126–127
    injuries of, 130, 144
    on Red Squad, 110, 112, 114,
        116, 126–127
    trial of Drolette and, 191–192
    Trial of the Bremen Six and, 155,
        156–160, 166, 167, 172–174

Southern Cross (ship), 41

Soviet Union, 72, 86
    Hitler-Stalin Pact with Nazi
        Germany and, 202–203, 206
    Hungarian Uprising and, 7, 219
    Spanish Civil War and, 197–198
    SS *Bremen* (ship) in, 203–204

Spanish Civil War
    Bailey, B., in, 195–196, 197–199,
        201, 211
    Battle of the Ebro in, 199
    Bianca in, 199
    Bremen Six in, 199
    fascism and, 196, 199
    Franco and, 195, 196, 200, 201

    Hakam in, 198
    Hemingway and, 198
    Hitler and, 196
    Jamieson in, 199–200
    Mussolini and, 196
    Neutrality Act and, 195
    Payne in, 198
    Soviet Union and, 197–198
    US Communist Party and, 197,
        200
    US volunteers in, 195–196
    White, P., in, 199
    Zaragoza offensive in, 199

Stahlhelm (Steel Helmets), 97–98

Sterling, Winthrop, 151

storm troopers, 58, 87, 95

storytelling, of Bailey, B., 7
    in early life, 15
    in later life, 224

Street, James, 104–105

Streicher, Julius, 58
    Der Stürmer and, 88, 94

Studnitz, Baron Jobst von, 28, 30

swastika
    anti-Semitism and, 50, 185
    Aryans and, 48, 50
    on Blood Flag, 51
    Ehrhardt Brigade and, 49
    flag on SS *Bremen* (ship), 4–5,
        52, 99–100, 116, 122–123,
        128–129, 170, 171, 175,
        186–187, 187 (photo),
        192–193
    flag on SS *Europa* (ship), 80
    flag reverence and, 51
    global activism against ship flags
        with, 64–65, 66
    history of, 47–50
    Hitler and, 48–52
    Krohn and, 49, 50
    Marcantonio on, flag, 192–193

as Nazi Germany official flag, 192–193
Nazi Party and, 49, 192–193
ship flags and activism against Nazi Germany, 64–65, 66
Trial of Bremen Six and, flag, 170, 171, 175, 177
Untermyer on flag with, 66
use of, 50–51

Tauber, Joseph, 147
Trial of Bremen Six and, 155–156, 158, 159–160, 165, 166
Tavenner, Frank, 216, 217
Tell, Irving J., 155, 170
Teller, Albert, 32
Thälmann, Ernst, 45, 117
Thule Society, 49
Treaty of Versailles, 22, 24
Trial of Bremen Six, 151
Bailey, B., at, 162–163, 167
Blair at, 174–175
Brodsky and, 156, 164, 165, 166–167, 168, 170–174, 177, 180–183, 189
decision in, 173–174, 177, 180–183, 189
Drolette and, 156, 157, 159, 162–164, 165–166, 167, 173, 174
final statement in, 170–174
Goebbels on, 175, 179
jury for, 174
Kuntz and, 155, 158–159
Luther on ruling of, 175–176
Marcantonio and, 155, 160–164, 165–168
McCormack and, 163
Moore and, 160, 162–163, 165–166, 174

moral purpose in, 161
Murphy and, 163, 164, 165
Nazi press on, 175
Pyke and, 165–167
setting of, 154–155
Solomon and, 155, 156–160, 166, 167, 172–174
swastika flag review in, 170, 171, 175, 177
Tauber and, 155–156, 158, 159–160, 165, 166
Tell and, 155, 170
Unger and, 155, 156
unlawful assembly and, 171–173
US media on, 175, 177–178
Truman, Harry S.
Communist Party and, 212–213
Korean War and, 213

Unger, Abraham
bail lowered and, 143
Bremen Six represented by, 131, 134–135, 141, 143
Trial of Bremen Six and, 155, 156
United States (US)
boycott of Olympic Games (1936), 148, 196
Catholic Church, 14–15, 96, 106, 112–113, 130
media, 54, 94, 137–138, 175, 177–178
Merchant Marine, 109, 207–209
politicians opposing Nazi Germany, 84, 101–102, 103–104, 149
volunteers, 195–196
See also activism (US), against Nazi Germany

Untermyer, Samuel, 197
    boycott of German goods and,
        65–66, 102, 196, 204
    death of, 204
    NSANL of, 62, 76, 102, 154, 196
    SS *Bremen* (ship) and, 62
    on swastika flag, 66
US. *See* United States

Velde, Harold, 215, 216, 217–218

Walker, Doris Brin, 25 (photo),
    215–216
Walker, James J., 31
Warning, Eric, 187
Weaver, Margaret
    bail for Bremen Six and,
        143–144
    Bailey, B., and, 92
    Blair and, 92, 140, 174, 199, 213
    Bremen Riot and, 105–106, 109,
        121, 123, 132, 133, 155
    Communist Party and, 92
Weidemann, Hans
    activism against Nazi Germany
        and, 62–63, 64
    Goebbels and, 64, 79
Weimar Germany
    Communist Party in, 45
    election of 1932 in, 44
    Hindenburg in, 23–24, 27–28
    National Socialist mob in, 45
    unemployment rate in, 42
Wels, Otto, 56

Wexler, Haskell, 37–38
White, E. B., 33
White, Paul, 199
Wilhelm, Kaiser, II, 21
Williams, Tennessee, 211
Winkler, Irwin, 222–223
Wise, James Waterman, 148
"Won't You Please Come Home,
    Bill Bailey," 10, 211
World War I, 21
    Drolette in, 109
    France in, 109
    Schulwitz during, 47
    Treaty of Versailles after, 22, 24
World War II, US in
    atomic bombs in, 208
    Bailey, B., and, 6, 207, 211–212
    Battle of the Bulge and, 208
    Gavin in, 208
    Pearl Harbor and, 206
    US merchant marines and,
        207–209
Wright, Edythe, 32
writing, of Bailey, B.
    fiction, 219–220
    The Kid from Hoboken as, 221, 223

Zellenleiter (cell leaders), 46–47
Ziegenbein, Leopold
    Bremen Riot and, 119–120, 131,
        139
    radio address by, 31
    as SS *Bremen* (ship) captain, 28,
        30, 31, 104

RAN GRAFF

PETER DUFFY is an author and journalist based in New York City. He has written three books of historical nonfiction— *The Bielski Brothers* (HarperCollins, 2003); *The Killing of Major Denis Mahon* (HarperCollins, 2007); and *Double Agent* (Scribner, 2014). His journalism has appeared in the *New York Times, New York* magazine, the *Wall Street Journal, Slate,* the *New Republic,* and many other publications.

PublicAffairs is a publishing house founded in 1997. It is a tribute to the standards, values, and flair of three persons who have served as mentors to countless reporters, writers, editors, and book people of all kinds, including me.

I. F. STONE, proprietor of *I. F. Stone's Weekly*, combined a commitment to the First Amendment with entrepreneurial zeal and reporting skill and became one of the great independent journalists in American history. At the age of eighty, Izzy published *The Trial of Socrates*, which was a national bestseller. He wrote the book after he taught himself ancient Greek.

BENJAMIN C. BRADLEE was for nearly thirty years the charismatic editorial leader of *The Washington Post*. It was Ben who gave the *Post* the range and courage to pursue such historic issues as Watergate. He supported his reporters with a tenacity that made them fearless and it is no accident that so many became authors of influential, best-selling books.

ROBERT L. BERNSTEIN, the chief executive of Random House for more than a quarter century, guided one of the nation's premier publishing houses. Bob was personally responsible for many books of political dissent and argument that challenged tyranny around the globe. He is also the founder and longtime chair of Human Rights Watch, one of the most respected human rights organizations in the world.

. . .

For fifty years, the banner of Public Affairs Press was carried by its owner Morris B. Schnapper, who published Gandhi, Nasser, Toynbee, Truman, and about 1,500 other authors. In 1983, Schnapper was described by *The Washington Post* as "a redoubtable gadfly." His legacy will endure in the books to come.

Peter Osnos, *Founder*